Gertrude Stein's
Theatre of the Absolute

Theater and Dramatic Studies, No. 21

Bernard Beckerman, Series Editor

Brander Matthews Professor of Dramatic Literature
Columbia University in the City of New York

Other Titles in This Series

Gertrude Stein.
(Photo: Estate of Carl Van Vechten by Joseph Solomon, Executor)

Gertrude Stein's
Theatre of the Absolute

by
Betsy Alayne Ryan

UMI RESEARCH PRESS
Ann Arbor, Michigan

Produced and distributed by
UMI Research Press
an imprint of
University Microfilms International
A Xerox Information Resources Company
Ann Arbor, Michigan 48106

Library of Congress Cataloging in Publication Data

Ryan, Betsy Alayne.
    Gertrude Stein's theatre of the absolute.

    (Theater and dramatic studies ; no. 21)
    Revision of thesis—University of Illinois, Urbana,
1980.
    Bibliography: p.
    Includes index.
    1. Stein, Gertrude, 1874-1946—Dramatic works.
2. Stein, Gertrude, 1874-1946—Stage history.
3. Experimental theater. I. Title. II. Series.

PS3537.T323Z8214 1984   812'.52   84-191
ISBN 0-8357-1548-5

for Evelyn Lehman and Leo Ryan

Contents

Acknowledgments

I wish to acknowledge the Collection of American Literature, the Beinecke Rare Book and Manuscript Library, Yale University for access to Gertrude Stein's unpublished manuscripts, typescripts, letters, and to newspaper reviews and photographs of productions of her works; the Estate of Carl Van Vechten for the use of play production photographs; the Estate of Gertrude Stein, Liveright Publishing Corporation, and Random House, Inc. for permission to quote from Stein's published works and letters; the University of Illinois Library, the New York Public Library at Lincoln Center, and George Ashley of Performing Artservices for locating hard-to-find reviews of Stein's productions; and Virgil Thomson and Lamont Johnson for illuminating interviews.

I also wish to thank those whose contributions are not easily measured: Burnet Hobgood, who encouraged this study of Stein's theatre from the beginning; Nicholas Mankovich, for generously aiding its progress; and Terry Ryan and Victoria Scott for giving support to the making of this book.

Preface

From the early part of this century to the 1940s, Gertrude Stein created an aesthetic for the theatre and a playwriting technique that joins with those of Brecht and Artaud in evoking the definitive qualities of the contemporary avant-garde theatre. Stein advocated, along with one or the other of these theorist-practitioners, a return to the physicality of theatre, an emphasis upon its function as well as its fiction, a new concept of time which came closer to a concept of space, a devaluation of language as it is traditionally used, and the practice of theatre for its own sake and toward its own ends.

Though the influence of Brecht and Artaud has been exhaustively reported during the past twenty years and more, Stein's contribution to dramatic art has been almost totally overlooked. Perhaps this is because she was so much of an outsider; her revamping of twentieth century literature in novels, stories, poems, and portraits was her major task as a writer, something she pointed out more than once. In addition, her theatrical art and her aesthetic seemed more tied to the world of painting than to theatre. What is not widely known, however, is that Stein considered the complete fulfillment of her aesthetic to lie in her plays and their performance.

Perhaps, too, Stein has been neglected because the aesthetic she posed in response to the needs of her time is more uncompromising than Brecht's and Artaud's. Her concepts of time and entity, for example, preclude the use of language for anything other than exploration of the moment. Investigations of social issues or political realities, of psychologies, metaphysics, or dreams comprise no part of her art. Uncompromising though this may be, it effectively freed Stein to create the most purely theatrical theatre of the three.

Though it is not to any single source that one may attribute the recent burgeoning of theatre as practiced by Richard Foreman, Robert Wilson, Snake Theatre, Hellmuth and Reynolds, Nightfire, Squat Theatre, Stuart Sherman, Laurie Anderson, Soon 3, The Wooster Group, Mel Andringa's

Drawing Legion, or Spalding Gray, surely Gertrude Stein is the most evocative one. While the worlds of painting, of the Happening, of Jarry and Mallarmé, of Maeterlinck and Tzara all come to mind, the theories and practices of Stein are tied less to any particular political climate, and more to the shaping of consciousness towards the making of art in its purest manifestation. They are thus able to express what is central to today's theatrical avant-garde: a concern, above all, with the formal aspects of theatre and art, and with the exploration of personal consciousness.

In light of this, and in recognition that a description of her art is a pressing need, this book investigates the nature of Gertrude Stein's theatrical art, the forerunner of the contemporary avant-garde theatre.

Introduction and Commentary

Introduction

In 1913, Georges Braque painted *Le Courrier,* one of the milestones in the development of cubism and modern painting as we now know it. In 1913, the first performance of Stravinsky's *Rite of Spring* caused a riot. And in 1913, Gertrude Stein wrote her first play.

While we have since grown accustomed to such innovations in painting and music — arts which integrate themselves quickly into the cultural fabric by virtue of their concreteness — Stein's equally innovative creations in literature and theatre continue to hit us with the force of the strange and unexpected. We are likely to see the strangeness of her writing as the outcome of some personal, anarchic quirk or iconoclastic urge, while we no longer take the works of Braque or Stravinsky to be other than genuine products of genius.

But the art of Gertrude Stein was addressed as completely and determinedly as the art of these modernists to the expression of her time, and it can in no way be characterized simply as an iconoclastic dismissal of existing forms. She devoted her aesthetic to an embodiment of the "now" and to the evolution of a style which could adequately express it. As she stated, "The business of art...is to live in the actual present the complete actual present and to completely express that complete actual present." The forms Ibsen created in response to his reality no more concerned her than the painting of Ingres concerned Picasso or Braque, or Wagner's music, Stravinsky. Ibsen did not exist for her; his forms were inadequate for a complete expression of Stein's present. She geared her own program for literature and the theatre to address directly that present.

This critical study seeks to establish Stein's playwriting aesthetic as a serious attempt to express her conception of the new landscape of the twentieth century and to reveal the techniques she used to realize that aesthetic in her seventy-seven plays.

Chapter one presents Stein's account of her literary aesthetic, as she herself explained it in works written from the 1920s to the 1940s: *Composition as Explanation* (1923), *The Autobiography of Alice B. Toklas* (1932), *Lectures in America* (1934), *Narration* (1935), *The Geographical History of America or the Relation of Human Nature to the Human Mind* (1935), *Everybody's Autobiography* (1936), *What are Masterpieces and Why are there so Few of Them* (1936), and *Four in America* (1947).

It is clear from Stein's writings on theory that she set out to deal uncompromisingly in terms of that new landscape as she formulated her aesthetic. After describing her position on the artist's depiction of the world, which culminated in a split of the artist's consciousness, the chapter considers the ramifications of that position for the artwork under the headings of *Time* and *Entity*, her major theoretical propositions.

Chapter two explains Stein's playwriting aesthetic and shows how the aesthetic operates in her plays. The chapter justifies Stein's isolation from the theatre world and her reasons for writing plays despite this isolation, and treats the aesthetic for the theatre as it emerged in plays of the three periods that Stein and her critics have promulgated. After demonstrating how her aesthetic concepts shape her plays, the chapter considers the adequacy of the distinct periods as the means of critically examining them. It suggests that a better way might be found: a detailed view of play traits, which may provide a new, cohesive view of her theatre art.

Chapter three seeks to establish the particular dramaturgical techniques Stein used to realize her aesthetic concepts in her plays. A thorough study of the plays makes it clear that the traits they possess must be defined in terms both rudimentary and extensive, ranging from the appearance of the text on the printed page to an examination of the author's perspective. The traits identified, then, must be consonant with a critical study of the play texts and informed by a respectful knowledge of her aesthetic. This is not to say that the traits are prescriptive, or even exhaustive; they are open-ended, allowing the plays either to exhibit them or not. Conceivably, other Steinian traits could be justified by other students following this path of scrutiny, but I would contend that any other traits would be in harmony with those identified here.

The results of this analysis are tabulated in Appendix B, which is composed of two parts: the list of play characteristics or traits as described in the chapter and a statistical summary that specifies in which texts the traits appear.

Chapter four summarizes Stein's contribution to the theatre through her aesthetic and technique as established in preceding chapters, describes the tenor of productions of her work, and relates her to contemporary theatricians who use the very techniques she introduced to playwriting and the theatre, to produce a similar art.

The study concludes with three more Appendices. Appendix A is devoted to the first chronological listing of Stein's plays by date of composition and tells the reader in what published volumes to find them. The plays also exist in original manuscript and typescript form at the Beinecke Library, Yale University, the former handwritten by Stein in paperbound lesson books used by French schoolchildren, and the latter mostly typed by Alice Toklas the morning after they were written. There are virtually no changes in any of the plays from manuscript to typescript to published version, and there are virtually no revisions in the manuscripts, some of which end on the last possible line in the book, and some of which are inspired by the picture that happens to appear on the cover. These lesson books are instruction in her aesthetic in themselves. Appendix C lists chronologically Stein's major play productions together with basic program information. Appendix D presents a bibliography of play reviews connected with those productions and should provide some helpful material for those interested in the production aspect of her plays.

This is the first study of Stein's work to give specific attention to the techniques exhibited by all seventy-seven of her play texts. Rather than focusing on a few plays in depth, it concentrates on the body of her plays, relating them to her theoretical propositions and to each other. Further, it attempts to approach the plays on the basis of the traits they exhibit in themselves, using traditional playwriting techniques as counterpoints to her unique style. This approach enables an indication in Chapter four of Stein's influence upon the contemporary avant-garde theatre, where Steinian techniques abound.

Commentary on Stein Criticism

Surprisingly, the body of critical writing associated with Stein's theatre — though it hardly represents a single point of view — would never suggest such an influence, even when the critics have a knowledge or concern with the current avant-garde. One group of Stein's scholars inevitably conclude that Stein, interesting though she was as a person, might have spared the theatre world her idiosyncratic theatrical creations. Often they contend that her plays are not dramatic at all, as if drama — their catchword for traditional crisis-centered theatre literature — must necessarily inhere in all types of plays. The intimation is that Gertrude Stein tried to write the traditional play and failed, due to her ignorance of the theatre and her unusual way of looking at things. Though many such critics proceed from an appreciation of Stein as a person and a writer, they feel compelled to reveal that they themselves know the difference between what Stein was satisfied to call plays and what plays really are.[1]

This attitude prevails in the theatre world as well, where knowledge of Gertrude Stein as a playwright is meager at best. Lamont Johnson, who was largely responsible for the first production of *Yes is for a Very Young Man* in 1946, still does not see her as a dramatist. Her texts, he believes, supply "the dynamics that a dramatist would take and transmit, transform, into a larger theatrical form... where the conflict would be truly opposed and... acted out in a dramatic action."[2] Stein rewrote that text according to the specifications of Johnson and others involved in the production with the result that it worked neither on his nor her terms:

> The Pasadena Playhouse premiere of "Yes" by Gertrude Stein was inordinately dull. One went expecting at least some of that fantastic alleged originality of the author as a fillip, but aside from a few early sorties in that direction, the play seemed shortly to settle down to a kind of pseudo-conventionality, and very little vitality was discernible either in plot or characters, while most of the situations even with the French wartime background carried little or no impact. The play can be written off as amateurish.[3]

A number of admirable general studies of Stein's works and aesthetic deal less effectively with the plays. Richard Bridgman's *Gertrude Stein In Pieces* presents *Yes is for a Very Young Man* in this fashion:

> The action is loose, often improbable and insufficiently developed, and rarely dramatic. The few successful moments come when Gertrude Stein deals with the tensions that wrung French men and women of good will.[4]

The plays, in his opinion, suffer from the lack of development and the lack of richness characteristic of her other works and integral to her aesthetic. And John Malcom Brinnin's *The Third Rose* describes *Yes* as a "play of types rather than of individually defined characters"[5] as if, like Bridgman, he is applying a set of demands for the plays which he does not apply to her other works. He concludes his introduction to a recent collection of Stein's plays, *Selected Operas and Plays,* by claiming her influence upon Beckett, Pinter, Ionesco, and N. F. Simpson—an influence he believes to be either admitted by the playwright, documented by his critics, or "otherwise obvious" to Stein's audience.[6] But these playwrights do not acknowledge such an influence, and they see no similarity in outlook or technique.[7] The art of Gertrude Stein, as we shall see, is demonstrably unlike the work of Beckett and Pinter in more ways than it is similar. Though they share the attention to a relatively static situation, Beckett and Pinter deal in levels of significance that are ultimately foreign to Stein and do not even approach her stringent attention to the present. These distinctions are important to note; such hastily conferred likenesses have resulted in the impression that Stein is a lesser light in a large school of playwrights and that better renditions of her theories and techniques exist in the repertory. But she was part of no school, and her plays are unique.

A number of writers deal more effectively with the plays. Thornton Wilder and Carl Van Vechten, both personal friends of Stein with knowledge of literature and theatre, contribute to an understanding of her personality and her writing technique through their introductions to collections of her works. Wilder gives Stein a central position in modern dramaturgy:

> I never doubted her conviction that she was the greatest writer of the Twentieth Century, and that her playwriting was our time's drama and was to show us where the theatre is to go.[8]

While he is able to go beyond Van Vechten's fascination with Stein's personality, he tends to share Van Vechten's view of the iconoclastic Gertrude Stein. For instance, he sees Stein's deliberate disjunction of traditional play structure as arbitrary, calling it her satirical jab at pedantry and formalism, her way of saying, "don't fence me in!"[9] But this aspect of Stein's plays is more than sheer arbitrariness, more than simple iconoclasm, as an examination of her plays in terms of her aesthetic will show.

Frederick Hoffman, Michael Hoffman, Norman Weinstein, William Gass, Wilford Leach, Bruce Kawin, and Donald Sutherland provide a coherent picture of her contribution to the theatre by recognizing that Stein was little concerned with traditional theatre modes. Weinstein's study marks a great advance in considering the plays as an integral part of Stein's literary canon which directly reflect her aesthetic. Michael Hoffman and Donald Sutherland share Weinstein's focus, Hoffman's study providing the best view to date of Stein's manipulation of structure and style. Donald Sutherland's study is one of the few that considers the theatrical consequences of this manipulation, though he does not deal as thoroughly with the actual manipulation. The plays, as he sees them, are movements in space — embodiments of theatre which are meant to be fulfilled in live performance.

Wilford Leach's dissertation, *Gertrude Stein and the Modern Theatre,* is the only full-length work devoted to the plays of Stein. Though it gives a larger section to play analysis than do any of the previously mentioned works and though it studies at great length Stein's aesthetic and its background, there is still no detailed attention to the structure and style of the plays in terms of that aesthetic. This may be attributed to his acceptance of the three general periods put forth by Stein, and his analysis of the plays in terms of periods rather than specific traits.

Despite these important advances in Stein scholarship, there is no study to date which treats her playwriting aesthetic and technique specifically enough for a genuine understanding of her art and for an indication of its influence upon the contemporary theatre. It is my hope that this study, launched from a knowledge of her aesthetic and concerned above all with the revelation of her playwriting technique, contributes that specificity. It is also my hope that its breadth of treatment at a time when most of Stein's plays are lost to the theatre may compensate for the necessarily brief treatment of any one play. I believe that students of Stein, and particularly those who would stage her work, will find her plays more accessible with the help of this study. It is a pity that the theatre has so rarely utilized the work of this genius of our time to make itself the contemporary vehicle of expression it could become.

1

General Aesthetic

Background

Each generation has to do with what you would call the daily life: and a writer, painter, or any sort of creative artist, is not at all ahead of his time. He is contemporary. He can't live in the past because it is gone. He can't live in the future because no one knows what it is. He can live only in the present of his daily life. He is expressing the thing that is being expressed by everybody else in their daily lives.[1]

In this disarmingly simple passage lies Gertrude Stein's aesthetic credo: the creative artist, who can live only in the present of his daily life, expresses that strict present in his work.

One would hardly anticipate that out of so simple an intention would emerge such writing as this:

Put the putty in before the door put the oil glass in with what is green. Put the mellow choice with all the test, rust with night and language in the waist. Praise the cat and show the twine the door, mention every scrap of linen carpet, see the eagle and behold the west, win the day light with the hat unpressed, show it in a shudder and a limp, make the best container with no speed, and a jacket and a choice and beets, beets are what there are when bets are less. Bets are less in summer. [*White Wines*, 1913][2]

First in a circle.
Papa dozes mamma blows her noses.
We cannot say this the other way.
Exactly.
Passably.
Second in circles.
A citroen and a citizen
A miss and bliss.
We came together.
Then suddenly there was an army.
In my room.
We asked them to go away
We asked them very kindly to stay.

How can Cailloux be dead again.
Napoleon is dead.
Not again.

[*A Circular Play,* 1920][3]

Pigeons on the grass alas.
Pigeons on the grass alas.
Short longer grass short longer longer shorter yellow grass
Pigeons large pigeons on the shorter longer yellow grass alas pigeons on the grass.
    If they were not pigeons what were they.

[*Four Saints in Three Acts,* 1927][4]

Obviously, Stein's credo is not as straightforward as it appears. Its effects are completely unlike those produced by the realists and naturalists of the late nineteenth century who, according to K. T. Baskerville, wished to escape the romantic distortion inherent in a concentration upon distant times and places. They are equally unlike those produced by the symbolists, who professed an even more stringent concept of the present.

The distinction between these artists and Stein resides less in a variable degree of dedication to the present than in a complete revision of the very concept of the present brought about by the revolution in man's understanding of the universe at the turn of the twentieth century. This revolution forged Stein's present and impelled her to create an aesthetic which directly responded to it. Stein's understanding of the present built directly from her perception that a new age had dawned:

> The only thing that is different from one time to another is what is seen and what is seen depends on how everybody is doing everything. This makes the thing we are looking at very different and this makes what those who describe it make of it, it makes a composition, it confuses, it shows, it is, it looks, it likes it as it is, and this makes what is seen as it is seen. Nothing changes from generation to generation except the thing seen and that makes a composition.[5]

According to Stein:

> The twentieth century is more splendid than the nineteenth century, certainly it is much more splendid. The twentieth century has much less reasonableness in its existence than the nineteenth century but reasonableness does not make for splendor. The seventeenth century had less reason in its existence than the sixteenth century and in consequence it has more splendor. So the twentieth century is that, it is a time when everything cracks, where everything is destroyed, everything isolates itself, it is a more splendid thing than a period when everything follows itself.[6]

Stein believed that the innate quality of the new century — which stemmed from an unprecedented diversity and spatial expanse — was staticity: she spoke of "distribution" and "equilibration" of isolated elements rather than of progress or causality.[7] Her first experience in an airplane gave her practical knowledge of this difference:

> One must not forget that the earth seen from an airplane is more splendid than the earth seen from an automobile. The automobile is the end of progress on the earth, it goes quicker but essentially the landscapes seen from the automobile are the same as the landscapes seen from a carriage, a train, a waggon [sic], or in walking. But the earth seen from an airplane is something else.... When I was in America I for the first time travelled pretty much all the time in an airplane and when I looked at the earth I saw all the lines of cubism made at a time when not any painter had ever gone up in an airplane. I saw there on the earth the mingling lines of Picasso, coming and going, developing and destroying themselves, I saw the simple solutions of Braque, I saw the wandering lines of Masson, yes I saw and once more I knew that a creator is contemporary, he understands what is contemporary when the contemporaries do not yet know it, but he is contemporary and as the twentieth century is a century which sees the earth as no one has ever seen it, the earth has a splendor that it never has had, and as everything destroys itself in the twentieth century and nothing continues, so then the twentieth century has a splendor which is its own.[8]

Stein's airplane travel is a model of what artists like herself had experienced with the coming of the new century: a new awareness of space. The airplane ride involved perception of a landscape from a distance, so that possibilities for interminglings and disappearances of lines and sections was the natural vision. Driving in a car within the landscape on a road naturally resulted in a vision of progress or development — travel through time — where points of the journey are perceived in order, according to the movement of the car. The airplane, on the other hand, freed the traveller to order the journey as he wished while hovering over the whole landscape. Stein's resistance to the automobile's deterministic movement is legendary: she wandered all over France in various automobiles without benefit of reverse gear or maps, neither of which she could bring herself to use.

The differences between the two modes of travel, as Stein saw them, are primarily differences in time and space. For the automobile traveller, the trip is not complete until the car has progressed from point a to point b. In addition, one point in the trip is likely to appear more or less important or interesting than another as items in the landscape approach and recede. For the airplane traveller, the trip is complete, in a sense, at every moment, since the landscape exists as a piece at every moment: the changes perceived from one moment to the next are so small relative to changes perceived from the car as to be non-existent, and may have as much to do with changes of consciousness as with changes in the landscape. For Stein, the difference between car and plane travel was no less than the difference between the nineteenth and twentieth centuries: an experience of time had become an experience of space.

It is interesting that the new field of subatomic physics had revealed a world as "unreasonable" as the one revealed in Stein's pragmatic observations, and one strikingly similar in character. Up to the middle of the nineteenth century, the accepted model of physical reality had been that of Isaac Newton. It described a three-dimensional, rigid world that appeared to progress as a unit in a separate dimension, time, and accepted a Cartesian duality of "objective" mind and "dead" matter, an ideal wherein the structured actuality of solid things could be absolutely described. Throughout the nineteenth century, however, revisions in this reasonable view accumulated. Faraday and Maxwell depicted a fluctuating order, and showed that matter was less a thing than a dynamic force exhibiting no fixed connections.[9] And Einstein theorized that time and space connect to form a four-dimensional continuum "space-time." It seemed, as a result, more reasonable to think of a static picture of space and time within which events do not develop, but just are: what in the old model seemed to unfold with the passage of time now existed all at once.[10] As a result of these changes, it was no longer useful to think of an inherent order existing independent of one person's observation, or one point in time.

The changes in the concepts of mind, matter, time and space, order, and perception that accompanied the new century and its way of life, its modes of travel, and its scientific expression would have profound effects upon art and literature. In the vast universe where multidimensionality, not directionality, seemed the defining characteristic, and where a subject was not easily distinguished from an object, many things once thought reasonable became matters for fundamental questioning: whether an objective description of a thing was possible (or useful), whether a thing—or an artist—should be torn from context for purposes of description, whether an artist could see the thing at which she looked, whether it was possible to convey a description to an audience, and so on. For Gertrude Stein, in the post-Einsteinian universe, the human self remained. Her work can be seen as an effort by one such human self to cope with a new experience of existence and articulate that experience in language. She believed that the modes which had characterized the Western literary tradition heretofore— single perspective, progressive development, transition, and causal connection—were no longer adequate. Moreover, she perceived that the very act of trying to comprehend or express the new situation seemed foredoomed to failure because it was an attempt to divide up what necessarily had to be viewed as a whole for true apprehension. The act of writing seemed compromised at base. Was there any way in which it could continue as an act of ordering, comprehending, and expressing human experience, or was she henceforth condemned to a situation which had gone permanently beyond her powers of comprehension or expression? This was the situation Gertrude Stein confronted, the challenge she endeavored to meet.

Aesthetic of Gertrude Stein

A consistent aesthetic informed the work of Gertrude Stein, which changed focus at various points throughout her long career. A brief summary of her overall writing periods will make these changes of focus clear and will avoid any suggestion that the aesthetic principles introduced in this chapter receive equal emphasis throughout her diverse body of work.

Breaking from a protracted description of relations and a "prolonged present" in her early writing (1903–1911), Stein formed concepts of "entity" and a "continuous present" in 1911 with *The Making of Americans,* which she used for the rest of her career, ending in 1946. In 1932, however, she became interested for the first time in narrative, which, according to her, was writing from someone else's point of view. In *The Autobiography of Alice B. Toklas* and *Everybody's Autobiography* she wrote expressly for an audience, contradicting, as we shall see, the principles set up in 1911. After that, she sought to use narrative in a way in which she could remain true to those principles. Her work after 1932 represents this combination; in her view, some works conformed more and some less to the "continuous present," "entity," and narrative. The late writings depend as much upon the 1911 principles as does a key early work, *Tender Buttons* (1912), though those writings display a clarity emerging from narrative that the early works lack almost entirely.

Personal Consciousness

In the landscape of the twentieth century, it was Gertrude Stein's belief than an artist must immerse herself in the world and experience it directly in order to know it. It was simultaneously her belief that the artist's highest aspiration is to present an objective picture of what is from a personal point of view. In the early thirties, she described the way in which the artist must operate to fulfill this dual purpose by posing a duality between participation and disengagement. In this division she joined a long tradition. George Santayana, whom Stein encountered at Radcliffe in the 1890's, termed the impulse toward participation the sense of existence, which is flux and non-being. It is opposed, according to him, by the impulse toward disengagement, or "the intuition of pure being."[11] Stein's aesthetic accommodates both in its duality of "existence" and "being" (Santayana's words), each representing a separate mode of personal consciousness, each having a special relationship to the questions of time and relations. Her most immediate source for this notion was very likely William James, her teacher and mentor at Radcliffe, whose theories of time and consciousness became an early stimulus. In the latter theory James distinguished between the self as "known," or the "Me," and the self as "knower," or the "I":

> Whatever I may be thinking of, I am always at the same time more or less aware of *myself*, of my *personal* existence. At the same time it is *I* who am aware; so that the total self of me, being as it were duplex, partly known and partly knower, partly object and partly subject, must have two aspects discriminated in it, of which for shortness we may call one the *Me* and the other the *I*. . . [12]

The Jamesian "Me" is an object in the world of objects, leaving the "I" to function as the subject who is aware of both.

The distinct elements of Stein's personal consciousness are identity and entity, or as she most often refers to them, "human nature" and "human mind." Roughly equivalent to the Jamesian "Me" and the Santayanan "existence," "human nature" is the social self which possesses personality and a sense of an audience, uses memory and association, and senses the passage of time. It is the subjective self whose sole identification lies in its relations with external characteristics, and which is thereby associated by Stein with identity. "Human mind," on the other hand, disengages itself from all such considerations and exists in itself. It possesses "entity," or final being, as opposed to transitory identity, and it requires nothing outside itself for completion or definition.

Like the Jamesian "I," the human mind is aware of human nature as an object in the world:

> They used to think that the world was there as we see it but this is not so the world is there as it is human nature is there as it is and the human mind. The human mind knows this, that everything is there as it is. [13]

Gertrude Stein believed it was possible and necessary for the creative artist to separate human mind from human nature while composing. Disengaged from the world, the human mind has a special ability to know it not as human nature sees it — through a veil of identity — but directly, as it "is." Disengaged from mere subjective considerations, the human mind directs itself solely toward the object of its attention. In this concentrated state the human mind attains the most detached perspective possible, and accordingly, can generate the creative process. It is the mind that writes:

> The human mind can write what it is because what it is is all that it is and as it is all that it is all it can do is to write. [14]

> The thing one gradually comes to find out is that one has no identity that is when one is in the act of doing anything. Identity is recognition, you know who you are because you and others remember anything about yourself but essentially you are not that when you are doing anything. I am I because my little dog knows me but creatively speaking the little dog knowing that you are you and your recognizing that he knows, that is what destroys creation. That is what makes school. [15]

I am not I any longer when I see
This sentence is at the bottom of all creative activity.
It is just the opposite of I am I because my little dog knows me.[16]

Concomitant with this disengagement of human mind from human nature and the world is a disengagement from the flow of time. Anticipation of future time and memory of past time lies within the liberal confines of human nature. The writing mind, however, is detached from the "flux" of existence, perceiving the world through the isolated instants of its attention. Unaware of development and incapable of memory, it is able to express only the absolute present moment of perception:

I meditated a good deal about how to yourself you were yourself at any moment that you were there to you inside you but that any moment back you could only remember yourself you could not feel yourself and I therefore began to think that insofar as you were yourself to yourself there was no feeling of time inside you you only had the sense of time when you remembered yourself. . . .[17]

There is no remembering and there is no forgetting because memory has to do with human nature and not with the human mind.[18]

The human mind knows what it knows and knowing what it knows it has nothing to do with seeing what it remembers.[19]

The human mind perceives anew with each moment, and each moment of perception contains all the significance it will ever contain. There is no causal relationship between these perceptual moments and no progressive sequence, since each moment is self-sufficient, containing, in effect, its own "beginning and ending."[20]
Once shorn of self-centered reverie and the flux of the world, the human mind can come to have intimate contact with the object of its attention. Stein called this contact "knowledge," and described it in this fashion:

How do you know anything, well you know anything as complete knowledge as having it completely in you at the moment you have it. That is what knowledge is, and essentially therefore knowledge is not succession but an immediate existing.[21]

This precise contact with the moment as it occurs produces "writing as it is being written." A writer who decides what he wants to write before he writes is "writing what he is going to be writing."[22] According to Stein, this writing lacks immediacy because it is not recorded at the moment of perception, journalism providing a prime example:

I said newspapers make things too easy and I said that once to a reporter and he said you have no idea I am sure how terribly hard we work. Yes I said but after you have done all that hard work you have to write it up as it would be if you had known it all beforehand and that is what really makes it too easy. There is no discovery there is mostly no discovery in a newspaper or in history, they find out things they never knew before but there is no discovery and finally if all this goes on long enough it is too easy.[23]

She thought that even Shakespeare's sonnets, as opposed to his plays, were "written as they were going to be written," according to prescription rather than immediate knowledge,[24] not to mention her own translation of George Hugnet's *Enfances*:

Hitherto I had always been writing, with a concentration of recognition of the thing that was to be existing as my writing as it was being written. And now, the recognition was prepared beforehand there it was it was already recognition a thing I could recognize because it had been recognized before I began my writing and a very queer thing was happening....no recognition as the words were forming.[25]

Stein termed such writing "serving Mammon," not God, since "the minute they all begin to think what they want to say and how they want to say it they no longer choose."[26] Writers who write what they are writing have a direct relationship with the object and the artwork. According to Stein, they are serving, not Mammon, but God:

Now serving god for a writer who is writing is writing anything directly, it makes no difference what it is but it must be direct, the relationship between the thing done and the doer must be direct. In this way there is completion and the essence of the completed thing is completion.[27]

Writing for Stein, then, is synonymous with knowing. It is not a separate activity to be performed subsequent to attaining knowledge; it is the coming to know something at the moment it is known. This view inheres in Stein's rejection of any attempt at re-writing:

I have never understood how people could labor over a manuscript, write and rewrite it many times, for to me, if you have something to say, the words are always there. And they are the exact word and the words that should be used.[28]

Rewriting implies experimentation, something she could not abide:

Artists do not experiment. Experiment is what scientists do; they initiate an operation of unknown factors in order to be instructed by its results. An artist puts down what he knows and at every moment it is what he knows at that moment. If he is trying things out to see how they go he is a bad artist.[29]

It follows from this that the challenge in "writing as it is written" lies not in shaping or polishing from the outside, but in developing from the inside. The most difficult thing in writing, as she told George Hugnet, was to be "true enough to yourself, and to know yourself enough so that there is no obstacle to the story's coming through complete."[30] Her own method lay in practicing her spontaneities, as Virgil Thomson has related.[31] Polishing her work would have been not merely extraneous, it would have destroyed "writing as it is written," and the rough quality in writing which proceeds from knowing a thing at the moment it is known. This roughness is not only the natural result of writing as it is written, it is the primary means the audience has of coming to know something. It is evident in the practice of artists since Cezanne who leave bare patches of canvas, or mere suggestions of relationships, compelling the spectator to collaborate actively for "completion." The same roughness is evident in the line of a sketch which charts the movement of an artist's hand and eye and draws the spectator to the very moment of composition. It is a palpable clue of the author's perspective. Stein has written:

> Ordinarily anybody finishes anything.
> But not in writing. In writing not any one finishes anything. That is what makes a masterpiece what it is that there is no finishing.[32]

> In a novel in a play no matter what it is that happens it is hoped that nothing will be smoothed over that every minute of that novel there is a beginning and ending that always any personality that anyone has there is one that no one can ever change into something that anyone can recover from.
> And the reason why is this. The more a novel is a novel the more a play is a play the more a writing is a writing the more no outside is outside outside is inside inside is inside.[33]

The "outside" shape of the work must proceed directly and organically from the "inside" content, that is, the disengaged present.

Time

The evolution of strategies for composition of a literature to correspond directly with the "now" — the exact moment of her perception — was Gertrude Stein's singular purpose during the first half of the twentieth century. Her resulting writing style represents a rejection of the Western literary tradition based on Aristotelian concepts of progressive time, causality, and single point perspective. As she explains:

> Each period of time not only has its contemporary quality, but it has a time-sense. Things move more quickly, slowly, or differently, from one generation to another. Take the Nineteenth Century. The Nineteenth Century was roughly the Englishman's Century. And their method, as they themselves, in their worst moments, speak of it, is that of "muddling through." They begin at one end and hope to come out at the other;

their grammar, parts of speech, methods of talk, go with this fashion. The United States began a different phase when, after the Civil War, they discovered and created out of their inner need a different way of life. They created the Twentieth Century. The United States, instead of having the feeling of beginning at one end and ending at another, had the conception of assembling the whole thing out of its parts, the whole thing which made the Twentieth Century productive. The Twentieth Century conceived the automobile as a whole, so to speak, and then created it, built it up out of its parts. It was an entirely different point of view from the Nineteenth Century. The Nineteenth Century would have seen the parts, and worked toward the automobile through them. Now in a funny sort of way this expresses, in different terms, the difference between the literature of the Nineteenth Century and the literature of the Twentieth. . . . in *The Making of Americans* I had this idea of a whole thing. But if you think of contemporary English writers, it doesn't work like that at all. They conceive it as pieces put together to make a whole, and I conceive it as a whole made up of its parts. I didn't know what I was doing anymore than you know, but in response to the needs of my period I was doing this thing.[34]

The nineteenth century's developmental time was reflected in its intricately plotted novels with their causally related events, melodramatic scenes, climaxes, and resolutions. Within such works, an ideal eye operating from a single, fixed perspective views parts progressively, element by element, until enough elements combine to make a whole. Combination is the key word here, the style relying less on the particular elements than on the ways in which they are combined. The progressive sequence builds at the expense of the work's constituent elements, which are necessarily altered to fall in line with it, and results in the impression that the significance of a work is buried in its ending, or in its development, rather than in its elements. The constituent elements serve, on the contrary, as mere stepping stones, drawing their identity from relations with surrounding elements and the singular perspective of the viewer, wherever it is placed. As Stein would say, the constituent elements of the nineteenth-century work lack entity. In addition, each element is in no way an adequate expression of the present moment. A full expression of the moment is suspended, rather, over a group of elements.

Gertrude Stein felt obliged to adopt a twentieth-century viewpoint of time as soon as she sensed what it was. According to her, the new century had no interest in events:

One thing which came to me is that the Twentieth Century gives of itself a feeling of movement, and has in its way no feeling of events. To the Twentieth Century events are not important. You must know that. . . . I was struck with it during the war: the average dough-boy standing on a street corner doing nothing—(they say, at the end of their doing nothing, "I guess I'll go home")—was much more exciting to people than when the soldiers went over the top. The populace were passionately interested in their standing on street corners, more so than in the St. Mihiel drive. And it is a perfectly natural thing. Events had got so continuous that the fact that events were taking place no longer stimulated anybody. . . . People are interested in existence.[35]

To capture this new, static universe in her writing, Stein approached it moment by moment, changing, in effect, perspective as the moment changed. As a result, her literature contains elements that do not combine, but isolate, as the following passage from *Old and Old* (1913) demonstrates:

> A whole eggs in stout muds. A vest sand, a lime eater, a cold saw, a kind of stammer, a little shade, a new opera glass, a colored mule, a best winter, a spoon, a wetness, a jelly, a window and a fruit season and a ripe pear and a point in pudding in a pudding being a pudding and sometime anytime, in being a pudding and necessary and reasonable and mostly judicious and particularly flattering and seasoned, really seasoned and almost always too bad.[36]

Contrary to the old work which buried its significance in its conclusion, the new work harbors it within each constituent element. In Stein's own terminology, the new artwork is "flat."

> The masterpieces always flatten it out, flatten human nature out so that there is no beginning and middle and ending, because if there is not then there is no doing and if there is no doing then there is no human nature.[37]

> The human mind has neither identity nor time and when it sees anything has to look flat. That is what makes a masterpiece what it is.[38]

> When you look at anything and you do not see it all in one plane, you do not see it with the human mind.[39]

The clearest example of a flat perspective is in the work of the cubists, who, as Wylie Sypher states,

> broke open the volumes of things by spreading objects upon shifting interrelated planes that did not violate the surface of the canvas, the space at the disposal of the painter as painter. This flat perspective meant also that painting would reintegrate itself with the wall, which could be treated like a cinematic screen.[40]

Just as the cubists avoided leading the eye away from the surface of the canvas, so Stein avoided leading it away from the surface — the particular moment — of the writing.

The full attention to the non-eventful moment and the lack of development in the work which issues from it was characterized by Stein and her critics as a "continuous present." This style did not emerge in one piece; in fact, Stein's writing in the eight years prior to *The Making of Americans* in 1911 was characterized as a "prolonged present" in which each successive moment was a slight variation of the preceding one, building toward the end for a total effect. Similar to the management of time one finds in Beckett, Faulkner, and Joyce, this method depended upon memory, and Stein abandoned it as her concepts of human nature and human mind solidified:

I wrote a Negro story called *Melanctha*. In that there was a constant recurring and beginning there was a marked direction in the direction of being in the present although naturally I had been accustomed to past present and future, and why, because the composition forming around me was a prolonged present...I created then a prolonged present naturally I knew nothing of a continuous present but it came naturally to me to make one, it was simple it was clear to me and nobody knew why it was done like that, I did not myself although naturally to me it was natural.[41]

Beckett and Faulkner rely on developmental structure: their novels and plays progress from point a to point b. Stein might argue that they remain one step behind the actual moment. Bruce Kawin has written:

Faulkner felt that once he had said it all, he would be finished writing; the Unnamable expects that once he is said, he will be able to be still; but life does not stop at being said: it continues to grow and change; Stein knew that "it all" needs always to be said anew, as it all is always new.[42]

Donald Sutherland has distinguished between the prolonged and continuous present in this fashion:

A prolonged present asserts a theme and then proceeds to complicate and elaborate it, in the manner of a fugal theme in Bach, so that the presence of the original theme, no matter how elaborately overlaid with variations, is maintained or prolonged as a going existence in each present passage or moment. It is as if one counted one two three four five six and so on, where the original unit of one is prolonged and present in the other figures in which it remains a component. But a continuous present...would be one in which each unit, even if identical or nearly with the previous one, is still, in its present, a completely self-contained thing, as when you say one and one, the second one is a completely present existence in itself, and does not depend, as two or three does, on a preceding one or two...[It] arrives in a continuous present, that is, the present is so continuous it does not allow any retrospect or expectation.[43]

And Stein herself compared her continuous present to the cinema:

In the beginning I continued to do what I was doing in the Making of Americans, I was doing what the cinema was doing, I was making a continuous succession of the statement of what that person was until I had not many things but one thing.... I said what I knew as they said and heard what they heard and said until I had completely emptied myself of all they were that is all that they were in being one hearing and saying what they heard and said in every way that they heard and said anything.[44]

Simultaneity, a concept promulgated by Stein's friend and associate Guillaume Apollinaire during the "banquet years" of 1885–1918, shared the stillness, the lack of overt movement between moments, of Stein's continuous present. It was a stillness accomplished largely through an absence of conventional transition, a characteristic element of traditional Western literature, applying, as Roger Shattuck says, to those works that rely upon clear articulation of the relations between parts at the places they join: connection at the edges (though other, inner connections may exist as well). It means one event, one sensation, one thing at a time, and is the effective result of the great Renaissance disciplines.... The copulative function of language used classically made every transition smooth and clear. In painting, linear perspective related every object to every other object along imaginary lines representing space. The whole "classic" idea of style in art arose from the undisputed supremacy of transition. It ruled that in any artistic experiment, each point must follow from the last.[45]

The supremacy of transition was challenged in the new age by Cezanne and the cubists in art, by Webern, Satie, Schoenberg, and Berg in music, and by Apollinaire and Stein in literature. Most of their work, however, should perhaps not be characterized as lacking transition so much as transforming transitive modes into substantive ones. William James suggested that transitive parts of speech should not be used as mere "connectors," but should be elevated to the status of substantives. They were at least as important, if not more, since his "stream of consciousness" inhered in transition, in "going on":

The first and foremost concrete fact which every one will affirm to belong to his inner experience is the fact that consciousness of some sort goes on. "States of mind" succeed each other in him.[46]

Grammar, according to James, should reflect this movement:

We ought to say a feeling of *and*, a feeling of *if*, a feeling of *but*, and a feeling of *by*, quite as readily as we say a feeling of *blue* or a feeling of *cold*. Yet we do not: so inveterate has our habit become of recognizing the substantive parts alone, that language almost refuses to lend itself to any other use.[47]

Substantive states of consciousness involve memory, as James has pointed out, while transitive states are too fleeting to last:

For a state of mind to survive in memory it must have endured for a certain length of time. In other words, it must be what I call a substantive state. Prepositional and conjuctival states of mind are not remembered as independent facts.[48]

Stein, concerned as much as James was with separating memory from attention, followed his suggestion by treating transitives as substantive parts of the sentence. She favored them no less than other parts, striving for an evenness throughout her writing:

Letting pin in letting let in let in in in in let in let in wet in wed in dead in dead wed led in led wed dead in dead in led in wed in said in said led wed dead wed dead said led led said wed dead wed dead led in led in wed in wed in said in wed in led in said in dead in dead wed said led led said wed dead in. [*Four Saints in Three Acts*][49]

> She writes excusing herself.
> But which may they do.
> Oh yes they do.
> Bertha Haviland has been held by her arm. Or they may go.
> Augusta Blaine for which they are well as they are well if they wish.
>
> [*A Manoir*][50]

These passages contain no transitions or connections as such, though transitive elements of grammar are used as substantives; they build not at the expense of their integral elements, but to their greater integrity. The purpose is to express not "identity," but "entity."

James's stream of consciousness did not interest Stein as much as her fixed consciousness: she wanted above all to render the exact moment of perception without exceeding the moment. At the same time, she wanted these static moments to be dynamic, like the existence of the doughboy on the street corner and the wandering lines of Masson seen from an airplane. This characteristic of Stein's art she called "self-contained movement," and it was an integral part of her aesthetic from *The Making of Americans*, completed in 1911, to the end of her career.

> I had to find out inside everyone what was in them that was intrinsically exciting and I had to find out not by what they said not by what they did not by how much or how little they resembled any other one but I had to find it out by the intensity of movement that there was inside in any one of them.[51]
>
> As I say a motor goes inside and the car goes on, but my business my ultimate business as an artist was not with where the car goes as it goes but with the movement inside that is of the essence of its going.[52]

It reached its culmination for Stein in later works of the 1920s–1940s, which were conceived entirely as self-contained movement:

> Instead of giving what I was realizing at any and every moment of them and of me until I was empty of them I made them contained within the thing I wrote that was them. The thing folded itself up inside itself like you might fold a thing up to be another thing which is that thing inside in that thing. If you think how you fold things or make a boat or anything else out of paper or getting anything to be inside anything, the hole in the doughnut or the apple in the dumpling perhaps you will see what I mean.[53]

Like a top which spins to the point of stillness, these works become absorbed in their own dynamics. They are not based on reference to the outside world.

This vibration is characteristic of the smallest elements of Stein's style, and is nowhere more clear than in her use of grammar and syntax, both of which emphasize the dynamic character of her aesthetic without violating its stillness. As a twentieth-century writer, she felt that her "choice" of language was limited to words which had been for so long associated with static meanings that they were hardly adequate to describe the "now."

> A language tires.
> A language tries to be.
> A language tries to be free.[54]

She felt things had come to a point at which authors could no longer choose words, but were forced to use them to indicate the dead meanings they had come to have. She insisted upon getting back to the innocence of earlier times in which words were still fresh: "Think well of the English literature of the Sixteenth Century and see how they choose the words, they chose them with so much choice that everything made the song they chose to sing."[55]

Her largest targets were nouns; she found their meanings fixed, and thus incapable of sufficiently expressing the present. Adjectives, by virtue of their modification of nouns, suffered similar inadequacies. As substantives, they inevitably involved memory, inevitably recalled antiquated connotations she did not want them to have. She wanted to "flatten" them as she flattened the progressive sequence, depriving them of familiar associations and contexts. During her disenchantment with them she abandoned them almost entirely, preferring to use verbs and adverbs which, as transitives, did not involve memory, did not carry the weight of unwanted associations, and were open to new usages. In various combinations they could come to have the freshness she desired:

> I recognize verbs and adverbs aided by prepositions and conjunctions with pronouns as possessing the whole of the active life of writing.[56]

> Verbs and adverbs are more interesting. In the first place they have one very nice quality and that is that they can be so mistaken. . . Nouns and adjectives never can make mistakes can never be mistaken but verbs can be so endlessly, both as to what they do and how they agree or disagree with whatever they do. The same is true of adverbs. . .
> Beside being able to be mistaken and to make mistakes verbs can change to look like themselves or to look like something else, they are, so to speak on the move and adverbs move with them and each of them find themselves not at all annoying but very often very much mistaken. That is the reason any one can like what verbs can do. Then comes the thing that can of all things be most mistaken and they are prepositions. Prepositions can live one long life being really being nothing but absolutely nothing but mistaken. . .
> Then there are articles. . . They are interesting because they do what a noun might do if a noun was not so unfortunately so completely unfortunately the name of something. Articles please, a and an and the please as the name that follows cannot please. They the names that is the nouns cannot please, because after all you know well after all that is what Shakespeare meant when he talked about a rose by any other name. . .
> Beside that there are conjunctions, and a conjunction is not varied but it has a force

that need not make any one feel that they are dull. Conjunctions have made themselves live by their work...

Of course there are pronouns. Pronouns are not as bad as nouns because in the first place practically they cannot have adjectives go with them. That already makes them better than nouns.

Then beside not being able to have adjectives go with them, they of course are not really the name of anything.[57]

Adverbs, verbs, prepositions, conjunctions, pronouns, and articles were capable of inherent movement. Unlike nouns and adjectives, which carried the weight of three centuries of meaning, these parts of speech were, for Stein, effectively disengaged from any rigid meaning, entities in their own right. By their ability to be "mistaken"—that is, by not being necessarily connected with a particular image or associated with "dead" meanings of long standing—and by appearing to modify more than one word, they kept the moment dynamic without exceeding it.

The literary unit which corresponded to the moment of perception was not always the word, however. By the time she wrote *Four Saints in Three Acts* in 1927 Stein had, in her words, "in hundreds of ways related words, then sentences, then paragraphs at the thing at which I was looking."[58] Her sentence, by virtue of its lack of transition, did not entail development or its inevitable concomitant, emotion. The paragraph did.

A sentence is not emotional a paragraph is.[59]

A succession if it has a beginning and middle and an ending as a paragraph has does form create and limit an emotion.[60]

The sentence was an entity capable of capturing the moment without exceeding it:

Sentences are contained within themselves and anything really contained within itself has no beginning middle or end.[61]

It existed by "internal balancing,"[62] requiring the addition of no other sentence to balance it. But a writer must inevitably face the consequence of putting one sentence down beside another to form a paragraph, and for Stein, the consequence of doing so was problematic. She proceeded to search for a method by which she could use the paragraph developmentally without destroying the internally balanced sentence and the integrity of the moment. She thought eventually that she discovered:

Something that had neither the balance of a sentence nor the balance of a paragraph but a balance a new balance that had to do with a sense of movement of time included in a given space which as I have already said is a definitely American thing.[63]

First, she fashioned long sentences which "had no longer the balance of sentences because they were not the parts of a paragraph nor were they a paragraph:"[64]

> Cold wets and cold woods and cold cow harness and cold in the stretch and more pleasing reason with the cheque in the book and a dress and a dress and a medium choice and a blooming chest and a passing supper and a little cheese and a white a white and a wet white tool and a pole and a straw and a little chicking bean and a little toe white and a little cow soon.[65]

Later she condensed further and composed shorter, more assured segments:

> He looks like a young man grown old.[66]

> A dog which you have never met before has sighed.[67]

> Once when they were nearly ready they had ordered it to close.[68]

These sentences display a combination of sentence balance and paragraph development, the former existing in the tension exhibited between all sentence elements, and the latter, in the juxtaposition of tenses provided by the clauses within the sentences. They are, first and foremost, spatial entities which contain time, and, like her writing as a whole, are more amenable to spatial than temporal analysis. Like the motor that moves without going anywhere, Stein's sentences move without leading to another sentence, even though they are arranged side-by-side. The sentence and paragraph, then, not only the word, became literary units corresponding to the human mind's moment of perception.

After the new balance of sentence and paragraph had been struck and condensed, nouns and adjectives were readmitted in a very special sense:

> But after I had gone as far as I could in these long sentences and paragraphs that had come to do something else I then began very short things and in doing very short things I resolutely realized nouns and decided not to get around them but to meet them, to handle in short to refuse them by using them.[69]

In that notorious line "a rose is a rose is a rose is a rose," for example, she "caressed completely caressed and addressed a noun"[70] with the result that "the rose is red for the first time in English poetry for a hundred years."[71] She "refused" the noun by repeating it until its associative meanings were lost and the thing itself could emerge, intensified. It was an activity generally reserved for poetry, and it was well represented in *Tender Buttons,* completed in 1912:

> The time when there are four choices and there are four choices in a difference, the
> time when there are four choices there is a kind and there is a kind. There is a kind.
> There is a kind. Supposing there is a bone, there is a bone. Supposing there are bones.
> There are bones. When there are bones there is no supposing there are bones. There are
> bones and there is that consuming.[72]

Stein believed she had by 1927 rendered the dynamic, present moment
without exceeding its confines through the use of words, self-contained
sentences and paragraphs, and through verbs as well as nouns.[73] According
to her, she had by then achieved the "self-contained movement" central to
her aesthetic, the goal she set for herself in 1911. By giving its full attention
to the new dynamic-static universe, Stein's human mind, she felt, captured
the world as it is, at each moment that it is.

Entity

> Anyone being one is one. Anything put down is something. Anything being down is
> something and being that thing it is something and being something it is a thing and
> being a thing it is not anything and not being anything it is everything and being that
> thing it is a thing and being that thing it is that thing. Being that thing it is that thing
> and being that thing it is coming to be a thing having been that thing and coming to be a
> thing having been that thing it is a thing being a thing it is a thing being that thing.[74]

In breaking up time into isolated moments for observation, the human
mind necessarily isolates the things residing within those moments, disengaging them from any context or association not born of the moment. As
Stein said, "being a relation is not a necessary thing."[75]

> The minute it means anything, it has nothing to do with the human mind, with human
> nature yes, but not with the way the earth is and looks and not with the human mind.[76]

> And the writing that is the human mind does not consist in messages or events it con-
> sists only in what is written and therefore it has no relation to human nature.[77]

Stein conceived of each element of a composition as complete entity: an
end-in-itself which requires no action from any other element for completion. As we have seen in her use of transitives, this results in an equal distribution of attention throughout the composition:

> Everything I have done has been influenced by Flaubert and Cezanne, and this gave
> me a new feeling about composition. Up to that time composition had consisted of a
> central idea, to which everything else was an accompaniment and separate but was not
> an end in itself, and Cezanne conceived the idea that in composition one thing was as
> important as another thing. Each part is as important as the whole, and that impressed
> me enormously....You see I tried to convey the idea of each part of a composition
> being as important as the whole. It was the first time in any language that anyone had

used that idea of composition in literature. Henry James had a slight inkling of it and was in some senses a forerunner, while in my case I made it stay on the page quite composed...

After all, to me one human being is as important as another human being, and you might say that the landscape has the same values, a blade of grass has the same value as a tree.[78]

This concept stems from her personal reflection upon the twentieth century landscape, a landscape so large and so diverse that its elements isolate temporally and spatially from one another. It is a landscape without inherent sequence or causal connection in which the isolated present moment, whatever it may contain, is all that is tangible:

If the stars are suns and the earth is earth and there are men only upon this earth and anything can put an end to anything and any dog does everything like anybody does it what is the difference between eternity and anything.[79]

That is to say, there is no difference between eternity and anything if all we can know of eternity resides in the present moment. As Stein's friend Alfred North Whitehead reasoned, "the part evidently is constitutive of the whole...the whole is evidently constitutive of the part."[80]

Stein's human mind is concerned with direct knowledge of the entity of a thing, a concern shared by William James, who distinguished in his theory of consciousness between "acquaintance" and "knowledge about:"

Knowledge about a thing is knowledge of its relations. Acquaintance with it is limitation to the bare impression which it makes.[81]

Stein uses a similar idea in reference to *Tender Buttons*:

I try to call to the eye the way it appears by suggestion the way a painter can do it. This is difficult and takes a lot of work and concentration to do it. I want to indicate it without calling in other things.[82]

She hoped that she could acquaint herself with a thing in an absolute sense; that is, not have to depend for full knowledge on the relations she remembers the thing to have with other things. In this sense, her knowledge of the thing strives for the absolute and not the relative. She tried to capture not the world and its relations (what it means, how it progresses) but the world in itself (how it is) moment by moment. To her, this would result in a literature that was more accurate, more objective, and less fleeting:

If it were possible that a movement were lively enough it would exist so completely that it would not be necessary to see it moving against anything to know that it is moving. This is what we mean by life and in my way I have tried to make portraits of this thing.[83]

She hoped that her concentration would uncover the essential nature of the isolated object. Henri Bergson's distinction between "intuition" and "analysis" can help to illuminate this:

> The absolute, which is the object and not its representation, the original and not its translation, is perfect, being perfectly what it is. . . . it follows from this that an absolute could only be given in an *intuition*, whilst everything else falls within the province of analysis. By intuition is meant the kind of *intellectual sympathy* by which one places oneself within an object in order to coincide with what is unique in it and consequently inexpressible. Analysis, on the contrary, is the operation which reduces the objects to elements already known, that is, to elements common both to it and other objects. To analyze, therefore, is to express a thing as a function of something other than itself. All analysis is thus a translation, a development into symbols, a representation taken from successive points of view from which we note as many resemblances as possible between the new object which we are studying and others which we believe we know already.[84]

The result of such specialized knowledge is that the object is not described or imitated, but in the words of Bergson, "touched and penetrated:"

> A true empiricism is that which proposes to get as near to the original itself as possible, to search deeply into its life, and so, by a kind of *intellectual auscultation*, to feel the throbbing of its soul.[85]

Gertrude Stein, unlike Bergson, believed that the unique quality of the object was not inherently inexpressible. She made it her lifelong task to capture that quality in language. But rather than transport the human mind into the thing to capture it, as Bergson suggested, Stein wished to transport the thing into the human mind.

Her definition of knowledge, it will be remembered, is "having [anything] completely in you at the moment that you have it."[86] Her initial impulse to control the world by drawing it within her gaze could allow nothing less, while her drive to dispassionately render the thing could allow nothing more. Once the thing is transported in this fashion, wrenched from its familiar context, the human mind can begin to see its essential character, what makes the thing what it is. That is what she means by entity.

Except for her first period of writing from 1903–1911, during which, as she states, "I became very interested in resemblances, in resemblances and very slight differences between people,"[87] Stein was more concerned with the peculiar quality of the thing than with the attributes it shared with a class of phenomena. As Stein has written, "That was for me the whole of *The Making of Americans,* it was the strengthening the prolonging of the existing of everything being inside in one."[88] She confined herself to an exploration of the entity, not the identity, of the thing, seeking to render the essence of the object, the "essence of the thing contained within itself:"[89]

I wrote portraits knowing that each one is themselves inside them and something about them perhaps everything about them will tell some one all about that thing all about what is themselves inside them.[90]

The realism of the people who did realism before me was a realism of trying to make people real. I was not interested in making the people real but, in the essence or, as a painter would call it, value. One cannot live without the other.[91]

In rendering a glass, for example, Stein would not be content to call it one but would seek to determine its unique quality—what makes it something as opposed to anything, a quality which could not be determined even through the most exhaustive attention to its external characteristics.

While casting about for a strategy through which she could successfully capture this unique quality, she encountered problems. Even her strict use of her chosen parts of speech was not enough, she felt, to capture the essential object, and as early as 1912 she began to "create without naming,"[92] "looking at anything until something that was not the name of that thing but was in a way that actual thing would come to be written."[93]

The result of this attempt was writing which was not in any sense a description of the object:

I became more and more excited about how words which were the words that made whatever I looked at look like itself were not the words that had in them any quality of description. This excited me very much at that time.

And the thing that excited me so very much at that time and still does is that the words or words that make what I looked at be itself were always words that to me very exactly related themselves to that thing the thing at which I was looking, but as often as not had as I say nothing whatever to do with what any words would do that described that thing.[94]

It was, rather, an embodiment of it, capturing the essential object so thoroughly that it subsumed it entirely. As Edward Burns put it, she describes

reality in terms of an iconography of such pervasive force that it commands aesthetically a position in the composition equal to the objects it describes. Gradually, the iconography becomes not the element that subsumes the composition, but itself the primary element out of which the composition is made.[95]

It is demonstrated well in *Tender Buttons*:

A CARAFE, THAT IS A BLIND GLASS

A kind in glass and a cousin, a spectacle and nothing strange a single hurt color and an arrangement in a system to pointing. All this and not ordinary, not unordered in not resembling. The difference is spreading.[96]

In capturing the thing in itself, the writing becomes so thoroughly separated from words that might describe the object, so meticulously parted from its familiar contexts, and so completely shorn of "associational emotion,"[97] that it comes, as much as any element of Stein's aesthetic, to have entity. Referring to nothing outside of itself, it concentrates on its own dynamics, spinning to the point of stillness.

The concept of entity led Stein quite naturally to a literature which expresses inherent value. By virtue of its intensity it attains a solidity as real as any thing in the world, as artificial as any artwork, and as isolated as any segment of her aesthetic. As Stein's friend, the cubist painter Juan Gris told Henri Kahnweiler, "My aim is to create new objects which cannot be compared to any other object in actuality.... My *violin*, being a creation, need fear no competition."[98] Or as Stein said of oil painting, "It must not only be in its frame but it must not, only, be in its frame."[99] It simultaneously exceeds and conforms to its boundaries, becoming more than an artwork (a thing in the world) by not referring to any reality but its own.

Stein has expressed her discomfort with artworks which do not share this balance, but which, once they are finished, do nothing but resemble the reality they describe. Such works reflect not entity but identity, depending for vitality upon their relationship to the world. Cazin, for example,

> made a field of wheat look almost like a field of wheat blowing in the wind. It did look like a field of wheat blowing in the wind and I was very fond of looking at fields of wheat blowing in the wind. In a little while I found myself getting a little mixed as to which looked most like a field of wheat blowing in the wind the picture of the field of wheat or the real field of wheat. When that happens one naturally gets discouraged. I may say one finally gets discouraged. One is not discouraged at first, one is confirmed in one's feeling about a field of wheat blowing in the wind and then gradually one is less pleased and at last one is discouraged. One does not like to be mixed in one's mind as to what looks most like something at which one is looking the thing or the painting. And so I rather lost interest in both.[100]

With Cezanne, however, there was no lack of interest:

> The apples looked like apples the chairs looked like chairs and it all had nothing to do with anything because if they did not look like apples or chairs or landscape or people they were apples and chairs and landscape and people. They were so entirely these things that they were not an oil painting and yet that is just what the Cezannes were they were an oil painting. They were so entirely an oil painting that it was all there whether they were finished, the paintings, or whether they were not finished.[101]

Such painting was the highest expression of Stein's concept of entity, a concept she insisted upon in any art:

> When I look at landscape or people or flowers they do not look to me like pictures, no not at all. On the other hand pictures for me do not have to look like flowers or people or landscapes or houses or anything else. They can, they often do, but they do not have to....the fact remains that for me it has achieved an existence in and for itself, it exists

on as being an oil painting on a flat surface and it has its own life and like it or not there it is and I can look at it and it does hold my attention.... Anything once it is made has its own existence and it is because of that that anything holds somebody's attention. The question always is about that anything, how much vitality has it and do you happen to like to look at it.[102]

Once created, the artwork needs resemblance to nothing, for it contains within itself the dynamics of Stein's art of stillness. No longer a window into another reality, it is an aspect of reality itself.

It is obvious that the more successfully this writing captures the thing in itself, the less it fulfills traditional demands of clarity. The human mind, whatever its special capacities, remains solely the mind of Gertrude Stein, and its perceptions of "essences" or of "words that...very exactly related themselves to that thing the thing at which I was looking" are very possibly not perceptions shared by or easily transmitted to her audience. But Stein's artwork, which contains, in effect, the thing within itself, commands that an audience face it or nothing. There is no object other than the word-object to refer it to. Ironically, then, it is precisely her objective approach to the essential thing which leads much of the world to regard Stein as incomprehensibly subjective, if not decadent. Her prevailing sentiment "if it can be done why do it?"[103] is testament to her dedication to the highest aims in her work, and indicates that her aesthetic may well have been devoted to the impossibility of simultaneously capturing a thing with the particularity she desired and allowing an audience to see it.

Stein's feelings about her audience, born of her original creation of a duality of human nature and human mind, were complicated ones. They led her on the one hand to dictate audience behavior within the framework of her aesthetic, and on the other hand to state to the *Partisan Review*:

An audience is pleasant if you have it, it is flattering and flattering is agreeable always, but if you have an audience the being an audience is their business, they are the audience you are the writer, let each attend to their own business.[104]

That she did not write with clarity for the audience in mind is plain from her thoughts on writing as it is written. A writer who concentrates upon her audience has no opportunity to concentrate on her work. Apart from some works written quite specifically for an audience—her "identity writing" of the 1930s, including such works as *The Autobiography of Alice B. Toklas* and *Everybody's Autobiography*—Stein wrote to fulfill no demands other than her own. Her regard for the object and her dedication to rendering its essential nature with precision took precedence over everything else:

Gertrude Stein, in her work, has always been possessed by the intellectual passion for exactitude in the description of inner and outer reality. She had produced a simplification by this concentration, and as a result the destruction of associational emotion in poetry and prose. She knows that beauty, music, decoration, the result of emotion should never be the cause of emotion nor should they be the material of poetry and prose. They should consist of an exact reproduction of either an outer or an inner reality.[105]

This is not to say that she ignored her audience. She sought to provide for communication with an audience in a way that would not compromise her concept of entity: by attaining clarity, paradoxical as it might seem, through opacity. According to Stein, no one can understand anyone else regardless of method or style of communication:

Nobody enters into the mind of someone else, not even a husband and wife. You may touch, but you do not enter into each other's mind. Why should you?[106]

She sought, in fact, a self-sufficient artwork which would capture a thing so completely that an encounter with it would be tantamount to an encounter with the thing itself. The artwork would impose itself directly on the audience with such force that the resulting confrontation would amount to an active experience comparable to Stein's own. It was force, not clarity, which was capable of transmitting knowledge to an audience:

Mr. Owen Young made a mistake, he said the only thing he wished his son to have was the power of clearly expressing his ideas. Not at all. It is not clarity that is desired but force. Clarity is of no importance because nobody listens and nobody knows what you mean no matter what you mean, nor how clearly you know what you mean. But if you have vitality enough of knowing enough of what you mean, somebody and sometime and sometimes a great many will have to realize that you know what you mean and so will agree that you mean what you know, what you know you mean, which is as near as anybody can come to understanding anyone.[107]

This was an aesthetic concept rooted in her perception of the new age, one in which, she felt, clarity failed to clarify. Stein noted in *Everybody's Autobiography* that the Oriental tradition was penetrating Europe:

I used to think the name of anybody was very important and the name made you and I have often said so. Perhaps I still think so but still there are so many names and anybody nowadays can call anybody any name they like. Sometimes the name they say they are has nothing to do with what they are they may have borrowed or gambled away their reference and they seem to be there or not there as well with any name and any way the Oriental, and perhaps a name there is not a name, is invading the Western world. It is the peaceful penetration that is important not wars.[108]

Changes in physics wrought by relativity theory and quantum theory had likewise eroded the possibility, even the value, of clarity. Absolute knowledge of an object, knowledge true at all times for all viewers, was reduced to subjective knowledge of a single aspect of the object, which has a tendency to exist, from a single point of view at a moment in time. Transmission of knowledge from one viewer to another is theoretically impossible, since viewers cannot share perspectives. Also, quantum theory had undermined the concept of the solid object, making perception of the object tantamount to perception of force.[109] In the dynamic universe of Einstein and Stein, force has priority over clarity. In the rigid, predictable Newtonian world, clarity reigned.

Clarity is associated by Stein with memory; it does not exist in "writing as it is written:"

> If you do not remember while you are writing, it may seem confused to others but actually it is clear and eventually that clarity will be clear that is what a masterpiece is, and if you remember while you are writing it will seem clear at the time to anyone but the clarity will go out of it that is what a masterpiece is not.[110]

The use of memory amounts to an explanation of the thing, not a forceful grasp of it, and explanations have nothing to do with the thing or with true clarity:

> Explanations are clear but since no one to whom a thing is explained can connect the explanations with what is really clear, therefore explanations are not clear. Now this is a simple thing that anybody who has ever argued or quarreled knows perfectly well is a simple thing, only when they read it they do not understand it because they do not see that understanding and believing are not the same thing.[111]

Explaining, after all, merely posits relations without touching the thing itself. She sought not to explain things, but to write things. Explanations, like commas,

> by helping you along holding your coat for you and putting on your shoes keeps you from living your life as actively as you should lead it.[112]

The artwork which avoids explanation should force itself upon an audience, like the sentence which lacks a comma —

> a long complicated sentence should force itself upon you, make you know yourself knowing it and the comma, well at most a comma is a poor period that it lets you stop and take a breath.[113]

The audience directly contacts the artwork as it unfolds, experiencing it as thoroughly as the human mind does the object of its attention. In the words of John Dewey, "to perceive, a beholder must create his own experience. And his creation must include relations comparable to those the original producer underwent."[114] The beholder comes to know the artwork in the same fashion in which Stein comes to know the thing: by disengaging himself from the passage of time to recognize it.

> Literature is the telling of anything but in telling that thing where is the audience. There is an audience of course there is an audience but where is that audience. Undoubtedly that audience has to be there for the purpose of recognition as the telling is proceeding to be written and that audience must be at one with the writing, must be at one with the recognition, must have nothing of knowing anything before or after the recognition.[115]

Conclusion

Born of her unflinching confrontation with the century in which she lived, Stein's concepts of time and entity culminated in writing which made a pure attempt to express that reality. Divorced from concerns of psychology, sociology, morality—from anything, in short, which did not directly proceed from the moment of perception, and freed from the altering effects of time, it was completely dedicated to the perception of the "now." By the disconnected arrangement of such moments she hoped to attain a total lack of progression, an art of stillness.

These concepts, although they naturally evolved over time, were established in general terms by 1911, at which time the continuous present, the self-contained movement, and stringent application of language typical of Stein's mature writing were beginning to emerge. In works of the 1920s–1940s the dynamics of self-contained movement intensified, resulting more and more in works which captured with precision the thing in itself and which, therefore, became more and more self-referring. Though these later works effectively embodied Stein's concept of entity through their forceful grasp of the object, the entire body of her work after 1911 reflected it.

The literature of Gertrude Stein, insofar as it conforms to its program of entity, is an absolute art, possessing *aseity*, or self-existence, as opposed to relations with the world. It exhibits an aestheticism in which the thing, the touchstone of her art, is finally superseded by the complete work.

2

Playwriting Aesthetic

Gertrude Stein and the Theatre

Gertrude Stein's oft-expressed lack of interest and commitment to the theatre, outside of her cloistered penmanship of 77 plays, is summed up in this passage from the lecture entitled "Plays" in *Lectures in America*:

> I practically when I wrote my first play had completely ceased going to the theatre. In fact although I have written a great many plays and I am quite sure they are plays I have since I commenced writing these plays I have practically never been inside of any kind of a theatre. Of course none of this has been intentional, one may say generally speaking that anything that is really inevitable, that is to say necessary is not intentional.[1]

She entered the theatre as a *naïf* and considered it, as much as she did literature, a wholly solitary pastime. In 1920 she declared in *Coal and Wood*, "I do not care to see plays. I like to write plays."[2] In *Everybody's Autobiography* she modified this: "and really there is no use in going to see a thing if you have not written it no use at all."[3] Such sentiments run counter to the notion of theatre as a collective experience, but they are entirely consonant with Stein's concept of communication in the modern world, established in Chapter one:

> In a created thing it means more to the writer than it means to the reader. It can only mean something to one person and that person the one who wrote it.[4]

While she knew personally many theatrical figures,[5] she skirted professional association with all but Avery Hopwood, to whom she dedicated *A List* (1923), and upon whose *The Demi-Virgin* she based her own *Saints and Singing* (1922). But she counted herself in the company of no playwright. Of her association with Hopwood, Virgil Thomson said, "I doubt very much if they talked about how to write a play. He wouldn't have told her how to write a play and she wouldn't have asked."[6] Thomson continued:

> After all, Gertrude was not part of a playwright's club...She was a literary woman
> interested in the theatre, but in the theatre as a memory and an idea.... She did not
> think of herself as a professional playwright. She thought of herself as a professional
> novelist and poet. In that case, theatre would have been a form or medium which she
> took on casually and by reference and by privilege, but not with any obligation to a
> paying audience, which she didn't have anyway.[7]

Virgil Thomson's own collaboration with her as composer of her operas
Capital Capitals, Four Saints in Three Acts, and *The Mother of Us All* was
initiated by him in the winter of 1925–1926;[8] he appeared at her door with
a setting for voice and piano of her portrait, "Susie Asado." But even their
association was not a true collaboration. As Thomson said of their work
on *Four Saints in Three Acts*:

> She didn't work with me, and I didn't work with her. We agreed on what we were going
> to make it about and then she had to do her work and then I had to do mine. It was not
> a constant adjustment in terms of theatrical production, as libretto and opera writing
> often is.[9]

Stein's isolation from theatre was deliberate, her indifference to it,
pronounced. In *Lectures in America* she addressed the question directly:

> As I say everybody has to like something, some people like to eat some people like to
> drink, some people like to make money some like to spend money, some like the
> theatre...Anyway some one is almost sure to really like something outside of their real
> occupation...and I, personally, I like all these things well enough but they do not hold
> my attention long enough. The only thing, funnily enough, that I never get tired of
> doing is looking at pictures.[10]

She did not consider theatre to be her métier. As she wrote of herself in
The Autobiography of Alice B. Toklas in the persona of Alice:

> She is passionately addicted to what the French call métier and she contends that one
> can only have one métier as one can only have one language. Her métier is writing and
> her language is English...
> She says it is a good thing to have no sense of how it is done in the things that amuse
> you. You should have one absorbing occupation and as for the other things in life for
> full enjoyment you should only contemplate results. In this way you are bound to feel
> more about it than those who know a little of how it is done.[11]

She professed to know nothing about the intricacies of staging plays. In
Byron a Play (1933), where she cavorts with play definitions, she attests to
her faith in the production expertise of others: "A play is this. They manage to stage this."[12] Her absolute faith in those who undertook productions
of her plays allowed Virgil Thomson's extensive internal cutting of *Four
Saints in Three Acts* in 1934; she told him, "the burden of making it a suc-

cessful performance lies upon you."[13] She rewrote substantially *Yes is for a Very Young Man* at the request of Lamont Johnson and the group of amateur actors connected with the Pasadena Playhouse to whom she had given production rights in 1945. Still, as her plays received more attention in the theatre, she began to think more in terms of production, and wrote some texts, particularly during the thirties and forties, which display some knowledge of theatrical conventions.

We may associate this progression with her move toward a greater use of narrative in her plays which, as Stein explained it, was writing according to someone else's point of view. Prior to this move, her texts were explorations, distillations, and projections of her own experience — written not necessarily for actors, directors, or anyone other than herself. During the late narrative years, she was not entirely lacking in critical awareness of the productions her plays were receiving. She abruptly withdrew permission from the American Army's Biarritz University production when she learned that *Yes* would be given merely a workshop production for a specially invited audience. That group meant to force it into a symbolic or mystical mold, but she insisted upon its reality and simplicity.[14]

Still, the bulk of her late plays can hardly be considered conventional. Her sure sense of her own plays was coupled, even then, with a permeating naïveté about the theatre evident in her delight in the *Yes* curtain calls:

> I kept asking everybody is eight curtain calls an awful lot and everybody kept telling me yes it is an awful lot, I knew it was but I wanted everybody to tell me that it was.[15]

Her innocence at this late stage of her career branded her an imposter to those who view a playwright unversed in production techniques as no playwright at all. But Stein's break from theatrical tradition was part and parcel of her break from any kind of tradition, and was typical of new experiments in any art. The respected Jean Cocteau, in his preface to *The Eiffel Tower Wedding Party*, spoke for Stein as much as he did for himself:

> The poet ought to disengage objects and ideas from their veiling mists; he ought to display them suddenly, so nakedly and so quickly that they are scarcely recognizable. It is that they strike us with their youth, as though they had never become official dotards.[16]

Playwriting Aesthetic

Stein's resolute lack of involvement and expertise in theatre practice leads inevitably to questions concerning her motives for writing plays in the first place. But isolated as she was from other theatricians, she undertook to write plays neither carelessly nor gratuitously. The timing of her entrance into theatre would seem to indicate that she did so for the effect it would have upon her emerging style.

By 1912 she had arrived at the beginning of what she considered to be her second phase of writing.[17] Through such works as *The Making of Americans* and, most particularly, *Tender Buttons*, she broke from the prolonged present and description of relations characteristic of her first phase of writing and began to forge her concepts of the continuous present and entity, as described in Chapter one. Concomitant with this break came a change in approach from "listening and talking at the same time"[18] to what she was satisfied to call "including looking."[19] "Listening and talking" was Stein's phrase for the concentration with which she was able to capture a thing in the present moment. As she stated in "Portraits and Repetition:"

> Nothing makes any difference as long as some one is listening while they are talking. If the same person does the talking and the listening why so much the better there is just by so much the greater concentration. One may really indeed say that that is the essence of genius, of being most intensely alive, that is being one who is at the same time talking and listening. It is really that that makes one a genius. And it is necessary if you are to be really and truly alive it is necessary to be at once talking and listening, doing both things, not as if there were one thing, not as if they were two things, but doing them, well if you like, like the motor going inside and the car moving, they are part of the same thing.[20]

But having firmly established the technique of "talking and listening" in her portraits, she found that she still had not adequately solved the problem of "remembering:"

> I had the habit of conceiving myself as completely talking and listening, listening was talking and talking was listening and in so doing I conceived what I at that time called the rhythm of anybody's personality. If listening was talking and talking was listening then and at the same time any little movement any little expression was a resemblance, and a resemblance was something that presupposed remembering.[21]

> Then slowly once more I got bothered, after all I listened and talked but that was not all I did in knowing at any present time when I was stating anything what anything was. I was also looking, and that could not be entirely left out.
> The trouble with including looking...was that in regard to human beings looking inevitably carried in its train realizing movements and expression and as such forced me into recognizing resemblances, and so forced remembering and in forcing remembering caused confusion of present with past and future time.[22]

But looking was what she had to solve in order to render the present moment:

> I had the feeling that something should be included and that something was looking, and so concentrating on looking I did the Tender Buttons because it was easier to do objects than people if you were just looking.[23]

Stein's first play was written in 1913, within a year after she found the way to combine the continuous present, entity, and "looking" in *Tender Buttons.*

When she wrote her last play in 1946, these concepts were still in effect. As Donald Sutherland stated:

> The problem of *Tender Buttons,* that of a thing existing in itself, of an absolute and absolutely present literary work, was the problem which dominated all of her later writing, even when it returned to reporting and ordinary intelligibility.[24]

The plays as a group are tied to the very concepts of time and entity evident in her other work. The distinction between the genres lay in the extent to which the theatrical medium was able to realize them. A comment she made in *Photograph* may well indicate her view of the matter:

> I can sigh to play.
> I can sigh for a play.
> A play means more.[25]

The theatre's concreteness, its relational movement within the limitations of the performance, and its purely present existence could not help but strengthen her concepts of entity and time. Those concepts had emerged in relation to literature, but she could incarnate them for the theatre in a way that literature never would. What better way of "giving what I was realizing at any and every moment of them and of me until I was empty of them"[26] — and of having it directly and immediately perceived by an audience as it occurred — than to do it through the theatre? What better way to insist upon the entity of a work than to isolate it from the world in a finite space and present its solid reality to an audience? What better way to preserve the internal vitality of a static art than to give it a live performance exhibiting spatial dynamics?

Gertrude Stein perceived the essential elements of theatre in just this fashion. To begin with, she equated plays with their embodiment on the stage, believing that their sheer physicality outweighed any other considerations. Anticipating a major tenet of the contemporary theatre, she insisted upon the entity of the theatrical experience. In the words of Tom Driver, the theatre "is its own positive datum and is fulfilled in the degree that it is concrete."[27] In Stein's inimitable lexicon:

> What is a play?
> A play is scenery.[28]

If a play depends for its existence upon sequentially numbered and logically partitioned acts and scenes, a linear story, and clearly marked boundaries between it and life—in short, upon conventions insuring effectiveness which are not necessary to achieve communication with an audience—then Stein wrote no plays at all. But such a conception of plays has never been absolute. Since the very origins of theatre, it has been clear that vital theatrical forms thrive without any text whatever. The notion of a play as performance score, as opposed to a self-sufficient literary text, gained wide acceptance beginning with the theatrical avant-garde of 1887-94.[29] By 1922 Jean Cocteau was speaking in favor of a theatrical theatre, one in which the poetry *of* the theatre overcame poetry *in* the theatre. As he described *The Eiffel Tower Wedding Party*:

> The action of my piece is pictorial, though the text itself is not. The fact is that I am trying to substitute a "theatre poetry" for the usual "poetry in the theatre." "Poetry in the theatre" is a delicate lace, invisible at any considerable distance. "Theatre poetry" should be coarse lace, a lace of rigging, a ship upon the sea. *Wedding Party* can be as terrifying as a drop of poetry under the microscope. The scenes fit together like the words of a poem.[30]

At the same time, there has been resistance to this concept of plays and the theatre. As late as 1959 critics were bewailing the literary incompetence of major American playwrights. Dubbing them members of a "cult of inarticulacy" such critics mistook, it seems, a simple emphasis upon the theatrical moment for literary inadequacy.[31] Contemporary theatre artists such as Robert Wilson, Richard Foreman, Suzanne Hellmuth and Jock Reynolds, Jean Tardieu, Peter Handke, Jean-Claude Van Itallie, and Tadeusz Kantor—not to mention performance artists, and companies like Mabou Mines, Snake Theatre, Soon 3, Nightfire, the Performance Group, the Wooster Group, and the Living Theatre, have traditionally emphasized the immediacy, the finality, and the vitality of the theatre experience at significant cost to the play's "literary" qualities.

To reject Stein's plays as plays on the grounds that they do not conform to pre-determined literary characteristics would be folly in light of such developments. She wrote plays in the sense in which we have been speaking, a sense well articulated by Stark Young:

> A play is a piece of literature about a section of life written in such a way that it will go over the footlights, in such a way that what it has to say it can say in the theatre. That is the sole test. If it can do this it is a play, good or bad. It is a play in so far as the idea, the content, of it is expressed in theatre terms—the space relationships, the time elements, the oral values, the personal medium of the actors, and so on—as distinguished from the terms of literature.[32]

Gertrude Stein believed that plays were the "things anybody can see by looking":

> Two things are always the same the dance and war. One might say anything is the same but the dance and war are particularly the same because one can see them. That is what they are for that anyone living then can look at them. And games do do both they do the dance and war and bullfighting and football playing, it is the dance and war anything anybody can see by looking is the dance and war. That is the reason that plays are like that, they are the thing anybody can see by looking.[33]

Despite the fact that her plays are unconventionally put forth in text, they are able to communicate effectively with an audience once they are given physical incarnation in the theatre. In the hands of genuine creative artists, they become concrete manifestations of her aesthetic.

> When a work is put on a stage of course everyone has to look at it and in a sense if it is put on the stage everyone is forced to look and since they are forced to look at it, of course, they must accept it, there is nothing else to do.[34]

As she noted, "A thing seen is necessarily successful."[35] Or, to take it to its logical end, "A play may not be removed."[36]

Emerging from the same immediacy of perception characteristic of her aesthetic as a whole, plays are what anybody can see but not what Stein can see:

> Whenever I write a play it is a play because it is a thing I do not see but it is a thing somebody can see that is what makes a play to me. When I see a thing it is not a play to me because the minute I see it it ceases to be a play for me, but when I write something that somebody else can see then it is a play for me. When I write other things not plays it is something that I can see and seeing it is inside of me but when I write a play then it is something that is inside of me but if I could see it then it would not be.[37]

"Seeing" a play involves its immediate perception, something Stein could not experience in the theatre if she had "seen" it before.

The emphasis on "seeing" erupts in most of the plays. *Byron a Play* reads:

> Could he look and see.
> In this is the essential of a play.[38]

It was a preoccupation of Stein's from her first year as a playwright. In 1913, Mabel Dodge wrote suggesting that Stein publish her plays and received a curt reply:

> No decidedly not. I do *not* want the plays published. They are to be kept to be played.[39]

It was a resolution she was ultimately unable to keep. Publishing her first collection of plays nearly ten years later, she would wait until 1934 for the first production of one of her texts, *Four Saints in Three Acts* (1927). Still, it was a resolution implicit in her thinking about her plays. Due to a lack of traditional extra-performance characteristics like story, stage directions, and clearly demarcated lines and characters, a reading of them does not promote ready visualization. The press release for the production of *Four Saints* says what would be repeated time and time again in relation to her plays:

> The charm of the opera lies not in its obvious literary dramatic values, but in the emotional content brought up in the individual by the fusion of sound, the dance, rhythmic movement, and the scenery and costumes.[40]

Plays, as distinguished from the novels and portraits which Stein had written up to 1913, are physical expressions whose realization lay not on the printed page, but in live performance. For full impact, they have to be seen. The plays seem to capture most simply and most absolutely Stein's concept of entity because in the theatre the plays exist as simple, concrete phenomena. In a medium whose defining characteristic is performance—simple projection of absolute existence—the concept of entity finds fulfillment.

"Looking" links the plays, too, with the general effort toward a continuous present which emerged in her novels and portraits of 1911. Culminating Stein's process of "talking and listening," looking succeeded, according to her, in capturing the essence of a thing in the absolute present. Emerging immediately after this discovery, the plays were direct reflections of the integrated technique, and embodiments of the continuous present. She sought from the very first to avoid telling stories:

> What is the use of telling a story since there are so many and everybody knows so many and tells so many...
> So naturally what I wanted to do in my play was what everybody did not always know or always tell.[41]

She believed plays should be conceived in opposition to the nineteenth-century novel which is based on a developmental story:

> One of the things that happened at the end of the Nineteenth Century was that nobody knew the difference between a novel and a play and now the movies have helped them not to know but although there is none there really is and I know there is and that is the reason I write plays and not novels.[42]

She even distinguished her plays from nineteenth-century plays, which had, according to her, too much of the novel in them:

The Nineteenth Century wrote a great many plays, and none of them are now read, because the Nineteenth Century wanted to put their novels on the stage. The better the play the more static. The minute you try to make a play a novel, it doesn't work. That is the reason I got interested in doing these plays.[43]

"In writing a story," she wrote, "one had to be remembering,"[44] and remembering, she asserted, was something her human mind was incapable of. Talking, listening, and looking, according to her, produced in themselves an intense concentration whereby she could record what was in front of her immediately. Plays were equated with this immediacy: "Anything that was not a story could be a play."[45] "[In] a novel...there is a middle and a beginning, in a play there is none."[46] A play, in other words, would have a vividness in every moment of its performance which is self-explanatory. Traditional, progressive playwriting technique to the contrary, Stein believed that a play needed neither a middle nor a beginning for clarity.

There was ample precedent for this attention to immediacy in plays and the theatre in the work of Chekhov, Craig, Pirandello, Cocteau, and Maeterlinck, and an environment conducive to it in experiments of Copeau, Reinhardt, Witkiewicz, and Jarry. As Maeterlinck described his art:

I have grown to believe that an old man, seated in his armchair, waiting patiently, with his lamp beside him; giving unconscious ear to all the eternal laws that reign about his house, interpreting, without comprehending, the silence of doors and windows and the quivering voice of the light, submitting with bent head to the presence of his soul and his destiny...I have grown to believe that he, motionless as he is, does yet live in reality a deeper, more human, and more universal life than the lover who strangles his mistress, the captain who conquers in battle, or "the husband who avenges his honor."[47]

It gained momentum in the work of playwrights like Beckett who forsook the linear movement of history for an investigation of personal consciousness. Martin Esslin has stated in *Anatomy of Drama*:

The introspective poetic playwrights such as Beckett or Ionesco tend to neglect the realities of social circumstances and their documentation in favor of an inner truth. Their plays are dreams rather than photographs of the external world. But these dreams are as real to them—and to audiences—as the external realities are to the Brechtians.[48]

In post-modern performance, it is a defining characteristic of the work of Richard Foreman and Robert Wilson, both of whom have been termed "painterly" artists, in part because of their abandonment of progressive time for investigations of space and consciousness. Through his distension of time, Wilson accomplishes a new kind of awareness in the theatre. According to him, "The brain begins to operate on a slower frequency.

Ideally, in our work, someone in the audience might reach a point of consciousness where he is on the same frequency as one of the performers —
where he receives communications directly."[49]

Gertrude Stein argued for this immediacy and embodied it in her plays
beginning in 1913. Her impetus for doing so, however, lay in the cinema,
not in the theatre of her day. By her account, the cinema was able, as she
was, to present each moment in full as it occurred, conforming to her continuous present in a way that no theatre she was aware of did: "By a contin-
uously moving picture of any one there is no memory of any other thing
and there is that thing existing."[50] In addition,

> I may say that as a matter of fact the thing which has induced a person like myself to
> constantly think about the theatre from the standpoint of sight and sound and its rela-
> tion to emotion and time, rather than in relation to story and action is the same as you
> may say general form of conception as the inevitable experiments made by the cinema
> although the method of doing so has naturally nothing to do with the other. I myself
> never go to the cinema or hardly ever practically never and the cinema has never read
> my work or hardly ever. The fact remains that there is the same impulse to solve the
> problem of time in relation to emotion and the relation of the scene to the emotion of
> the audience in the one case as in the other.[51]

While her plays were the opposites of dramatic stories, they were not,
as she pointed out, unconcerned with "what happened." After all, she
wrote, "something is always happening."[52] Her early plays, in fact, were
dedicated to uncovering "what happened" without telling a story, and were
distinguished from the portraits in this way:

> In my portraits I had tried to tell *what each one is* without telling stories and now in my
> early plays I tried to tell *what happened* without telling stories so that the essence of
> what happened would be like the essence of the portraits, what made what happened be
> what it was.[53]

If Stein had used developmental stories in her plays, she would have vio-
lated her strict time sense. As it was, she presented the essences of stories
and avoided such violation.

Stories violate not only the time sense of Stein's aesthetic but its concept of entity, since they describe an event instead of incarnating it. She
wanted to produce something "that was not description"[54] of an event but
the event itself, in essence.[55] It was an intent shared by abstract expression-
ist painters, whose pictures are less pictures of something than pictures
with their own validity. In attempting this in the theatrical medium she
allied herself with a major modern movement which centered around
Appia, Craig, and the new stagecraft. As Robert Edmond Jones summed
up their program, "all art in the theatre should be, not descriptive, but
evocative."[56]

According to Stein, then, her plays from 1913–1946 were static compositions. As still as her other writing, they referred to no reality but their own, as she related during her 1934 tour of America to Charlie Chaplin:

> We naturally talked about the cinema, and he explained something. He said naturally it was disappointing, he had known the silent films and in that they could do something that the theatre had not done they could change the rhythm but if you had a voice accompanying naturally after that you could never change the rhythm you were always held by the rhythm that the voice gave them. We talked a little about the Four Saints and what my idea had been, I said that what was most exciting was when nothing was happening, I said that saints should naturally do nothing if you are a saint that was enough and a saint existing was everything, if you made them do anything then there was nothing to it they were just like anyone so I wanted to write a drama where no one did anything where there was no action and I had and it was the Four Saints and it was exciting, he said yes he could understand that, I said the films would become like the newspapers just a daily habit and not at all exciting or interesting, after all the business of an artist is to be really exciting and he is only exciting, when nothing is happening, if anything happens then it is like any other one, after all Hamlet Shakespeare's most interesting play has really nothing happening except that they live and die but it is not that that is interesting and I said I was sure that it is true that an interesting thing is when there is nothing happening, I said that the moon excited dogs because it did nothing . . . he wanted the sentiment of movement invented by himself and I wanted the sentiment of doing nothing invented by myself, anyway we both liked talking but each one had to stop to be polite and let the other one say something.[57]

But Chaplin, in fact, had no monopoly on movement. Stein herself insisted upon the vitality of her static art. Movement within stillness was her aim more than stillness itself, and she turned to the theatre for its ability to express it: "Then I began to do plays to make the looking have in it an element of moving."[58] The plays grew out of her interest in portrait writing:

> I wrote portraits knowing that each one is themselves inside them and something about them perhaps everything about them will tell some one all about that thing all about what is themselves inside them and I was then hoping completely hoping that I was that one the one who would tell that thing.[59]

> I came to think that since each one is that one and that there are a number of them each one being that one, the only way to express this thing each one being that one and there being a number of them knowing each other was in a play. And so I began to write these plays.[60]

In theory, a play could be distinguished from a portrait by the fact that it considered more than one person. Most important, it could be distinguished by its ability to relate individuals to one another, to move within itself, as opposed to the portrait's ability to refer to a single subject outside of itself. As Stein wrote in *Byron a Play*: "A play is when there is not only so but also."[61] This capacity for movement could be literally embodied in the plays. As Donald Sutherland indicated, the plays bring a "greater liveliness" and a "greater movement" to the "thing existing in itself."[62]

Stein distinguished her plays from other genres by their concreteness or "entity," their perfect present tense, and their relationality. The theatrical medium, as Stein conceived it, was the perfect receptacle for such works. But she stripped it of extraneous notions traditionally associated with it just as she stripped plot and time from literature. The traditional theatre as Stein knew it depended more upon the alternate reality of a story than on its own reality. It shifted the attention of its audience from the all-important present moment to that of fiction and resulted, according to her, in a distancing of audience and actor. It created a gap between what happened on stage and what the audience perceived, which she called "syncopation:"

> The thing that is fundamental about plays is that the scene as depicted on the stage is more often than not one might say it is almost always in syncopated time in relation to the emotion of anybody in the audience.
> What this says is this.
> Your sensation as one in the audience in relation to the play played before you your sensation I say your emotion concerning that play is always either behind or ahead of the play at which you are looking and to which you are listening. So your emotion as a member of the audience is never going on at the same time as the action of the play.[63]

Needless to say, Stein did not look upon syncopation as anything of value, even though she noted that jazz had made of it a positive "thing in itself." For her, syncopation described the inability of the static audience to merge at any point with a relentlessly moving reality on the stage. The syncopation of the action on stage and the emotional response of the audience resulted, according to Stein, in nervousness, which "consists in needing to go faster or to go slower so as to get together."[64] The nervousness inheres in the structure of the fictional play, which is built according to the Renaissance ideal; that is, it builds up to and recedes from a climax. To her, this nervousness was not a satisfying condition.

In life, according to Stein, an individual experiences "completion" of excitement at a climax; in theatre one knows "relief" at having finally reached the substance of the play.[65] Similarly, if an individual is recalling an exciting experience of which he has been a part he can obtain "relief" but not "completion," the difference being that memory of an experience turns it into the "thing seen or heard and not the scene felt."[66] The difference between a climax in life and in the theatre, then, is that the emotion of the individual keeps time with the real scene as it builds, providing "completion" at its climax, while it cannot keep time with the fictional reality in the theatre as it builds. Even in remembering a real scene, or in reading a book, while the individual cannot experience completion he has some control over the movement of his emotion in relation to the real scene. A person can go back and forth in memory or in reading until ready to go on. But the stage, Stein thought, "is different, it is not real and yet it is not within your control as the memory of an exciting thing is or the reading of an exciting book."[67] In reading a book the reader becomes familiar with its characters, for instance, through a "forcing process or incubation." But:

> It is not possible in the theatre to produce familiarity which is of the essence of acquaintance because, in the first place when the actors are there they are there and they are there right away.[68]

Stein realized the rift between stage and audience during her first theatre experiences;[69] it built throughout her youthful theatre-going and emerged, full blown, when she reached adolescence:

> Then gradually there came the beginning of really realizing the great difficulty of having my emotion accompany the scene and then moreover I became fairly consciously troubled by the things over which one stumbles over which one stumbled to such an extent that the time of one's emotion in relation to the scene was always interrupted. The things over which one stumbled and there it was a matter both of seeing and of hearing were clothes, voices, what they the actors said, how they were dressed and how that related itself to their moving around. Then the bother of never being able to begin over again because before it had commenced it was over, and at no time had you been ready, either to commence or to be over. Then I began vaguely to wonder whether I could see and hear at the same time and which helped or interfered with the other and which helped or interfered with the thing on the stage having been over before it really commenced. Could I see and hear and feel at the same time and did I.
>
> I began to be a good deal troubled by all these things, the more emotion I felt while at the theatre the more troubled I became by all these things.[70]

Before she came to this acute awareness of "syncopation" as an adolescent, she saw a lot of theatre as a child in Oakland and San Francisco. At that time she rested undisturbed in the "moments" of the plays she saw, which is all a child, according to Stein, can retain. A child's feeling of the theatre, she summarized, is two things:

> One which is in a way like a circus that is the general movement and light and air which any theatre has, and a great deal of glitter in the light and a great deal of height in the air, and then there are moments, a very very few moments but still moments. One must be pretty far advanced in adolescence before one realizes a whole play.[71]

It is only with adolescence, Stein found, that these qualities began to give way to nervousness in the face of having to "realize a whole play."

Soon after she reached adolescence and began to experience "syncopation," however, Sarah Bernhardt came to San Francisco:

> And then I was relieved...I knew a little french of course but really it did not matter, it was all so foreign and her voice being so varied and it all being so french I could rest in it untroubled. And I did.
>
> It was better than the opera because it went on. It was better than the theatre because you did not have to get acquainted. The manners and the customs of the french theatre created a thing in itself and it existed in and for itself as the poetical plays had that I used so much to read, there were so many characters just as there were in those plays and you did not have to know them they were so foreign, and the foreign scenery and actuality replaced the poetry and the voices replaced the portraits. It was for me a very simple direct and moving pleasure.[72]

It was very similar, in fact, to her conception of theatre as a child except that instead of facing a single moment of a play she faced a series of them, disembodied and concrete. The French theatre created in Stein an interest in melodrama

> because there again everything happened so quietly one did not have to get acquainted and as what the people felt was of no importance one did not have to realize what was said.[73]

The interest culminated in Civil War dramas like William Gillette's *Secret Service* which contained, according to her, a new technique of "silence, stillness, and quick movement."[74] More than the melodrama, Gillette in his plays, she thought,

> made the whole stage the whole play this technique...One was no longer bothered by the theatre, you had to get acquainted of course but that was quickly over and after that nothing bothered.[75]

Having thus taken the theatre of Gillette and Bernhardt to heart as the only true theatre, Stein lost interest in the medium. She regained it years later through experiences at the dance and at bullfights:

> There was of course Isadora Duncan and then the Russian ballet and in between Spain and the Argentine and bullfights and I began once more to feel something about something going on at a theatre.[76]

Stein's youthful theatre experience led her to reject wholeheartedly the traditional theatre, its alternate reality of fiction, and its climactic structure. She embraced instead a theatre which was either not based on an alternate reality at all (the dance, bullfights) or based on a story that was so obvious (melodrama) or so foreign (Bernhardt) that it could be ignored in the face of the physical relationship of actor and audience. The theatre that she enjoyed and respected was concrete, dynamic, and absolutely present, capturing in essence what traditional theatre was content to describe linearly. Her own plays would be based strictly upon this conception, and would embody it. Her conception of them in performance was identical to her delighted description of the theatre as a child. In *Everybody's Autobiography* she writes of her ballet, *A Wedding Bouquet*:

> And then we went to the Sadlers Wells Theatre for the rehearsal I had never seen a rehearsal a dress rehearsal, and there were so many there, not only on the stage but everywhere and they do make them do it again and I liked hearing my words and I like it being a play and I liked it being something to look at and I liked their doing it again and I like the music going on.[77]

Stein herself claimed that her efforts to embody the continuous present, entity, and self-contained movement in the theatre fell into three distinct phases: plays as the essence of what happened, plays as landscapes, and plays as narration. Whether these phases are distinct, as Stein and certain other commentators have claimed, is open to investigation. To begin with, Stein thought of all her plays, as we have seen so far in this chapter, as having no story, consisting of relational movement, and capturing the thing it refers to in essence. Secondly, as we shall see, certain of her plays seem to conform as well to one of her periods as they do to another, begging a more flexible approach to the question of periods. Still, the question of periods has bearing on the fashion in which Stein approached theatre, and it is for this reason that Stein's explanation of her art within these distinct phases and her demonstration of her theories with the plays themselves will be examined here.

Plays as the Essence of What Happened

In 1913, having freed herself from the grip of stories through her mastery of "talking, listening, and looking," and having rejected a description of the thing at which she looked in favor of an incarnation of its entity, Gertrude Stein began writing plays. Her first period of playwriting, lasting from 1913–1921, was spent in creating "the essence of what happened," according to Stein.[78] In these plays she sought to create not the essence of one thing, as she had in her portraits, but the essence of a relationship between things, and to express this relationship "without telling what happened, in short, to make a play the essence of what happened."[79] Unconcerned with telling a story, she focused on the core of a situation, in order to reveal "what everybody did not always know nor always tell."[80] She realized it would be difficult to realize this aim.

> I have of course always been struggling with this thing, to say what you nor I nor nobody knows, but what is really what you and I and everybody knows and as I say everybody hears stories but the thing that makes each one what he is is not that.[81]

In her lecture entitled "Plays" Stein demonstrated her dedication to the present moment by citing from *What Happened* (1913), *A Curtain Raiser* (1913), and *Ladies' Voices* (1916). She quoted at length from *What Happened*, a play whose title casts it as a prototype for her first period of playwriting. As Stein described it, "I think and always have thought that if you write a play you ought to announce that it is a play and that is what I did. What Happened. A Play."[82] Written after a dinner party at the home of Harry and Bridget Gibb,[83] it rendered the images, rhythms, and qualities of the evening in relationships without ever suggesting a story:

> (ONE.)
> Loud and no cataract. Not any nuisance is depressing.
> (FIVE.)
> A single sum four and five together and one, not any sun a clear signal and an exchange.
> Silence is in blessing and chasing and coincidences being ripe. A simple melancholy clearly precious and on the surface and surrounded and mixed strangely. A vegetable window and clearly most clearly an exchange in parts and complete.
> A tiger a rapt and surrounded overcoat securely arranged with spots old enough to be thought useful and witty quite witty in a secret and in a blinding flurry.
> Length what is length when silence is so windowful. What is the use of a sore if there is no joint and no toady and no tag and not even an eraser. What is the commonest exchange between more laughing and most. Carelessness is carelessness and a cake well a cake is a powder, it is very likely to be powder, it is very likely to be much worse.
> A shutter and only shutter and Christmas, quite Christmas, an only shutter and a target a whole color in every centre and shooting real shooting and what can hear, that can hear that which makes such an establishment provided with what is provisionary.[84]

Stein's attention to the evening as it unfolded was meant to rivet the attention of the audience upon the present moment. And the relationship between words, textures, and rhythms keeps the perceiver aware of the dynamics of the work itself, along with possible links to the "outside." It evokes an easy, comfortable ambience, whether it once existed or could exist outside of the piece.

The point was made even more strongly by *A Curtain Raiser*, which reads in its entirety:

> Six.
> Twenty.
>   Outrageous.
> Late,
> Weak.
>   Forty.
> More in any wetness.
> Sixty-three certainly.
> Five.

Sixteen.
Seven.
Three.
More in orderly. Seventy-five.[85]

Here, the juxtaposition of non-referential numbers with referential adjectives increases the possibility of finding relationships between them, again confining the perceiver's attention to the work in itself.

In a slightly different vein Stein composed *Ladies' Voices* (1916) using snatches of conversation, dramatizing relations in a new fashion while maintaining the attention to qualities and rhythms at the expense of a developing story.

Ladies' voices give pleasure.
The acting two is easily lead. Leading is not in winter. Here the winter is sunny.
Does that surprise you.
Ladies' voices together and then she came in.
Very well good night.
Very well good night.
(Mrs. Cardillac.)
That's silver.
You mean the sound.
Yes the sound.[86]

Every Afternoon. A Dialogue (1916) presents conversation that appears to display more attention to logical connections:

I get up.
So do you get up.
We are pleased with each other.
Why are you.
Because we are hopeful.
Have you any reason to be.
What is it.
I am not prepared to say.
Is there any change.
Naturally.
I know what you mean.[87]

Still, the play cannot be considered to progress. Rather, sections of dialogue isolate themselves from each other, not leading anywhere. In addition, though the "situation" might be imagined to be more clear in this play at first glance, it is actually more veiled. "I" and "you" are the only references we have to protagonists, and there is no action even implied. Dialogue here enforces relationships within the text, and isolates *Every Afternoon* as effectively as it did *Ladies' Voices* from the outside world. Stein's impulse toward conversation in this early period is summed up in *I Like It to be a Play* (1916) as follows: "I liked it to be a play and so cleverly spoken."[88]

The focus of these first plays upon the dynamics of the work and not upon links to the outside is epitomized by *IIIIIIIIII* (1913), in which there is a more complete lack of development and reference. As Stein states in the text, the play was a high point in her development: "forward and a rapidity and no resemblance no more utterly."[89] It reads, in part:

> INCLINE.
> Clinch, melody, hurry, spoon, special, dumb, cake, forrester. Fine, cane, carpet, incline, spread, gate, light, labor.
> (. . . .)
>   M-n H-
> A cook. A cook can see. Pointedly in uniform, exertion in a minimum. A cook can see.
> Clark which is awful, clark which is shameful, clark and awful.
> A pin is a plump point and picking and combined and more much more is in fine.
> Rats is, rats is oaken. Robber. Height, age, miles, plaster, pedal, more order.[90]

In the two previous examples, relationships with the text itself were more clear. In this text, we are not to know the subject in the author's mind, not even to guess at it. We are to accept the succession of words and make of it what we may.

At the opposite pole stands *A Movie* (1920), structured in a straightforward story of intrigue and suspense, yet revealed shot by shot, as in a scenario:

> American painter sits in cafe and contemplates empty pocket book as taxi cabs file through Paris carrying French soldiers to the battle of the Marne. I guess I'll be a taxi driver here in gay Paree says the American painter.
> Painter sits in studio trying to learn names of streets with help of Bretonne peasant femme de menage. He becomes taxi driver. Ordinary street scene in war time Paris.
> Being lazy about getting up in the mornings he spends some of his dark nights in teaching Bretonne femme de menage peasant girl how to drive the taxi so she can replace him when he wants to sleep.
> America comes into the war american painter wants to be american soldier. Personnel officer interviews him. What have you been doing, taxiing. You know Paris, Secret Service for you to go on taxiing.[91]

This work shares with other plays of this early period the attention to the moment. It is accomplished through juxtaposition of elements whose logical links are minimized. It does not conform, however, to Stein's signal definition of plays in this early period as things that capture "without telling what happened the essence of what happened."[92] Rather, it tells us what happened while capturing its essence. *A Movie* represents an anomaly of sorts, leading some to regard it and her other movie, *Film*, as needing to be seen apart from her plays. Though Stein herself did not refer to these texts as plays, she did not refer to some of her normally accepted play texts as plays either. (See Appendix B.) Her avowed use of cinematic techniques and theory in the writing of her plays leads me to reject such a distinct separation. By virtue of the relative clarity of these movies, in fact, it becomes simpler to demonstrate the juxtaposition and attention to the present inherent in her less clear plays. (See Chapter three.)

As Stein describes them, then, the characteristics of "plays as the essence of what happened" from 1913–1921 are that they render the essence of an occurrence with its attendant qualities and textures without telling a story and that they deal with more than one person or thing in relation. The focus is upon a timeless reality within which various relationships are posed. The early plays embody this focus. By eliminating developing situations and emphasizing relations in the work, Stein created in her first period of playwriting a flat world. A spectator is compelled to consider this flat world as a set of related elements with which a subjective projection is not possible. These works posit only a presence, an ineffable and somewhat mysterious here and now to be experienced by the willing spectator, who knows that this presence stands quite aloof from other moments and other realities.

Plays as Landscapes

Stein's second period of playwriting was devoted to the landscape play. Growing naturally from the first period, it is an extension and refinement of an already established aesthetic, and represents her ultimate reaction against "syncopation" in the theatre. In "Plays" she related that in 1922:[93]

> I began to spend my summers in Bilignin in the department of the Ain and there I lived in a landscape that made itself its own landscape. I slowly came to feel that since the landscape was the thing...a play was a thing and I went on writing plays a great many plays. The landscape at Bilignin so completely made a play that I wrote quantities of plays.
>
> I felt that if a play was exactly like a landscape then there would be no difficulty about the emotion of the person looking on at the play being behind or ahead of the play because the landscape does not have to make acquaintance. You may have to make acquaintance with it but it does not with you, it is there and so the play being written the relation between you at any time is so exactly that that it is of no importance unless you look at it. Well I did look at it and the result is all the plays I have printed in Operas and Plays.[94]

Stein quoted from from *A List* (1923), among other plays, to demonstrate her conception of a landscape play:

Martha.	If four are sitting at a table and one of them is lying on it and there are pomegranates on it and one of the five is leaning on the table it does not make any difference.
Martha.	It does not make any difference if four are seated at a table and one is leaning upon it.
Maryas.	If five are seated at a table and there is bread on it and there are pomegranates on it and one of the five is leaning on the table it does not make any difference.
Martha.	If on a day that comes again and if we consider a day a week day it does come again if on a day that comes again and we consider every day to be a day that comes again it comes again then when accidentally when very accidentally every other day and every other day every other day and every other day that comes again and every other day comes again when accidentally every other day comes again, every other day comes again and and every other and every day comes again and accidentally and every day and it comes again, a day comes again and a day in that way comes again.
Maryas.	Accidentally in the morning and after that every evening and accidentally every evening and after that every morning and after that accidentally every morning and after that accidentally and after that every morning.
Maryas.	After that accidentally. Accidentally after that.
Maryas.	Accidentally after that. After that accidentally.
Maryas and Martha.	More Maryas and more Martha.
Maryas and Martha.	More Martha and more Maryas.[95]

A List, as Stein saw it, did not result in syncopation for an audience because it reflects sheer physical, spatial presence. It can be said to operate on a number of levels, but whether one conceives the play to be based on the immediate relationship of Maryas and Martha or on the relational reality of tables, days, pomegranates, bread, and evenings described in the "dialogue," it is clear that the play has been expressed in the physical terms of a landscape in which elements relate to one another but ultimately remain static. The spatiality of this play is emphasized by the technique of modifying or qualifying an existing line in a later line, relating it yet distinguishing it from later manifestations, fulfilling Stein's ethic of self-contained movement.

Objects Lie on a Table (1922) describes the same physicality and spatiality without depending upon such modifications. It, too, is a landscape play, but does not share the intense vibration in the lines brought about by modification evident in *A List*:

The objects on a table have been equal to the occasion. We can decorate walls with pots and pans and flowers. I question the flowers. And bananas. Card board colored as bananas are colored. And cabbages. Cabbages are green and if one should not happen to be there what would happen, the green would unhappily unhappily result in hardness and we could only regret that the result was unfortunate and so we astonish no one nor did we regret riches. Riches are not begun. They have a welcome in oceans. Oceans can not spread to the shore. They began description and so we relish seas. Over seas objects are on the table that is a wooden table and has not a marble top necessarily. So thank every one and let us begin faintly.[96]

The physical and spatial relationships of green cabbages, pots, pans, flowers, and cardboard colored bananas brought from overseas evoke a domestic landscape as perceived by Gertrude Stein. It is a private perception which has to be accepted as such without further justification, as if Stein insists that the willing spectator get in touch with her perception, since she is not about to get in touch with his. It was her feeling that she could not capture this landscape with the particularity it deserved if she were preoccupied with transmitting it to someone else.

The landscape play is spatially arranged, not vertically progressive, and depends, according to Stein, upon relationships, like a scene from nature.

The landscape has its formation and as after all a play has to have its formation and be in relation one thing to the other thing and as the story is not the thing as any one is always telling something then the landscape is not moving but being always in relation, the trees to the hills the hills to the fields the trees to each other any piece of it to any sky and then any detail to any other detail; the story is only of importance if you like to tell or hear a story but the relation is there anyway.[97]

The concept of a play as a spatial configuration is borne out by theoretical musings in the plays themselves. *A Play a Lion. For Max Jacob* (1932) begins:

As a play is a lane for a lion
Who makes paws purr.
    An invitation to a space.[98]

Objects Lie on a Table (1922) reveals:

When I appeal I appeal to their relation. . . I find that milk salt flour and apples and the pleasant respective places of each one in the picture make a picture.[99]

The relationality of the landscape play reinforces its physicality. Generated by personal dynamics, and offered to the view of others, it does not move away from the spectator, but moves within itself at a distance from his gaze. As Stein has written of *Four Saints in Three Acts*:

Anyway I did write Four Saints an Opera to be Sung and I think it did almost what I wanted, it made a landscape and the movement in it was like a movement in and out with which anybody looking on can keep in time. I also wanted it to have the movement of nuns very busy and in continuous movement but placed as a landscape has to be because after all the life in a convent is the life of a landscape, it may look excited and a landscape does sometimes look excited but its quality is that a landscape if it ever did go away it would have to go away to stay.

Anyway the play as I see it is exciting and it moves but it also stays and that is as I said in the beginning might be what a play should do.[100]

As Stein described it, the self-containment of the landscape play increased as the period wore on, reaching its most intense point around 1925-1926.[101] She stated in the persona of Alice Toklas:

She began at this time to describe landscape as if anything she saw was a natural phenomenon, a thing existent in itself, and she found it, this exercise, very interesting and it finally led her to the later series of operas and plays. I am trying to be as commonplace as I can be, she used to say to me. And then sometimes a little worried, it is not too commonplace.[102]

The later series of operas and plays, then, as Stein herself described it, is consonant with the move in her general aesthetic toward the concept of self-contained movement, a concept well demonstrated, she thought, in *Say it with Flowers* (1931), within which characters engage in no overt action, yet remain active.

Time Louis XI.

Place Gisors.
Action in a cake shop and the sea shore.
Other interests.
The welcoming of a man and a dog and the wish that they would come back sooner.
George Henry and Elizabeth Henry and Henry Henry ruminating.

Elizabeth and William Long.
Waiting.

Who has asked them to be amiable to me.
She said she was waiting.
George Henry and Elizabeth Henry and Henry Henry.
Who might be asleep if they were not waiting for me.
She.
Elizabeth Henry and Henry Henry and George Henry.
She might be waiting with me.
Henry Henry absolutely ready to be here with me.[103]

Landscape plays, then, extend principles introduced in Stein's first playwriting phase such as staticity and vibratory movement, by casting them for the first time in the overtly spatial terms of a physical landscape.

That landscape, particularly in the later plays, moves within itself, not away from the spectator, and charts relationships in a flat world that asks to be taken on its own terms.

Plays as Narratives

It is usual to speak of Stein's last period of playwriting as her "narrative" period, beginning in 1932, within which she depended for the first time upon some kind of story.[104] Stein's lecture "Plays" ends with landscapes, her clearest reference to plays as narratives appearing in a letter to Carl Van Vechten in July 1938 regarding *Doctor Faustus Lights the Lights* (1937):

> I have been struggling with this problem of dramatic narrative and in that I think I got it.[105]

Narrative, for Stein, was an occupation differing greatly from her usual style. It came perilously close to "writing as it is going to be written," or writing according to prescription, an activity she singled out for censure in such divergent theoretical works as *Four in America,*[106] *Narration,*[107] and *Lectures in America.*[108] (See Chapter one.) It lacks the immediacy of artist and object inherent in "writing as it is written." She writes in "A Transatlantic Interview" that Shakespeare's plays

> have a roughness and violence in their juxtaposition which the sonnets do not have, and this brought me to a great deal of illumination of narrative, because most narrative is based not upon your opinions but on someone else's.
>   Therefore narrative has a different concept than poetry or even exposition, because you see, the narrative in itself is not what is in your mind but what is in somebody else's.[109]

Since plays "use it less"[110] she decided to attempt narration in *The Autobiography of Alice B. Toklas,* a novel in which she recreated the view of somebody else so well that the agent for the publisher had to call to see who had actually done the writing, Stein or Toklas. In that book, as she said,

> I had recreated the point of view of somebody else. Therefore the words ran with a certain smoothness. Shakespeare never expressed any feelings of his own in those sonnets. They have too much smoothness. He did not feel "this is my emotion, I will write it down." If it is your own feeling, one's words have a fullness and violence.[111]

This "smoothness" must have seemed enormously attractive at this time to Stein, who had long been criticized for her incomprehensibility. Still, she did not leap foolishly into ordinary comprehensibility, but, as she wrote in "A Transatlantic Interview," became "interested in how you could tell this thing in a way that anybody could understand and at the same time keep true to your values."[112] Specifically, she sought the smoothness, the clarity which comes from the presentation of another's point of view while maintaining the immediacy of the present moment.

> In narration your great problem is the problem of time in telling a story of anybody. And that is why newspaper people never become writers, because they have a false sense of time. They have to consider not the time in which to write but the time in which the newspaper is coming out...
>
> I found that in the essence of narration is this problem of time. You have as a person writing, and all the really great narrative has it, you have to denude yourself of time so that time does not exist. If time exists, your writing is ephemeral. You can have a historical time, but for you the time does not exist, and if you are writing about the present, the time element must cease to exist.... There should not be a sense of time, but an existence suspended in time.[113]

An existence suspended in time is precisely what Stein seems to have accomplished in some plays of her late period.

While containing recognizable, sequential stories, these plays depend less upon causal connections between story elements than on sustained views of each element. In very much the same manner as Chekhov, Stein subordinates overt movement or progression between scenes to the texture and quality of the scene at hand. In *Doctor Faustus Lights the Lights,* for instance, although the play moves gradually toward Faust's trip to hell, it is rooted in the present. Stein deflates the overt movement of the play by using a very late point of attack; in the first twenty lines we learn that Faust's soul has already been sold. In addition, she distends and prolongs the remainder of the play, minimizing overt changes and maximizing gradual ones. The "entrance" of Marguerite Ida and Helena Annabel (one character) demonstrates this:

> Faustus half turns and starts
> I hear her
>   he says
> I hear her say
> Call to her to sing
> To sing all about
>   to sing a song
> All about
> day-light and night light.
> Moonlight and star-light
> electric light and twilight
> every light as well.

The electric lights glow and a chorus in the distance sings
Her name is her name is her name is Marguerite Ida and Helena Annabel.
Faustus sings
I knew it I knew it the electric lights they told me so no dog can know no boy can know
I cannot know they cannot know the electric lights they told me so I would not know I
could not know who can know who can tell me so I know you know they can know her
name is Marguerite Ida and Helena Annabel and when I tell oh when I tell oh when I
when I when I tell, oh go away and go away and tell and tell and tell and tell and tell, oh
hell.
The electric lights commence to dance and one by one they
go out and come in and the boy and the dog begin to sing.
Oh very well oh Doctor Faustus very very well oh very well, thank you says the dog oh
very well says the boy her name her name is Marguerite Ida and Helena Annabel, I
know says the dog I know says the boy I know says Doctor Faustus no no no no no
nobody can know what I know I know her name is not Marguerite Ida and Helena
Annabel, very well says the boy it is says the boy her name is Marguerite Ida and
Helena Annabel, no no no says Doctor Faustus, yes yes yes says the dog, no says the
boy yes says the dog, her name is not Marguerite Ida and Helena Annabel and she is not
ready yet to sing about day-light and night light, moonlight and star-light electric light
and twilight she is not she is not but she will be. She will not be says Doctor Faustus
never never never, never will her name be Marguerite Ida and Helena Annabel never
never never never well as well never Marguerite Ida and Helena Annabel never Marguerite Ida and Helena Annabel.
There is a sudden hush and the distant chorus says
It might be it might be her name her name might be Marguerite Ida and Helena
Annabel it might be.
And Doctor Faustus says in a loud whisper
It might be but it is not, and the little boy says how do you know and Faustus says it
might be it might not be not be not be, and as he says the last not be the dog says
Thank you.

Scene II

I am I and my name is Marguerite Ida and Helena Annabel.[114]

Stein also deflates the progressive story through attention to the quality of
the language in the present moment, utilizing modification and repetition
to emphasize gradual change rooted in the present:

And you wanted my soul what the hell did you want my soul for, how do you know I
have a soul, who says so nobody says so but you the devil and everybody knows the
devil is all lies, so how do you know how do I know that I have a soul to sell how do
you know Mr. Devil oh Mr. Devil how can you tell you can not tell anything and I I
who know everything I keep on having so much light that light is not bright and what
after all is the use of light, you can see just as well without it, you can go around just as
well without it you can get up and go to bed just as well without it, and I I wanted to
make it and the devil take it yes you devil you do not even want it and I sold my soul to
make it. I have made it but have I a soul to pay for it.[115]

Equivocality and ambiguity are also utilized to produce gradual change rooted in the present. As Faustus cures Marguerite Ida and Helena Annabel what would be the crisis of a traditional play sounds like this:

A viper has bitten her
And if Doctor Faustus does not cure her
It will go all through her
And he what does he say
He says he cannot see her
Why cannot he see her
Because he cannot look at her
He cannot look at Marguerite Ida and Helena Annabel
But he cannot cure her without seeing her
They say yes yes
And he says there is no witness
And he says
He can but he will not
And she says he must and he will
And the dog says thank you
And the boy says very well
And the woman says well cure her and she says she is Marguerite Ida and Helena Annabel.
   There is silence the lights flicker and flicker, and Marguerite Ida and Helena Annabel gets weaker and weaker and the poison stronger and stronger and suddenly the dog says startlingly
Thank you
   Doctor Faustus says
I cannot see you
The viper has forgotten you.
The dog has said thank you
The boy has said will you.
The woman has said
Can you
And you, you have said you are you
Enough said.
You are not dead.
Enough said
Enough said.
You are not dead.
No you are not dead
Enough said
Enough said
You are not dead.
   All join in enough said you are not dead you are not dead enough said yes enough said no you are not dead yes enough said, thank you yes is enough said no you are not dead.
   And at the last
   In a low whisper
   She says

I am Marguerite Ida and Helena Annabel and enough said I am not dead.

Curtain[116]

In Act II we are informed that Doctor Faustus indeed cured Marguerite Ida and Helena Annabel in Act I, though the action presented previously did not point directly to that conclusion. Stein, then, deflated her crisis before it could occur.

She accomplished a similar suppression of overt action in *The Mother of Us All* (1946), relating events through expository writing and confining the dramatic action to investigations of the quality of the moment. Act II Scene VI, for example, presents a group of people trying to coax Susan B. into working on their behalf:

> Chorus.   Do come Susan B. Anthony do come nobody no nobody can make them come the way you make them come, do come do come Susan B. Anthony, it is your duty, Susan B. Anthony, you know you know your duty, you come, do come, come.
>
> Susan B.   I suppose I will be coming, is it because you flatter me, is it because if I do not come you will forget me and never vote my laws, you will never vote my laws even if I do come but if I do not come you will never vote my laws, come or not come it always comes to the same thing it comes to their not voting my laws, not voting my laws, tell me all you men tell me you know you will never vote my laws.
>
> Men.   Dear kind lady we count on you, and as we count on you so can you count on us...
>
> Susan B.   I am not well
>
> Chorus.   But you look so well and once started it will be all right.
>
> Susan B.   All right

Curtain[117]

Act II Scene VII does not, as might be expected, deal with the scene in which Susan B. defends the cause, but begins with Anne and Susan B. at home:

> Anne comes in.   Oh it was wonderful, wonderful, they listen to nobody the way they listen to you.
>
> Susan B.   Yes it is wonderful as the result of my work for the first time the word male has been written into the constitution of the United States concerning suffrage. Yes it is wonderful.[118]

This does not destroy the linear movement of the play, or even disrupt it to a great extent; it merely subordinates it to the tensions and qualities of the moment.

Three Sisters who are not Sisters (1943) can be considered a paradigm for Stein's spatial treatment of narrative. Like the earlier plays, all overt action takes place in the dark, so to speak. Here, however, Stein uses the cover of actual darkness to shield a series of murders witnessed by neither character nor audience. Even the murderer is not aware that he is the murderer. When the lights appear once again, the characters and the audience see the body simultaneously. In this fashion Stein has achieved a rather perfect present tense and a signal lack of syncopation. The audience knows what the characters know, no more and no less, at the exact moment they know it. At the same time, Stein has told a progressive story, though she has avoided dramatizing the central action.

Analysis of Periods

As much as the landscape play may have extended and refined concepts existing in Stein's earlier plays, it remains an integral part of the original effort to produce a relational, physical, present-tense theatre. The only substantial difference between landscape plays and plays as the essence of what happened lies in a subtle change of approach. *Lend a Hand or Four Religions* (1922), Stein reveals, was "the first attempt that later made her Operas and Plays, the first conception of landscape as a play."[119] It was the first time that Stein *conceived* a play in the overtly spatial terms of a physical landscape, even though her earlier plays, by virtue of their abandonment of progressive time, may be said to be equally spatial. These first plays, conceived as essential expressions of an occurrence, emerged as expressions of space which stirred Stein to conceive of plays as landscapes. *A Curtain Raiser,* in particular, is an expression of spatial relations written in 1913, nine years before she "conceived" plays as landscapes. In addition, many of Stein's early plays share the modification of lines we have seen in *A List* which had the effect of spatializing the play. *Old and Old* (1913) ends this way:

> Baby mine, baby mine, have a cow come out of have a cow come out of baby mine baby mine have a cow come out with time, baby mine baby mine have a cow come neatly have a cow come sweetly baby mine baby mine have a cow come out in mine. Baby mine baby mine have a cow come out of have a cow come out of baby mine baby mine have a cow come out of have a cow come out of, have a cow come have a cow come have a cow come come come come.[120]

Not Sightly (1915) reads:

> When I stood and measured distances when I stood and measured distances I bowed I bowed to the reasonable interpretation of plain stairs bent together and when I meant to

go away I did not leave out of that, consideration. I did not leave out of that, consideration.[121]

In *The Autobiography of Alice B. Toklas* Stein herself supports the view that landscape as a term and as a theory describes the early plays too. In the persona of Alice she wrote:

> It was during this winter [1913] that Gertrude Stein began to write plays. They began with one entitled, It Happened a Play. This was written about a dinner party given by Harry and Bridget Gibb. She then wrote Ladies' Voices. Her interest in writing plays continues. She says a landscape is such a natural arrangement for a battlefield or a play that one must write plays.[122]
>
> It was during this stay at Palma de Mallorca (1912) that most of the plays afterwards published in Geography and Plays were written. She always says that a certain kind of landscape induces plays and the country around Terreno certainly did.[123]

All of the plays published in *Geography and Plays* were, according to Stein, plays as the essence of what happened.

The issue of separating Stein's early plays from her landscape plays becomes even more complicated when one realizes that she gave conflicting accounts of the division. She states in "Plays" that her landscapes are all the plays included in the volume *Operas and Plays*,[124] and in *The Autobiography of Alice B. Toklas* that *Lend a Hand or Four Religions* (1922) was her first conception of landscape as a play.[125] Aside from the fact that *Lend* was published separately from *Operas and Plays*, the latter includes four plays written in the years 1921 and 1922, preceding, according to the Gallup and Haas catalogue compiled under Stein's supervision, *Lend* in 1922. *Reread Another, Objects Lie on a Table,* and *Saints and Singing,* all published in *Operas and Plays,* were all written before *Lend*. So was *Saints in Seven,* published elsewhere, where she used to explain her theories in her Oxford and Cambridge lectures. In addition, the *Operas and Plays* volume includes *A Movie,* written in 1920, which, though described at length by Stein in the *Autobiography,* is not described as a landscape.

To avoid this confusion it is necessary to either take Stein's statement about *Lend* to heart, thus rejecting the earlier plays in *Operas and Plays* as landscapes, to accept all plays in the volume as landscapes, including *A Movie* or to take heed from her less stringent references to landscape as a unifying characteristic of all her plays and argue for a more flexible approach to the question of periods. In light of the evidence here examined, I believe the latter to be the better solution. If there is any difference between the plays of the two periods, it is that landscape plays take an established aesthetic a bit further, realizing it more completely, and that they attack the question of space in a more forthright and unified manner.

They are conceived as physical landscapes and demonstrate landscapes as finished theatre pieces. There is no divergence from this mission within the group as there was in the early period, where some plays were exclusively concerned with conversation, for instance.

She gave conflicting accounts of her narrative period, as well. In "A Transatlantic Interview" she wrote:

> As soon as the war was over I settled down and wrote the whole of the Geography and Plays. That turned into a very strong interest in play form, and then I began to be slowly impressed by the idea of narration.
>
> After all, human beings are interested in two things. They are interested in the reality and they are interested in telling about it. I had struggled up to that time with the creation of reality, and then I became interested in how you could tell this thing in a way that anybody could understand and at the same time keep true to your values, and the thing bothered me a great deal at that time. I did quite a few plays and portraits, and that ended roughly with the Four Saints, 1932. Most of the things that are in the Useful Knowledge...were constant effort, and after that I was beginning the narration consisting with plays at first, ending with the Four Saints.[126]

Four Saints was written in 1927, not 1932, and is described by Stein in "Plays" as an example of a landscape play, as we have seen. Yet not only does Stein seem to claim in this passage that *Four Saints* involved narrative, but that previous plays did as well. This would seem to indicate that narrative was a wider-ranging aesthetic principle than heretofore believed. Later in the same interview Stein said that the bulk of her work since *The Autobiography of Alice B. Toklas* (1932) has been "largely narration,"[127] and later still, that "the narrative phase began in the middle thirties and has continued to the present time."(1946)[128]

It seems reasonable to accept the latter since by 1936 she had perfected, she thought, narrative in *Doctor Faustus*. We may then disregard her misdate of *Four Saints*, leaving it in the company of the landscape plays. Still, it is probably correct to assume that narrative informed some of the earlier landscape plays such as *Four Saints*, though it was not their determining characteristic.

As we have seen, in some plays from the narrative period Stein attained clarity and smoothness for the first time in her career, while maintaining the spatial quality of her landscape plays and the immediacy of the present moment. But, if we are to give credence to Stein's claim that narrative occupied her thoughts from the time of *The Autobiography of Alice B. Toklas*, we should say the same for all of the plays written between 1932 and 1946. Wilford Leach, whose 1956 dissertation remains the most comprehensive consideration of her plays to date, avoids the question by not considering nine plays written between those dates, five of which do not contain narrative, and by stating that the final period consists of only six plays: *Doctor Faustus, Yes is for a Very Young Man, The Mother of Us All, Three Sisters who are not Sisters, Look and Long,* and *In a Garden.* In fact, there are fifteen plays which fall within those years, only ten of which — *Lesson 16, Lucretia Borgia, John Breon,* and *Identity a Poem,* in addition to the six Leach mentions — exhibit definite narrative. *Scenery and George Washington* (1932), *Byron a Play* (1933), *Listen to Me* (1936), *A Play Called Not and Now* (1936), and *Daniel Webster* (1937) do not display the consistent narrative of some of the later plays in this period. For this reason it is most important to consider them for a full view of Stein's progress toward narrative in her plays.

The period question is further complicated by the fact that two earlier efforts, *A Movie* (1920) and *Film* (1929), exhibit narrative structure. As we have seen, though, Stein was always interested in stories. As she said in relation to her earliest plays, "something is always happening."[129] That story or narrative would emerge in the medium of film was natural since Stein felt that it had tried, as she was trying, to solve "the problem of time in relation to emotion and the relation of the scene to the emotion of the audience." It utilized narrative while solving these syncopatory problems. Stein's approach to narrative in her plays was, as I see it, a slow process wherein she attempted to balance the spatial quality of a landscape play with the clear, smooth quality of a story.

Her first play written after the completion of *The Autobiography of Alice B. Toklas* in 1932 showed the tension of the struggle in its very title: *Scenery and George Washington. A Novel or a Play.* Stein tried to point out the relationship of landscape to narrative within the text:

A play and an event. Also a story and their birth. Possibly the men and their arrival. May be they will.[130]

and succeeded in juxtaposing them:

The George Washington is not a memory.
He has been in the country.
Autumn scenery is lovely and as it is a good season and there is little money it is easy to find men workers.
George Washington was the father of his country. He was first in war first in peace and first in the hearts of his countrymen his life is not a memory.
The scenery of autumn is very lovely. There are many walnuts and the marshes are not empty nor are the rocks of trees nor of their color nor is there any lack of plenty.[131]

But she never quite accomplished in this early "narrative" play the treatment of landscape-as-narrative which succeeded so well in the later plays *Doctor Faustus* and *The Mother of Us All.*

A Play Called Not and Now displays a similar struggle with narrative.

In fact, it plays with the possibility of characters being simultaneously distant (in a story) and immediate (in the now). Are the characters here or are they not? Are they who they are or are they someone else? Are they not *and* now?

Act I

The ones who look like Dashiell Hammett Picasso Charlie Chaplin and Lord Berners stand around.

They hesitate about making witty remarks to each other but they do it just the same. This is what they say.

The one who looks like Dashiell Hammett looks at the one that looks like Picasso and both together look at the one that looks like Charlie Chaplin and the three of them then look at the one that looks like Lord Berners, and then they all say, we do not look like any other one and they did not and do not. And they say they say all together we will look at the women and then each one of them says each one as he sees each one and another one, at which one. They all answer as they look as if they did look like them.

Yes they say one says yes. Then one says if you say yes and I do not say yes will he say yes.

The one that looked like Dashiell Hammett said he was saying yes. The one that looked like Picasso said yes he did say he had been to say yes and the one that looked like Charlie Chaplin said if not no one had not said yes and the one who looked like Lord Berners said yes, yes he said yes. And then they all looked at the women. None of them who looked like Anita Loos or Gertrude Atherton or Lady Diana Grey or Katharine Cornell or Daisy Fellowes said yes.

That is it.

And so they all began again to look like another one.

The one that looked like Dashiell Hammett said.

If I look at you you will not look like me.

The one that looked like Picasso said, I said I did not look at two and three.

The one that looked like Charlie Chaplin said.

Charlie Chaplin looked like me.

The one that looked like Lord Berners said.

I do not look at me.

And all of them then came to be nearly ready to stay where they were as they stayed where they were.[132]

Between *George Washington* and *Doctor Faustus,* the play in which Stein felt she first succeeded in creating a narrative play, *Identity a Play* is the only one which exhibits a definite, though limited, narrative. It is a narrative in the sense that something is resolved in its telling. By its end a decision has emerged from a play among the three forces of human nature, human mind, and the dog.

Scene II

I am I because my little dog knows me even if the little dog is a big one and yet a little dog knowing me does not really make me be I no, not really because after all being I I am I has really nothing to do with the little dog knowing me, he is my audience, but an audience never does prove to you that you are you.[133]

Stein's movement into narration in 1932 with *The Autobiography of Alice B. Toklas* was her first deliberate employment of a sequential story with its inherent smoothness. Though she had earlier thought about story constructs, expressing as she did the essence of what happened in her first plays, she consciously used story only in her late plays beginning in 1932 with *Scenery and George Washington,* which I have singled out as a transitional work. Conscious use of a technique, however, has no inherent relation to its manifestation in an artwork, and it is clear from the plays of this period that it took some time to arrive at a happy balance between landscape and narration. Once the balance was struck the plays could emerge, as Stein believed they did, as narratives distributed through space, sequential but not causally connected, lacking overt action—in short, narratives treated as landscapes.

Recognition of the standard three periods is useful in defining and distinguishing trends in Stein's thinking as she approached the art of playwriting. It is clear from her theoretical writings and from the plays themselves that she progressed from an intent to express occurrences and relations between people and things in an essential manner, to a desire to express relations in the overtly physical terms of a landscape—including self-contained movement—and then on to an attempt to strike a balance between landscape and the comprehensibility inherent in narrative. However, this development took place less sequentially than organically; plays did not suddenly metamorphose into a new form. For this reason, strict adherence to such general periods can be confusing.

The plays from 1913–1946 emerged from Stein's reaction against theatre as a syncopatory experience, and all of them conform to a simple performance time. Even in the later plays of narration, the audience is not asked to immerse itself in the fiction of the play; rather, the fiction is presented in terms of the audience's reality in the present moment. In addition, the plays as a whole fulfill the three major trends of her aesthetic—the continuous present, self-contained movement, and entity—in a way in which her other writings never could. They do so by the implicit assumption of performance, by representing relational movement with no links to the outside world, and by creating a self-sufficient universe which has final, physical significance.

I submit that the plays are better approached through a consideration of the myriad techniques employed by Stein, and manifested within the plays' texts, to produce this immediate, dynamic, and self-contained theatre. Regardless of periods and intent as revealed in theoretical works, it is important to isolate and demonstrate the actual techniques which produce these effects—techniques which may well surpass the notion of periods and provide a unified view of her theatre art.

3

Play Analysis

Gertrude Stein's disruption of the alternate reality — or fiction — of the traditional theatre is the unifying principle of all her plays, regardless of period. Insofar as she was able to accomplish this disruption, she rooted the experience of the spectator in the theatrical present, avoiding what she termed "syncopation," and established an immediate relationship between the spectator and the physical world of the stage. This relationship involved no identification with a fiction on stage, but a detachment from it and a focus upon the surface of the theatre experience.

If this description seems to bear some resemblance to the intent of Brecht, it is best to take the analogy no further, for Brecht rendered social and political realities for overtly utilitarian ends. Stein's concerns, on the other hand, lay solely in the realm of epistemology. Interested less in political and social questions than in everyday reality, she sought to transmit her knowledge simply and directly to another mind. This is not to say that her position was not political. As Marcuse has said,

> The political potential of art lies only in its own aesthetic dimension. Its relation to praxis is inexorably indirect, mediated, and frustrating. The more immediately political the work of art, the more it reduces the power of estrangement and the radical, transcendant goals of change. In this sense, there may be more subversive potential in the poetry of Baudelaire and Rimbaud than in the didactic plays of Brecht.[1]

Stein made demands — through the "flatness" of her language; her preoccupation with horizontal, not vertical movement; her denial of narrative in her narrative plays and of stories in her essential plays; her interest in vibratory, not overt movement; her focus upon a series of disembodied presents; and her use of ambiguity and equivocality as a means of achieving balance within those presents. Above all, she demanded that the spectator encounter the work in itself, minus referents and ramifications.

This conception of plays and the theatre differs from the traditional one in its concentration upon theatre as an act in and of itself, rather than as an "imitation of an action" — the dominant view from the time of Aristotle. Life consists in action, Aristotle tells us, and its end is a mode of action, not a quality. But in attempting to cope with the changing landscape of the new century, Gertrude Stein found that life was indeed a quality and not an action. Furthermore, the only way to capture this quality, she decided, was to approach it moment by moment. Such an attitude contradicts directly the traditional view of plays and the theatre expressed by Bernard Beckerman[2] and Sam Smiley[3] — which is that the structure of the theatre experience inheres in action — and sums up Stein's iconoclastic position in traditional dramaturgy. Every aspect of her theatre art stems from this position, and every segment of her technique adheres to it.

Her plays, as a result, defy any attempt to analyze them according to traditional modes, which were, after all, set up to describe traditional drama. We may take Smiley's *Playwriting: The Structure of Action* to represent the orthodox views, which that book summarizes effectively. Though those views have little application to the work of Gertrude Stein, as we shall see in detail in this chapter, they help to delineate her general approach by their sheer opposition to it. For this reason, the characteristics of the traditional play as Smiley explains them will be used as counterpoints to aspects of Stein's technique as they are examined in this chapter. This is not to say that Stein's technique will be examined in the same fashion as Smiley examines traditional technique. Dialogue, for instance, since it is often lacking or inconsistent in Stein's plays, will appear not as a separate category under diction, as Smiley structures it, but as an aspect of perspective and text format, where it emerges in the most clear light.

In forcing audience attention upon the simple present moment, Stein evolved a style which completely disrupted traditional, consequential stage reality. The specific techniques used to accomplish this style vary widely, but we can consider them with clarity and ease by associating them under the concepts of form and subject matter.

Form

To say that Gertrude Stein's plays exhibit random form is to deny her seriousness of purpose regarding this aspect of her plays: she engaged in a systematic attempt to render non-traditional subject matter — the disengaged present moment — in a style appropriate to it. The chronological progression and dialogue structures in the traditional play are replaced in the plays of Stein by a structure-less, or paradoxically, a structure-conscious text which has to be taken on its own terms or not at all. Assumptions about the worlds of plays and of dramaturgy, of orthodox dramatic constructs or principles, go for nought in her plays. One must come to them openly and actively, ready to perceive them in whatever way they emerge at the moment they emerge. Stein was dedicated to the evolution of a style which would adequately express not the old world, but the new world of her experience. Her plays do not share the conventions of the traditional play; nor should they if they are describing a static world. The conventions of playwriting, after all, do not constitute the core of the playwright's craft, though they may be useful means for easy translation in the traditional theatre.

In order to establish the form—the style and its emergent structure—of Stein's plays I have applied to them a number of traits which enabled an examination of them in two categories we are familiar with, stillness and entity. In the category of stillness, we shall consider such aspects of her plays as juxtaposition, time, character, repetition, modification, and rhyme to establish the particular techniques Stein used to capture the isolated moments of her perception. Finally, we shall examine the ramifications of these aspects of style upon her structure by considering text divisions, and see to what extent it actually contradicts traditional methods of ordering plays.

In the category of entity we shall examine clarity vs. hermeticism, relationship of logical to non-logical expression, author's perspective, stage directions, and textual interpolations to see exactly how Stein confines the attention of the spectator to the work in itself and how she provides for movement within the static play. Additionally, we shall look at play format, where the most concrete evidence for this self-contained movement is found.

Stillness

Juxtaposition. Sam Smiley tells us that the structure of the traditional play inheres in its action. The structure of Gertrude Stein's plays inheres in a greater or lesser degree of stillness. She rarely presents through-action in Smiley's sense, but a series of disconnected moments which may or may not include even the smallest segment of action in his sense, the incident.[4] Because of her adherence to these moments, the plays do not exhibit causality, as linearly structured plays do.[5] Nor do they align themselves with the works of Beckett and selected other modernists which exhibit, according to Smiley, not linear but vertical structure—plumbing in depth discrete moments.[6] Rather, they present the essence, and only the essence, of the moment. Besides, as we saw in Chapter one, Beckett utilizes a style that "takes time," gradually rendering his singular object over a series of moments, while Stein renders a series of objects at each moment that she renders them. The art of these "vertical" dramatists is not so static as that of Gertrude Stein.

By setting down side by side text elements within a sentence or paragraph and by omitting or transforming transitive elements of grammar Stein created an arrangement of images in her plays that was quite unlike the traditional sequential arrangement with its logical transitions and resulting smoothness. This juxtaposition enabled her to root the spectator's experience in the sentence or paragraph itself, to avoid any suspension of the experience over a larger section of text. It is the technique she used to realize her "continuous present." *What Happened* (1913) reflects juxtaposition of elements within the sentence:

> A wide oak a wide enough oak, a very wide cake, a lightning cooky, a single wide open and exchanged box filled with the same little sac that shines.
> The best the only better and more left footed stranger.
> The very kindness there is in all lemons oranges apples pears and potatoes.[7]

A wide oak, for instance, can hardly be said to lead to a wide enough oak, a very wide cake, etc. Rather, it is a distinct sentence element retaining its identity at the expense of any forward movement or transition. It is there to relate with, not lead to, the other phrases. Even the final sentence containing the transitive verb "is" sacrifices the transitive capabilities of that verb for its substantive quality. "Is" does not link kindness to lemons, exactly, but produces a juxtaposition of kindness and lemons, a new conjunction, a fresh relationship.

Juxtaposition within the sentence in the fashion of *What Happened* occurs from 1913 to *Not Sightly* in 1915; in 1923 with *Am I To Go*; with all three plays in 1928, *A Lyrical Opera Made by Two, Paiseau,* and *A Bouquet. Their Wills*; with *Madame Recamier* in 1930; with the five plays of 1932, *A Play of Pounds, A Manoir, A Play a Lion, Short Sentences,* and *Scenery and George Washington*; and with *Doctor Faustus* in 1937. Though these nineteen plays share this intense juxtaposition, they give quite different effects, depending on whether the images arising from such juxtaposition are homogeneous or heterogeneous. *What Happened* can be said to reflect heterogeneity of images:

> Suggesting a sage brush with a turkey and also something abominable is not the only pain there is in so much provoking. There is even more. To begin a lecture is a strange way of taking dirty apple blossoms and is there more use in water, certainly there is if there is going to be fishing, enough water would make desert and even prunes, it would make nothing throw any shade because after all, is there not more practical humor in a series of photographs and also in a treacherous sculpture.[8]

Whereas, *Doctor Faustus* possesses images which are mostly homogeneous, a characteristic of most traditional literature:

D.F. What do I care there is no here or there. What am I. I am Doctor Faustus who knows everything can do everything and you say it was through you but not at all, if I had not been in a hurry and if I had taken my time I would have known how to make white electric light and day-light and night light and what did I do I saw you miserable devil I saw you and I was deceived and I believed miserable devil I thought I needed you, and I thought I was tempted by the devil and I know no temptation is tempting unless the devil tells you so.[9]

This passage possesses images which are similar in character and which have been traditionally grouped together, yet shares the level of juxtaposition within the sentence characteristic of *What Happened,* and reflects what Stein believed to be her "continuous present."

Another group of plays displays juxtaposition between sentences, the sentences themselves retaining conventional transitions. This group of twenty-two plays from *He Said It* in 1915 to *Lucretia Borgia* in 1938 displays juxtaposition much less intensely, as *A Circular Play* (1920) demonstrates:

A citroen and a citizen
A miss and bliss.
We came together.
Then suddenly there was an army.
In my room.
We asked them to go away
We asked them very kindly to stay.
How can Cailloux be dead again.
Napoleon is dead.
Not again.
A morning celebration.
And a surprising birthday.
A room is full of odd bits of disturbing furniture.
Guess again.[10]

Although the first sentence can be said to be juxtaposed within itself, the rest are juxtaposed with another sentence. The passage possesses heterogeneous images in the manner of *What Happened*, describing a series of continuous presents not usually connected. *He Said It* (1915) reflects juxtaposition between sentences, and results in heterogeneous images, too:

I consider it very healthy to eat sugared figs not pressed figs I do not care for pressed figs.

I consider it necessary to eat sugared prunes and an apple. I have felt it be the only advice I could give. It has been successful. I really feel great satisfaction in the results. No one can say that short hair is unbecoming.[11]

Please do not Suffer (1916) reflects the same extent of juxtaposition, but possesses homogeneous images:

(Mrs. Marchand).   I do not write often. I say I will mention it if a man pays attention to a woman and so I can say that I have not written. I will do as I like. I find that my baby is very healthy. I hope he will not talk the language spoken here but I can not say this to him. He is too young. He is not walking. If the Dardanelles are not taken perhaps they will open. I hear myself speaking. I have an orange tree that is open. The sun comes in. For ten days during ten days it rains and then until December we will have good weather. There is no fire in the house. I do not like to look at that map. Will you excuse me while I give my baby his luncheon.[12]

The plays containing heterogeneous images appear to be more disjointed than those with homogeneous ones, as is clear from this example, as though the latter are constructed according to a strictly adhered-to context. They tend to stay within some kind of obvious boundary. This would clash with Stein's aesthetic precepts were it not for the fact that she avoids transition within that context as she does here, juxtaposing a variety of sentences which conform to wartime perspectives on child-rearing, to produce a series of present moments. The transitions that would mark the conventional paragraph are absent. Still, the plays which reflect juxtaposition between sentences and homogeneous images are closer to the structure of the traditional play. They are more readily understood and perceived by the spectator attuned to patterns in Western literature and theatre since they reflect a consistent context. But traditional patterns are nevertheless challenged in these plays, for they force the spectator to begin anew with each statement.

A number of plays are closer still to accepted patterns, containing one or more paragraphs within which there are no juxtaposed sentences. *Bonne Annee* and *Captain Walter Arnold* (1916), *Lesson Sixteen* (1941), *In a Garden* (1943), *Three Sisters who are not Sisters* (1943), and *Look and Long* (1943) share this type of structure. *Bonne Annee* develops smoothly and logically from sentence to sentence most of the way through:

We do understand our pleasure. Our pleasure is to do every day the work of that day, to cut our hair and not want blue eyes and to be reasonable and obedient. To obey and not split hairs. This is our duty and our pleasure.[13]

Here, we begin to see transitive parts of speech actually working as transitives. *Lesson Sixteen* displays the structure more consistently:

A little boy was standing in front of a house and opposite him was a blackberry vine.
The blackberry vine had a very pleasant expression.
    How do you do little boy, it said.
    Very well I thank you said the little boy only I am all alone.
    Not like me said the blackberry vine I am never alone.
    No said the little boy not even in winter.[14]

As does *Look and Long*:

<pre>
              Jenny: Look at the chair.
              Helen: Which chair.
              Jenny: The only chair.
              Ellen: I can't see the only chair.
Jenny (*with a shriek*): Look at the only chair.
  All Three Together: There is no chair there.
             Samuel: No there is no chair there because I am sitting on it.
          Sylvester: And there is no him there because I am sitting on him.[15]
</pre>

This group of plays reflects a smoothness in the lines atypical of her aesthetic as a whole, and though it corresponds to some extent with her move toward narrative (the last five are narrative plays), it does not include all of the narrative plays, most of which involve juxtaposition to some degree.

The greatest number of plays, thirty, involve some combination of juxtaposition within and between sentences. *A Movie* (1920), *Photograph* (1920), eight plays between *Reread Another* (1921) and *A Village* (1923), *Four Saints* (1927), *Parlor* and *At Present* (1930), eleven plays from *Weighed* (1930) to *Civilization* (1931), *Scenery and George Washington* (1932), *Byron* (1933), *Daniel Webster* (1937), *Yes* (1944–1946), *The Mother of Us All* (1945–1946) and *John Breon* (1946) are all examples of this combination. *A Movie* alternates this way between internal and external sentence juxtaposition:

> Its snowing but no matter we will get there in the taxi. Take us two days and two nights you inside and me out. Hurry. They start, the funny little taxi goes over the mountains with and without assistance, all tired out he is inside, she driving when they turn down the hill into Avignon. Just then two American motor cycles come on and Bretonne femme de menage losing her head grand smash. American painter wakes up burned, he sees the two and says by god and makes believe he is dead. The two are very helpful. A team comes along and takes American painter and all to hospital. Two Americans ride off on motor cycles direction of Nîmes and Pont du Gard.[16]

"The two are very helpful" and "A team comes along and takes american painter and all to hospital" contain transitions; the other sentences are juxtaposed within themselves at some point. *Capital Capitals* is another example:

> First Capital. In sight of the first capital because of this capital beside this as a capital because of this as their capital and becoming this becoming their possession by way of this and their having the possession, permit to credit you with an excellent reason for remaining here. Permit me to do this and also permit me to assure you that coming again is not as pleasant as coming again and again and coming again and again is very nearly the best way of establishing where there is the most pleasure the most reasonable-

ness the most plenty the most activity, the most sculpture the most liberty the most meditation the most calamity and the most separation. If rose trees are cut down again and again he can be busily engaged and if he is busily engaged can he nourish hope and if he nourishes hope can he converse and if he converses can he say he hopes that some day he will supply the same that he did supply when the sun heated and the sun heated. When the mountains are near by and not high little mountains made at the right angle are not high and yet we can imply that they are neither nearby nor high and they are near by and they are near high. The capital was nearly eight hundred miles away. This gives me no idea of its distance of the distance from here to there.[17]

The Mother of Us All alternates this way:

> Susan B.   On the Platform. Ladies there is no neutral position for us to assume. If we say we love the cause and then sit down at our ease, surely does our action speak the lie.
> And now will Daniel Webster take the platform as never before.
>
> Daniel Webster.   Coming and coming alone, no man is alone when he comes, when he comes when he is coming he is not alone and now ladies and gentlemen I have done, remember that remember me remember each one.
>
> Susan B.   And now Virgil T. Virgil T. will bow and speak and when it is necessary they will know that he is he.
>
> Virgil T.   I make what I make, I make what I make, I make a noise, there is a poise in making a noise.[18]

All but six of Stein's plays contain a significant extent of juxtaposition, most of them reflecting some combination of intense juxtaposition within the sentence and a more relaxed one between sentences. The appearance of texts within these categories is modified by their reflection of homogeneous or heterogeneous images. Obviously, the most traditionally structured plays reflect this juxtaposition within the paragraph (or not at all) and homogeneous images, like the following fifteen: *Every Afternoon. A Dialogue* (1916), *Bonne Annee* (1916), *Please do not Suffer* (1916), *Polybe in Port* (1916), *Accents in Alsace* (1919), *A Movie* (1920), *Film* (1929), *Identity. A Play* (1935), *Listen to Me* (1936), *A Play Called Not and Now* (1936), *Lucretia Borgia* (1938), *Lesson Sixteen* (1941), *In a Garden* (1943), *Three Sisters* (1943) and *Look and Long* (1943). But the vast majority of Stein's plays, sixty-two in all, avoid the structure of the traditional play through her technique of juxtaposition and keep the spectator attuned to the present tense of the theatre experience.

Time.   Most of Stein's plays, then, are constructed according to horizontal (present) time, the extent of juxtaposition dictating the structural component (sentence or paragraph) to which the present conforms. "Horizontal" here is not meant in the sense that Smiley uses it. For him, the term refers to causally structured plays, plays which progress in time; and "vertical" refers to plays which stand on one spot of that time to focus in depth upon the particular moment.[19] We can hardly use the term "vertical" to describe the plays of Stein: as I have suggested, she focuses not on the depth but on the surface of the moment. In addition, we have seen that this "vertical" structure actually involves time. Playwrights like Beckett suspend the moment in the telling of it, and his texts all reflect at least limited movement from point A to point B. Stein describes one moment thoroughly then moves to the next, always adequate to the moment as it occurs, and her texts rarely reflect movement in even Beckett's sense. We might say that Stein's plays involve no time discrepancy in the rendering. But rather than say that Stein's plays are timeless, we can use the term "horizontal" as it might be applied to perspective in painting. By changing perspective with each pictorial component, a painter will make a flat canvas, one that does not tempt the spectator's attention away from its surface. It is horizontally, not vertically, constructed. A painter who operates according to the Renaissance tradition, from a single perspective, makes a painting which draws the spectator's eye away from the surface of the canvas into a fictional reality. It carries the attention of the spectator away on a vertical line, rather than letting it stay on the surface of the flat canvas. Stein's plays are constructed horizontally in this fashion and reflect a present tense.

But many of her plays reflect some amount of spiral (turning back on itself) or vertical (progressive) time as well as horizontal time. Plays reflecting spiral time in addition to horizontal are *Lend a Hand or Four Religions* (1922), *A List* (1923), *Capital Capitals* (1923), *A Village* (1923), *Four Saints* (1927), *A Play of Pounds* (1932), *Listen to Me* (1936), and *The Mother of Us All* (1945–1946). Spiral time in these plays is reflected in a fugue-like pattern wherein motifs are repeated and varied throughout the text. Time moves forward and turns back on itself at intervals, becoming fuller as the play progresses. At the same time, each moment occurring as the play progresses can be said to be discrete, as it fully expresses the present moment. *Lend a Hand or Four Religions* demonstrates this:

First religion As she advances is she led.
First religion Is she led as she advances.
That is the name of a house isn't it.
And a well.
First religion as she advances. Furnish a house as well.
Second religion as they advance. They furnish a house as well.
Third religion as she has advanced. Has she furnished a house as well or has she furnished a house as well as she has furnished a house.
Fourth religion as she is advancing and she will furnish a house as well.

Fourth religion Very well to advance to see some one then and to furnish a house as well.

Third religion, third religion to advance and to see some one or to furnish a house as well or to advance and furnish a house as well or to see someone or furnish a house as well.

Second religion They advance and as they advance they see some one and they furnish a house as well. As well furnish a house. They might furnish a house as well.[20]

Listen to Me is constructed less intensively, though more completely, according to this pattern — the motifs of Sweet William looking for his Lillian, the identity of the Fifth Character, the dog who can no longer bark at the moon because lights are too bright, and the presence of too many people on the earth to ever locate one appear rhythmically through the text and become fuller with each recurrence, but remain rooted in the present tense.

A Movie (1920), *Identity a Play* (1935), *Doctor Faustus* (1938), *Lucretia Borgia* (1938), *Lesson Sixteen* (1941), *In a Garden* (1943), *Three Sisters* (1943), *Look and Long* (1943), *Yes* (1944-1946), *The Mother of Us All* (1945-1946), and *John Breon* (1946) all reflect progressive time in addition to horizontal time. But in all eleven, the qualities, textures, and rhythms of the story as it unfolds are explored at the expense of a progression typical of most traditional plays. These plays can be contrasted with the horizontally structured plays by comparing at some length *A Movie* with *Film*. Though both of these plays are organized according to a series of events, only *A Movie* presents causal connections between events and a resulting forward momentum. As a rule, *A Movie* displays juxtaposition within a sentence and transition between sentences, allowing for development. *Film* displays the reverse, and stands still.

In *A Movie*, an American painter/taxi driver turned secret service agent investigates the disappearance of a sum of money from a quartermaster's department with the help of a Bretonne *femme de menage*. Her fifth cousin, upon prompting, reveals a suspicious and possibly related visitation of a wounded American soldier by two American officers in an Avignon hospital. The painter and the Bretonne f.m. drive to Avignon in the taxi to investigate and collide en route with two Americans on motorcycles. The American painter and the Bretonne f.m. are taken to the Avignon hospital where they learn that the two Americans on motorcycles are the very same Americans who have been visiting the wounded soldier. They leave the hospital in the direction the two Americans were travelling in their mended taxi, and catch up with them at Pont du Gard. There ensues an "exciting duel" among the American painter, the Bretonne f.m., a French Gendarme, and the two American "crooks" on motorcycles. The crooks are captured as they try to escape over the Pont du Gard, and it is revealed that they have been the receivers of the stolen money. The American painter and the Bretonne f.m. keep up their exploits, and bring up the rear of the procession at the final triumph of the allies at the request of General Pershing.

Though the incidents of *Film* can be recounted as easily as those of *A Movie*, their causal arrangement is missing entirely. As a result, time is purely horizontal, no one incident developing into another but each occurring independently. The film opens on the corner of a street on the outskirts of Paris. A mature laundress holding her package of linen is looking intensely at a photograph of two white dogs. A two-seater car is parked along the pavement. Suddenly, two women approach the laundress from the car and demand to see the photo. She and the two women look, full of admiration, until the moment when a young woman who looks like a beauty queen wanders down the street, passes the empty car, enters it quickly, and begins to cry. At that moment, the two women enter the car and cast the young woman outside. She falls against the laundress who starts to question her, and the car, driven by the two women, leaves. All of a sudden the laundress realizes she no longer has the photo. She sees a young man and tells him the story immediately.

A few hours later in front of the lost and found on Dragon Street, there is another laundress, younger, with her packet of laundry. The car of the two women approaches, stops, and the two women descend, showing the photo of the two white dogs to the laundress. She regards it with pleasure and excitement, but that's all. Just at that moment the young beauty queen approaches, utters a cry of joy, and dashes towards the car. The two women enter their car and upon entering, drop a little packet. They leave abruptly, with the photo in their possession.

The next day the first laundress is again on the street with her packet of laundry, and she sees the young beauty queen approach with a little packet in her hand. At the same time she sees the young man. They are all three together and all of a sudden the car with the two women passes. With them there is a real white dog with a little packet in its mouth. The three on the sidewalk watch it pass and understand nothing.

This play exemplifies the self-contained movement described in Chapters one and two which emerged in Stein's aesthetic in 1911 and intensified later in her career. By leaving out causal connections Stein increases the number of possible links between isolated story elements to such an extent that we have a network of possibilities and nothing more. There is a possible connection, for example, between the small packet dropped by the two women, the small packet in the possession of the beauty queen when she next appears, and the packet in the mouth of the dog, but no overt connection. There is a possibility that the white dog has been lost and the photo is connected with an attempt to find it, that the beauty queen has something to do with its disappearance or recovery, but in the end all we have are possibilities and relationships between two women, two laundresses, the beauty queen, the man, the photograph of the dogs and the real dog, the three laundry packets, the three small packets, the three confrontations, and the group of three on the corner who watch the three pass by in the car. As was the case in *Three Sisters who are not Sisters* (see Chapter two) neither the character nor the spectator comprehends what goes on because the connections are simply not there. Rather, a series of discrete story elements stand alone in a continuous present, moving within and among themselves, but connecting with nothing, progressing nowhere.

While the plays organized according to progressive time represent a move toward more traditional playwriting, even they remain ultimately in the realm of the present. Any plot they can be conceived to contain remains minimal and static enough to avoid transporting the spectator from the actual theatre experience into a progressive, fictional reality.

Other techniques of stillness.   Gertrude Stein emphasizes the continuous present brought about through juxtaposition of text elements by using repetition, modification, and rhyme, all of which have the effect of rooting the text where it begins. Sometimes these techniques are used to such an extent that they become the virtual determinants of style in a play. Modification is rampant in *Am I to Go or I'll Say So* (1923):

Interlude

The war.
Why is paper scarce.
Paper is not very scarce

Interlude

Not the war.
Or not the war
Indeed or not the war.
Or indeed or not the war.
Drawing paper is not scarce.
Or in drawing paper drawing paper is not scarce.
Nor is drawing paper scarce.
Or in or not in the war.
Either or.
Or the war.
Or not the war.
Or drawing paper.
Or scarce paper.

Or paper is not scarce.
Or drawing paper.[21]

and in *A List* (1923):

> Martha   A second list makes one day, a second list makes some day, a second list makes Monday, a second list makes Sunday, a second list makes more than one day a second list makes one day and makes one day.[22]

By taking an original statement and modifying it Stein comes up with a series of discrete statements which capture the object of her perception at the moment she renders it. At times, however, these statements can be said to combine with surrounding statements to suspend the present.

Modification is exhibited in sixty-six plays and is tied closely to her technique of repetition which, as she explained in *Captain Walter Arnold* (1916), was not repetition at all:

> Can you recollect any example of easy repetition. I can and I can mention it. I can explain how by twice repeating you change the meaning you actually change the meaning. This makes it more interesting.[23]

Repetition, while creating a series of discrete statements, actually intensifies the original statement, isolating it from traditional associations and references, and makes it a new statement. In the tradition of "a rose is a rose is a rose" we have in *Four Saints* (1927):

> Saint Plan.
>   Once in a while.
> Saint Therese.   Once in a while.
> Saint Plan.   Once in a while.
> Saint Chavez.   Once in a while.
> Saint Settlement. Once in a while.
> Saint Therese.   Once in a while.
> Saint Chavez.   Once in a while.
> Saint Cecile.   Once in a while.
> Saint Genevieve. Once in a while.
> Saint Anne.   Once in a while.
> Saint Settlement. Once in a while.
> Saint Therese.   Once in a while.[24]

Fifty-one plays rely on repetition in this manner.

A combination of modification and repetition is evident in many passages, the most intense occurring in *Four Saints* and *The Mother of Us All*:

> Pigeons on the grass alas.
> Pigeons on the grass alas.

> Short longer grass short longer longer shorter yellow grass Pigeons large pigeons on the shorter longer yellow grass alas pigeons on the grass.[25]

> Susan B. Anthony. Susan B. Anthony is my name to choose a name is feeble, Susan B. Anthony is my name, a name can only be a name my name can only be my name, I have a name, Susan B. Anthony is my name, to choose a name is feeble.[26]

Fifty-one plays reflect this combination.

Rhyme is used in forty-eight plays to punctuate Stein's present, *Am I to Go or I'll Say So* and *Four Saints* being prime examples:

> There was no check upon which to put the blame. There was the check and there was a frame and it was not to blame. It was not shame shame fie for shame nobody nobody will know the name. And all the same he was to blame and blame as to circumstance shame as to circumstance resemble as to the same. The same. All the same. All the same as to this circumstance it was not to blame nor as to the mention of a frame.[27]

> Letting pin in letting let in let in in in in in let in let in wet in wed in dead in dead wed led in led wed dead in dead in led in wed in said in said led wed dead wed dead said led led said wed dead wed dead led in led in wed in wed in said in wed in led in said in dead in dead wed said led led said wed dead in.[28]

Other techniques have the effect of focusing the spectator upon his experience in the theatre. Her implementation of simple language as opposed to lyrical in sixty-seven of the plays and of monotonous, not variegated, sentence structure in thirty-six makes a composition which works against spectator involvement. *Accents in Alsace* (1919) is one exception to this, lulling the spectator by the richness of its images and rhythms:

> Sing so la douse so la dim.
> Un deux trois
> Can you tell me wha
> Is it indeed.
> What you call a Petide.
> And then what do I say to thee
> Let me kiss thee willingly.
> Not a mountain not a goat not a door.
> Not a whisper not a curl not a gore
> In me meeny miney mo.
> You are my love and I tell you so.
> > In the daylight
> > And the night
> Baby winks and holds me tight.
> In the morning and the day and the evening and alway.
> I hold my baby as I say.
> Completely.

And what is the accent of my wife.
And accent and the present life.
Oh sweet oh my oh sweet oh my
I love you love you and I try
I try not to be nasty and hasty and good
I am my little baby's daily food.[29]

A Manoir (1932), on the other hand, throws the spectator's attention back on itself for sheer lack of lyricism and variety:

A manoir is a temporary home.
They are very well placed there.
The object of it is that there is no envy.
All who are around come there.
Could history find a time.
Could it matter that which they may ask
Did they have no one to be sure
Could it be a change once for all.[30]

The same occurs in *Byron a Play* (1933):

Italy and Italian a wife cooking and a husband cleaning.
This may make it as seeming.
That Byron was lying leaning.
And a foot had that attention
From which not only which to mention.
That they will ask after they answer
No in no way if they look well
Do they see that he could dwell
Except in seeking warmth and heating
Which they can call
Which they can manage
Better manage can call.
Byron.
And he comes
And he comes appealing
And she is meaning.
To have feeling.
Which she does.[31]

Character.   Since Gertrude Stein's plays do not chart action, they do not exhibit character in the traditional sense either. The absence of consistent characters engaged in consistent action in her plays also has a disruptive effect upon the fictional reality of the stage. Though she ostensibly spoke through the persona of character as soon as she used dialogue or monologue, the emergent character was expressed in essence only.

    White Wines (1913) contains the first direct reference to character of any kind, listing in the introduction the following specifications:

1. All together.
2. Witnesses.
3. House to house.
      (5 women)[32]

Here, the references to "All together," "Witnesses," and "5 women" are ambiguous, amounting possibly to mere descriptions of personages not in the play itself. *For the Country Entirely* (1916) contains the first deliberate naming of characters and the first evidence of any kind of characterization. Through a series of letters written in the course of the play, we learn that Mrs. Henry Watterson finds it necessary to worship individuality, that Isabel Furness heard her hurrying, that Frederick and Harriett Beef like Latin and often spell together, and that Young Bonnet does not expect Mr. Lindo Webb to change his coat. Moreover, it is fairly obvious that these characters are present in the play itself and not merely described by a disembodied narrative voice. Attention to character in this play is sporadic, at best, however, most passages being unconnected with any particular character and no character ever being mentioned more than once. Character for Stein is just another convention to use for her own purposes. *Ladies' Voices* (1916), while following *Country* in its inconsistency, accomplishes an expressiveness of character through dialogue and attention to language:

> Honest to God Miss Williams I don't mean to say that I was older.
> But you were.
> Yes I was. I do not excuse myself. I feel that there is no reason for passing an archduke.
> You like the word.
> You know very well that they all call it their house.
> As Christ was to Lazarus so was the founder of the hill to Mahon.
> You really mean it.
> I do.[33]

Louis XI and Madame Giraud (1930) attains some depth of character, not to mention wit, in the following exchange:

Louis XI

> I knew I saw Madame Giraud.
> I knew her when I saw her.
> I knew she would like a republic.
> I knew it when I saw her.

Madame Giraud

> I knew I would not like a republic.
> I knew it when I heard that I had liked it.
> I do not like a republic.

But I prefer it.
I prefer a republic.
I knew it when I saw it.[34]

Though Stein at her best captures the essential qualities of her characters, as we can see in these plays, such exchanges do not make for deep understanding of character. Lack of depth and inconsistency in character presentation prevent the involvement a spectator would normally have in a character, short or long term.

It is not until *A Movie* (1920) that characters are presented consistently throughout the text. The American painter, the Bretonne f.m., and the two American crooks on motorcycles have consistent voices throughout and take part in a series of events which reflect upon them in various ways. Still, they can hardly be said to develop. They are as complete and detailed in the beginning as they will ever be; the only thing that changes is the background against which they react. As will be the case in all the plays that treat character consistently, there is no attempt on Stein's part to present or describe characters before they present themselves again and again throughout the play. Moreover, there is no attempt to posit their existence or behavior outside the discrete moments of the play. Characters exist for Stein only insofar as they act within the confines of the play as it is being written. She wrote in *The Geographical History of America*:

> There need be no personages in a play because if there are then you do not forget their names and if you do not forget their names you put their names down each time that they are to say something.
> The result of which is that a play finishes.[35]

The very concept of a sustained or developing character is a denial of her nonlinear art. According to Stein, character must be expressed, and fully expressed, at each moment in the composition. If her audience attempts to combine those moments and argue for consistency, it has nothing to do with her and has no effect upon her technique.

In addition, her plays rarely exhibit the conventional distancing of author from character which allows, in Smiley's words, "the character to speak about what he himself feels and thinks."[36] Rather, they often include what is obviously the feeling and opinion of Gertrude Stein above and beyond her characters. Stein's position as an observer in the new world, it will be remembered, was as close to any one moment of the writing as it was to the next, and called for her own attitudes to be presented along with any fiction. But inevitably, character provided a means whereby Stein could escape occasionally from the narrative voice so dominant in her other work. In *They Weighed Weighed-Layed* (1930) she lists all the characters and states, "they think with me."[37] And in *Saints and Singing* she seems to address her characters when she states, "Converse with me. In a play you converse with me."[38] It is even doubtful to what extent Stein felt she should control her characters. In *Madame Recamier* (1930) she writes:

> Plays as they like
> They play as they like[39]

Though character traditionally provides a way for an author to vary her voice within the parameters of her art, it is rarely considered on these purely formal grounds in modern dramaturgy; rather, character is often considered to be an end in itself in this age of psychology. If a playwright can create a character with whom the spectator can identify, she has little else to do to ensure his interest in her play. It is safe to say that Stein never immersed herself or wanted to immerse her audience in character to this degree. She wanted to present character as it emerged during the course of the play and desired that the spectator see the presentation as much as the character itself. She was concerned first and foremost with character as a formal construct.

Subsequent to *A Movie* (1920), consistent, named characters emerge in *Saints and Singing* (1922), *A Saint in Seven* (1922), *Lend a Hand or Four Religions* (1922), *Capital Capitals* (1923), *Four Saints in Three Acts* (1927), *Film* (1929), and in the great majority of plays written after 1929. The most complete treatment of character comes in *Four Saints, Daniel Webster* (1937), *Lesson Sixteen* (1941), *In a Garden* (1943), *Look and Long* (1943), *Yes* (1944–1946), *Mother* (1945–1946) and *John Breon* (1946). In these plays, Stein balances the amount stated about characters by narrator, other characters, and the characters themselves with enough actual interaction to present a detailed individual. Still, her later characters remain essential expressions of character more than fully developed characters in Smiley's sense. Emerging from Stein's typical moment-by-moment presentation, they do not so much develop as emerge full-blown at the start. Stein avoided the peaks and valleys of her characters' experience just as she did those of action. As a result, the characters seem to disengage from the very lines they speak. Susan B., the crowning glory of Stein's efforts toward characterization, is detached at the height of her struggle. Her indictment of men is a reasoned, even one:

> Susan B.   Yes but, what is man, what are men, what are they. I do not say that they
> haven't kind hearts, if I fall down in a faint they will rush to pick me up, if
> my house is on fire, they will rush in to put the fire out and help me, yes
> they have kind hearts but they are afraid, afraid, they are afraid. They fear
> women, they fear each other, they fear their neighbor, they fear other

countries and then they hearten themselves in their fear by crowding together and following each other, and when they crowd together and follow each other they are brutes, like animals who stampede, and so they have written in the name male into the United States constitution, because they are afraid of black men because they are afraid of women, because they are afraid afraid. Men are afraid.

Anne.   And women.

Susan B.   Ah women often have not any sense of danger, after all a hen screams pitifully when she sees an eagle but she is only afraid for her children, men are afraid for themselves, that is the real difference between men and women.[40]

What would be her aria occurs at the end of the play:

Susan B.'s voice.

We cannot retrace our steps, going forward may be the same as going backwards. We cannot retrace our steps, retrace our steps. All my long life, all my life, we do not retrace our steps, all my long life, but.
(*A silence a long silence*)
But-we do not retrace our steps, all my long life, and here, here we are here, in marble and gold, did I say gold, yes I said gold, in marble and gold and where—
(*A silence*)
Where is where. In my long life of effort and strife, dear life, life is strife, in my long life, it will not come and go, I tell you so, it will stay it will pay but
(*A long silence*)
But do I want what we have got, has it not gone, what made it live, has it not gone because now it is had, in my long life in my long life
(*Silence*)
Life is strife, I was a martyr all my life not to what I won but to what was done.
(*Silence*)
Do you know because I tell you so or do you know, do you know.
(*Silence*)
My long life, my long life.[41]

Though this restraint makes for a powerful passage, it issues from Stein's desire to present the essential Susan B. Detached from the struggle herself, the character dictates that the spectator detach himself too.

Text divisions.   The appearance of the traditional play text on the printed page gives a reader or director a clear indication of how that play proceeds from moment to moment through dialogue, scenes, and acts. Traditional dialogue, according to Smiley, is "a means of expressing thoughts which characters employ as they participate in an action."[42] He goes on to say that "the dialogue of a play should present items of plot and story, reveal the nature of characters, communicate thoughts, set moods, and form basic rhythms."[43] Though Stein's dialogue accomplishes some of these tasks, it is obvious that, to the extent she uses it, it deals less with story or plot than it does with the essential quality of the moment. And because of the lack of action and traditional dialogue in most of her plays, Smiley's "beats," "segments," "scenes," and "acts" — all of which emerge progressively from the smallest portion of the script, dialogue — can hardly apply to the art of Stein. Though "beat," which he describes as a thought unit, could describe some of Gertrude Stein's discrete moments, the other divisions, which he describes as providing a coherence for intentions and climaxes occurring within them, could not.[44] In the plays of Gertrude Stein, text divisions such as acts and scenes rarely serve the function he describes. Only occasionally providing coherence for events or intentions occurring within them, they often appear as pure manifestations of play. Since this is the case, we need to proceed on a more basic level than Smiley does and pose the following questions: when do Stein's acts and scenes function as brackets in Smiley's sense, when do they progress from Act One to Act Two and so on as a traditional play would, and when do they serve no apparent function but exist as independent entities?

In eleven of the plays, text divisions are entirely absent, the text organized solely according to sequences of sentences, no one section of the text having a greater unity than any other. The unity inheres in the moment of composition and nothing more, in the whole within the part, unaltered by the imposition of larger acts or scenes.

Short Sentences (1932), organized according to 545 different names attached to short sentences, provides the clearest example of this absence of text divisions:

> The scene is one in which nicely they go.

Madame Bucher.	Will you come
Nathalie.	Oh yes will you come
Amelia.	But I know you will come
Barbette.	I ask you to come
Eugene.	Will you.
Joseph.	I have been able to come
Edmund.	Is he better because you bring what you bring when you do come

> Chorus
> And so they are all not alike.[45]

The use of 545 characters, each one having a line of sorts, works against structuring the play in segments any larger than the actual line, and successfully keeps the attention of the spectator on the moment.

The point is made less dramatically in *He Said It. Monologue* (1915), a straightforward dialogue between, for all appearances, Stein and Alice Toklas:

I feel that there must be a regular time for the oranges.
Oh yes indeed.
It was a surprise to you.
I say that I am certain that a great many things can be said.
Call it a fan love.

The piece continues with Toklas' standard objection to Stein's moment-by-moment construction:

I don't care to see pieces.
Don't you.
Indeed you don't.

But Stein continues determinedly:

Leaving stones aside what do you think of the weather and the country.
I think them both delightful.
So do I.
And we enjoy ourselves.
Oh very much.
Yes and what time do you wake up.
At half past seven.
I don't wake up till nine.[46]

The lack of larger structures within these plays emphasizes the moment-by-moment ordering which is the defining characteristic of her work, and to which she referred time and time again within the plays themselves:

Don't you understand trying.
Don't you understand trying to stammer.

[*I Like It*, 1916][47]

I master pieces of it. Exercise in Mastering Pieces of it.

[*Saints and Singing*, 1922][48]

We almost think in meters.

[*Reread Another*, 1921][49]

Think in stitches.

[*Paiseau*, 1928][50]

Of the sixty-six plays which contain text divisions, only forty-nine are structured in what Stein calls acts or scenes. The remaining seventeen, composed from 1913–1946, are organized according to titles which violate traditional play terminology to a greater or lesser degree.

Capture Splinters (1920), for example, is a play in two pages divided into "A Second Play" and "Play Three," titles which share the organizing function of acts and scenes. The divisions in *Capital Capitals* (1923) and *John Breon* (1946) merely distinguish between a fanciful introduction and the body of the play itself. *A Saint in Seven* (1922) shares this organization, while its second section is divided rather inconsistently according to the names introduced in the first section.

Am I to Go or I'll Say So (1923) and *Will He Come Back Better. Second Historic Drama. In the Country* (1930) are organized according to places. In the former, Stein plays consciously with the places she sets up in the following introductory passage:

A Play in Places

Near Annecy, Paris, Vence, Tahors, Some more.
In the first place.
Objects on a table and a survey of bridges and roads.
Interlude. In general, The general likes his coffee cold.
Interlude. The War.
Interlude. Not the War.
In the second place.
Paris. How do they occupy their room. In a way. They say that some time in the day, a whole day. A whole day every day. Twice a day, Two days, At least two days a week. At least two. Not as might be expected an incident, any such incident. And a use and a use for it.
In the third place.
Vence. Correctly on the road to Vence and once there, are we to admit that Shakespeare was as it were immodest, immodestly acquired. Are we to admit, that there is no drop and drop again drop it again. He'll say so.
In the fourth place.
Tahors, and very much more.[51]

In the second section of this play, Stein keeps, initially, to distinct divisions based on the places, Annecy, Paris, Vence and Tahors, established in section one. As she proceeds, however, playing with sectioning replaces the sectioning itself. Seven pages into the script there appear a number of titles not planned for in the beginning such as "In between" and "Not in-between." After another page, divisions disappear entirely in favor of a sequence of lines like this:

No place.
A place.
Place.

To place.
In a place.
In the fifth place.
No fifth place.
Fourth place.
A fourth place.
In the fourth place.
In place.
In that place.
Place to place a place my place, my place you place we place I place, I place you place, we place, my place, my place, why place, you place my place. I place my place, they place a place, for a place as for a place, to and as for the place, in their place in my place. I and my, to place and my place.[52]

Form thus merges with content in this piece.

Will He Come Back Better is organized more consistently according to places. Titles such as "Still in the Country," "Back in the country," and "near the country" divide a series of lines or sentences which are attached to character names. The change in place with each division gives a sense of movement to the piece, the divisions themselves allying Stein's present with a larger section of script.

A Circular Play (1920) provides the best example of Stein's use of titles as virtual acts or scenes. By avoiding play terminology Stein breaks with tradition, yet uses the divisions rather conventionally as she would acts or scenes to define a place or a situation. On the other hand, some of these titles do more than "act" could in rendering the series of occurrences within it, often describing them in essence rather than serving as a general title for them:

A Play In Circles

First in a circle.

Papa dozes mamma blows her noses.
We cannot say this the other way.
Exactly.
Passably.

Second in circles.

A citroen and a citizen.
A miss and bliss.
We came together.
Then suddenly there was an army.
In my room.
We asked them to go away.
We asked them very kindly to stay.

The third circle.

Round as around as my apple.
An apple is out of season.
So are raisins.
We rise above it.
A circle is contained in there.[53]

After two pages, Stein abandons her serial numbering of circles and gets more specific:

Circle Hats.

My color.
Their color.
Two.
One.
Two won.
I can think so quickly.
Silent and thoughtful. Crimson rambler and a legion post legion, a poor post legion.
Crimson rambler or star.
. . . .

The idea of a circle

I bind myself to exercise only in one way.

Beauty in a circle

A beauty is not suddenly in a circle. It comes with rapture. A great deal of beauty is
rapture. A circle is a necessity. Otherwise you would see no one. We each have our circle.
How old is America. Very old.[54]

Once again, form merges with content, this time in the construction of a play around the concept of circles, or self-contained segments within a whole piece. The circles in this play serve as virtual scene divisions, there being a specific character to each circle which is not continued into the next circle.

Violating the traditional play structure to a greater extent than any of these plays are those which rely on titles in the same fashion as her portraits do. *One. Carl Van Vechten* (1913) is divided by a series of numbers ("one," "four") to which the underlying text refers. The text can be said to be a presentation or description of "one" (Carl Van Vechten). *IIIIIIIIII* (1913) combines fragments of actual names (M-N H- for Marsden Hartley, etc.) with such titles as "Incline," "Banking," for the same effect. The text appears to be a realization of the title, not an occurrence within the *données* implicit in the title as with plays heretofore considered.

Plays organized according to pages violate traditional play structure even more. *The King or Something. The Public is Invited to Dance* (1917), *Monday and Tuesday. A Play* (1919), and *Scenery and George Washington. A Novel or a Play* (1932) move progressively from Page One to Page Two and so on. The divisions do not break up the text as the traditional act would, but sustain it as pages in a novel would. *The King or Something*, for instance, proceeds in this fashion:

Page IV.

Letting me see.
Nellie has a gift.

Page V.

Do you mind whose presents.
We didn't bring them up.

Page VI.

By hand.

Page VII.

Nellie.

Page VIII.

Now then yesterday.
No, then for today.
Nellie is poor that is to say she is not spending more money.
Josephine and Genevieve.
A cup.
I am so happy
In counting gifts.
Yes.
And in mixing ceramics.
You don't mean to make them.
Oh no to give them.
Oh yes.[55]

Of the plays which are sectioned into standard divisions of a play, only a very few reflect an orthodox progression from Act One to Act Two and so on. Of the 49 plays with acts and scenes, 32 represent a definite departure from the standard set-up. Some of them combine a regular, progressive act and scene structure with a further division according to titles of some kind. *They Weighed Weighed-Layed* (1930), *Madame Recamier. An Opera* (1930), and *The Five Georges* (1931) are organized according to character names placed at the center of the page with lines and descriptions below them. *What Happened. A Play* (1913) displays the same ordering, but character names are generalized like they were in *One. Carl Van Vechten* (1913), the underlying text providing a description of the generalized name ("One," "Five," "Two," "Three," "Three," "The same three"). Progressive acts divide segments of descriptions with no apparent rhyme or reason for particular placement.

Other plays are divided not only by acts or scenes but by straight titles, as in *White Wines* (1913), *A Lyrical Opera Made by Two* (1928), and *A Bouquet. Their Wills* (1928).

A very complicated structure emerges in *For the Country Entirely. A Play in Letters* (1916), which combines traditional act progression with divisions into chapters, and further, into letters composed during the course of the play. *Counting her Dresses. A Play* (1917) and *An Exercise in Analysis. A Play* (1917) are divided into parts, thirty-eight in the former and sixty in the latter, within each of which appears from one to four acts. In the former, each act is composed of one line, in the latter, from one to four or more lines. These plays have been literally chopped to pieces by the intensive act structuring.

Many of these plays carry the disruption of conventional structure further by toying with the order and number of acts and scenes. In *Four Saints in Three Acts* (1927), Stein places a large number of saints in the frankly theatrical setting of Acts, and moves them through seven Acts, though she mentions only four by number. The progression is as follows: "Act I," "Repeat First Act," "Enact end of an act," "Scene Two," "Scene III," "Scene III," "Scene IV," "Act Two," "Scene One," "Scene One," "Act One," "Scene V," and so on. *Civilization. A Play. In Three Acts* (1931) has forty-three Act Is, one Act, fifty-six Act IIs, and sixty-five Act IIIs, all in order. As early as 1919, Stein toyed with acts in this fashion. *Accents in Alsace* proceeds from Act II to Act 54 to Scene II to Scene III to Act 425 to an Interlude to Act in America to February XIV.

This intensive playing with order seems to be particularly characteristic of plays composed between 1931–1938, before and after which she uses conventional act divisions more consistently. The plays written before 1931 tend to combine act ordering with chapter and part or letter structuring, after which they rely on conventional play divisions alone. Interestingly, this corresponds to some degree with her preoccupation with narrative in her later years. *Doctor Faustus* (1938), it will be remembered, was considered by Stein to be her first successful use of narrative in a play. Prior to her use of narrative, however, she was concerned first and foremost with the presentation of a present moment, beginning literally again and again throughout a piece of literature. Calling a text division act three and the next act one may conflict with traditional methods of structuring a play but it makes sense in light of Stein's aesthetic. Her acts or divisions were never conceived of as "next," but as "now." As she said in *Byron A Play* (1933): "It is very strange but there is a difference between act one."

Act function is toyed with in a number of the plays. The whole of Play III of *Play I–(III)* (1930) reads:

Play III

In which Louise the wife.[56]

It is further toyed with in most of the plays which, though divided into acts and scenes, have little apparent reason for being so. Some of the divisions merely emphasize a present which is already created moment-by-moment in the lines. And some plays, as we have seen in *A King or Something,* march straight through act and scene divisions as if they weren't there. Most of the plays are not consistent in this, however; some sections conform to divisions and start a new subject with the next division, and other sections continue with the same subject despite divisions. *Ladies' Voices* (1916), *I Like It* (1916), and *Reread Another* (1921) are exceptions to this in her early plays, confining particular subjects to particular divisions.

A typically playful Stein scene is set up in this manner in *Daniel Webster* (1937). It is obvious that it brackets no action in Smiley's sense, though it may well bracket an "intention" as he describes it:

A great many came upon the stage among them Wilbur Wright and Henry James and Hiram Grant. They do not see each other but they see that they are there.
They do not lean away together.
Each one speaks and Irene and Dolene and Martha and Mattie decide to be side by side and Abigail and Sarah have their place.
That makes a scene.
Mr. and Mrs. that makes a scene.[57]

Late in her career text divisions begin to have a conventional function — bracketing actions occurring in the text — beginning with *Identity A Poem* in 1935, in which each new scene is a new attempt at understanding the relationship between human nature, human mind, and the dog:

Play 2
Try a play again
Every little play helps
Another play.[58]

A Play Called Not and Now (1936) presents relationships between characters who may or may not look like or be Charlie Chaplin, Anita Loos, Katharine Cornell, and so on, in progressive acts or scenes. Each division is a separate, progressive ordering of the reality of and relationships between these characters in the manner of *Identity*, though there is no sure conclusion as there was in that play. *Doctor Faustus* (1938) marks the beginning of what I would term conventional play ordering: a series of events divided into acts and scenes progresses toward a conclusion, the divisions providing the specific location and a structural coherence for events occurring within them. But though the later plays demonstrate this to a degree, they never completely do so, since even her narrative plays rely less on events than on qualities. *Doctor Faustus,* for example, has sections devoted to a ballet and one entitled "Let Me Alone." Still, the occurrences in each section are confined to that section alone, and sections are numbered progressively. As far as Stein accomplishes this in her late plays, she utilized traditional play structure. Of the late plays, *Lesson Sixteen. A Play* (1941), *Three Sisters who are not Sisters* (1943), *Look and Long* (1943), *Yes is for a Very Young Man* (1944-1946), and *The Mother of Us All* (1945-1946) reflect this structure.

Text divisions, then, are used in Stein's plays in various ways to emphasize her art of stillness, not to fulfill traditional play structure. Whether she uses them not at all or abuses them by calling them parts, chapters, or pages, confounding their progressive order, or combining acts and scenes with other titles or letters, she disrupts the ordering which might lead a spectator to perceive a play in a predetermined way. The spectator is not lulled by the structure of Stein's plays, where, even within a given play, there is rarely a consistently observed structure. It was simply not in keeping with Stein's aesthetic constructs to set up at the beginning of a piece a structure to which it would conform throughout. The very idea of a continuous present dictated that structure grow out of the content of the moment, that it be created as it is being created. It is not surprising however, that the later plays and a select few of the early ones are based on a more or less orthodox structure, the later plays being narratives constructed according to someone else's point of view, the early ones reflecting her familiarity with the construction of traditional plays. Interestingly, the writing of the later plays followed close on the heels of Virgil Thomson's 1934 production of *Four Saints in Three Acts,* for which Maurice Grosser provided a scenario divided neatly into four progressive acts. Though this may have stirred her toward greater clarity—at least in terms of structure—in her late plays, it is obvious that she understood playwriting conventions to some degree when she penned the conventionally structured plays during 1916 and 1921. She consciously chose to not use that structure in most of her plays to keep the spectator's attention rooted to the play in itself in the present moment.

Entity

Perspective.   Stein's manipulation of perspective within the plays short-circuits any involvement the spectator may have in any single perspective aspect of her plays. Of the seventy-seven plays, just eighteen display a single consistent perspective, fourteen reflecting narrative perspective, an unorthodox perspective for a play, and four reflecting the conventional author-character-speech perspective. The two categories contrast in this fashion:

> Its beginning in twenty twenty two.
> Nobody counts poplars.
> Nobody counts poplars.
> Nobody.
> Counts.
> Poplars.
> Nobody counts poplars as counts counts poplars.
> Next.
> Poplars and act as at went in presently preening incoherent ally.
> Philip in rain.
> Pointed in an absently mentioning whenever oppositely done with out.
> The Rhone fails. The Rhone fails.
> Not at all.
>
> [*Paiseau,* 1928][59]
>
> LUCY WILLOW: It would be lovely to be a queen, I must be a queen, I will be a queen.
>   (*Philip Hall and Kit Raccoon rush forward each one on a side and they fall on their knees and they stretch out their hands and they both say:*)
> Be a queen be a queen be my queen.
> LUCY WILLOW: What do you mean. I am a queen but not your queen, you (*pointing at Philip Hall*) you are Philip Hall and that is all, how can you be a king, but I (*she gives a sigh*) I am a queen oh it is so lovely to be a queen.
> PHILIP HALL: (*jumping to his feet*) I am a king and how can I tell I can tell because when I hit my chest I ring like a bell, that is what happens when you are a king, (*and then falling on his knees*) oh queen be a queen be my queen.
>
> [*In a Garden,* 1943][60]

The majority of the plays, however, exhibit multiple perspective. In them, Stein keeps a running commentary on the progress of the play and her feelings about it by including the narrative voice in what would otherwise appear to be a conventional play. Thus, the plays are as much chronicles of the writing experience as they are dramatizations of discrete events. Unlike the playwright operating traditionally by means of character dialogue strictly separated from narrative in the form of stage directions, Stein treated the process of playwriting as an integral part of the play itself. As she writes in *A Saint in Seven* (1922):

> I make fun of him of her.
> I make fun of them.

They make fun of them of this. They make fun of him of her.
She makes fun of of them of him.
He makes fun of them of her.
They make fun of her.
He makes fun of them.
She makes fun of him.
I make fun of them.[61]

As a result of this approach the plays are continually brought back to the moment of their creation from the suspended reality of any fiction. They display a frame (life) within a frame (art), fulfilling her aesthetic assertion that a picture must not only be in its frame but it must not, only, be in its frame. A Stein play can be best understood as a perspective continuum, each perspective vibrating steadily with those around it. She wanted the spectator to be made aware of multiple possibilities.In *Monday and Tuesday. A Play* (1919), for example, it is nearly impossible to say from what perspective Stein is operating at any particular point:

In the meantime what can we do about wishes.
Wish the same.
Agreed for dinner.
And for my niece. What are you doing for my niece.
Baby clothes.
And milk.
Malted milk.
And the omnibus.
We do not use that word.

Second Page

Indeed you may speak.
The baron.
You mean a woman.
I mean a divorced woman.
She is not divorced.
Can you think quickly.
Pray say Miss Filers.
Can you think quickly.
Can you think very quickly.[62]

It is simply not clear whether Stein speaks throughout as narrator, whether she speaks from one or more character perspectives, or whether she combines perspectives.

Her attempt to capture the present moment of perception/composition compelled her to record what she saw with no thought to consistent perspective. It is well established that Stein often wrote in the midst of daily household business, recording statements and proceedings as they occurred. If no dialogue was forthcoming she could either invent her own or continue with her side of the discussion. The latter shift seems to characterize *Captain Walter Arnold* (1916), which might be seen as a rendition of a conversation between her and Alice Toklas:

> Do you mean to please me.
> I do.
> Do you have any doubt of the value of food and water.
> I have not.
> Can you recollect any example of easy repetition.
> I can and I can mention it. . . .
> Do you really mean you have no preferences.
> I can not visualize the condition.
> By that time I am free to say that we have made offers of finding the right name for everything.
> Do you know that you are careful.
> Do you see the state of your purse.
> Have you been told that I will give you more if you ask for it.
> Or do you not care to receive a favor.
> Certainly you wish to be helped.
> Let me help you.
> Do not refuse me.
> You can regulate your expenditure.[63]

The spectator can either conclude from this passage that Stein strays from the straightforward character perspective and dialogue set up in the beginning, and lasting until "Do you know that you are careful," or that she continues as she started, true to the moments as they unfold. Why invent dialogue when it is not occurring, remain true to a character set-up when the character no longer exists, or sublimate an accurate portrayal of an event for purposes of mere consistency?

Unlike *Monday and Tuesday,* switches of perspective in other plays can be clearly and easily established. *Listen to Me* (1936) begins like this:

> There are three characters.
> The first one says. No noun is remown
> The second one says. Forget the air
> The first one says. But you need the air
> The third one says. For has nothing to do with get.
> > They giggle
> And then they are not through with three.
> And then they are solemn and they know that the world will.
> If they know that the world will.
> It is not used that they need where.
> > Three characters.
> There are always more than three characters because air is where.

Now I ask you if you listen to me do you say as air is there.
And so no longer three characters but all who are there say this.
Listen to me
A soliloquy[64]

There are only six lines constructed according to author-character-speech perspective here, the second through fifth, and the last two. The other lines reflect narrative perspective. *For the Country Entirely* (1916) provides some clue of how Stein began to ascribe her own thoughts to a character voice. In this play she often throws out a line, then assigns it to a particular character, or otherwise changes its form by putting it in a letter, as she does here with "Of course I have heard" and "They didn't leave the book:"

Of course I have heard.
Dear Sir. Of course I have heard.
They didn't leave the book.
Dear Sir.
    They didn't leave the book.
Yes Yes.
I know what I hear. Yes sir.
Dear Sir.
    I heard her hurrying.
    We all did.
    Good night.
        Isabel Furness.[65]

In some plays she did not so much switch perspectives as bury one within the other. *Listen to Me* and *The Mother of Us All* show a definite attempt to express the singular voice of the author through a multitude of characters. This passage from *Listen* is clearly constructed from one point of view despite the fact that lines are assigned to separate characters. Stein was not so much getting into her characters as individuals as getting them to speak for her:

Scene II

The moon
First character.   No dog barks at the moon.
Second character.   The moon shines and no dog barks
Third character.   No not anywhere on this earth.
Fourth Character.   Because everywhere anywhere there are lights many lights and so no dog knows that the moon is there
Fifth character.   And so no dog barks at the moon now no not anywhere.
First character.   And the moon makes no one crazy no not now anywhere.
Second character.   Because there are so many lights anywhere.
Third character.   That the light the moon makes is no matter.
Fourth character.   And so no one is crazy now anywhere.

Fifth character. Because there are so many lights anywhere.
First character. And so then there it does not matter
Second character. The sun yes the sun does matter
Third character. But the moon the moon does not matter
Fourth character. Because there are so many lights everywhere that any dog knows that lights any night are everywhere.
Fifth character. And so no dog bays at the moon anywhere.[66]

She expresses the author's perspective through characters in *The Mother of Us All* (1945–1946), too. A vast majority of the apparent dialogue is plainly an author's description of the other characters:

Jo the Loiterer. Anybody can be accused of loitering.
  Chris Blake
  A Citizen. Any loiterer can be accused of loitering.
Henrietta M. Daniel Webster needs an artichoke.
Angel More. Susan B. is cold in wet weather.
Henry B. She swore an oath she'd quickly come to any one to any one.[67]

These character-narrators do not confine themselves to presentations of other characters, but often present themselves, as in this passage from *The Mother of Us All*:

Anne. I will never marry.
Jenny Reefer. If I marry I will divorce but I will not marry because if I did marry, I would be married.
    (*Ulysses S. Grant pounds his chair*)
Ulysses S. Grant. Didn't I say I do not like noise, I do not like cannon balls, I do not like storms, I do not like talking, I do not like noise. I like everything and everybody to be silent and what I like I have. Everybody be silent.
Jo the Loiterer. I know I was silent, everybody can tell just by listening to me just how silent I am, dear General, dear General Ulysses, dear General Ulysses Simpson dear General Ulysses Simpson Grant, dear dear sir, am I not a perfect example of what you like, am I not silent.
    (*Ulysses S. Grant's chair pounds and he is silent*)
Susan B. I am not married and the reason why is that I have had to do what I have had to do, I have had to be what I have had to be, I could never be one of two I could never be two in one as married couples do and can, I am but one all one, one and all one, and so I have never been married to any one.[68]

The same occurs in *Do Let Us Go Away* (1916):

(Nicholas.) I used to be hurried. Now I imagine I will not be.
(Theodore.) It is not necessary to dance or sing. Let us sing that song. Let us call them their names Nicholas. Theodore we will. We are dishonored. We visit one another and say good-bye.

(Nicholas.)   I do not like to be teased. It is so easy to kill mosquitos but what is the use when we are discouraged by the war. We are so are the Japanese. We will never mention them.

(Theodore.)   My principle idea is to eat my meals in peace.[69]

When the characters are not presenting themselves, they often describe their physical activity as an author would, like Virgil T. does in *The Mother of Us All*:

> (*Virgil T. after he has sung his prelude begins to sit*)
> Virgil.   Begin to sit.
>   Begins to sit.
>   He begins to sit.
>   That's why.
>   Begins to sit.
>   He begins to sit.
>   And that is the reason why.[70]

The conventional author-character-speech perspective is confined to the four plays written between 1943–1944, *In a Garden, Three Sisters who are not Sisters, Look and Long,* and *Yes is for a Very Young Man.* In these plays the author's voice finds expression only within the character persona and in separate, distinct stage directions. The process of writing so evident in other works is present only through general techniques of repetition, modification, and so on which characterize her art without exception. *Yes* demonstrates the orthodox perspective in this way:

CONSTANCE.   Is it really all over?

FERDINAND.   Yes, really all over. You will go back to the quays of Paris and sooner or later to roasted chickens.

CONSTANCE.   And you, Ferdinand?

FERDINAND.   Ah, this time I do disappear.

CONSTANCE.   Disappear, where to?

FERDINAND.   Hush, you did say that yes is for a very young man. You must not ask but I'll tell you just the same, to Germany. No I do not go back there to work, but I am being sent to organize my fellow countrymen.

CONSTANCE.   Ferdinand.

FERDINAND.   Yes, Constance, this is our war, you have done your share, your countrymen will fight some more, but this is our war, our war, and we will fight it and we will win.

CONSTANCE. Yes, I know, and so it is all over.

FERDINAND. Yes, look facts in the face, Constance, for you it is all over, for Henry it is all over, but for me it is just beginning, yes is for a very young man.

CONSTANCE. Yes, Ferdinand, yes Ferdinand.

FERDINAND. I won't have time to think so I won't think about you and the quays of Paris and the roast chickens and Henry and Denise and the little girl who looks like me, no I won't have time to think. Goodbye, Constance.

CONSTANCE. (*Extending her hand*) Goodbye Ferdinand.
         (*FERDINAND shakes her hand, then kisses it and leaves*)

CURTAIN[71]

Intimately bound up in the question of perspective is Stein's use of textual interpolation or injection of information irrelevant or disruptive to the story at hand, having to do with the process of writing or with the world outside of the play. It is present in varying degrees in fifty-three of the plays and is an expression of the author's voice. Such explorations as the following are common:

I will not cease a play
Just when a play
Is not a play
To-day.

[*Byron a Play*][72]

...now a theatre is a place. It arranges itself as a purse at most or a rest. At rest.

[*Byron a Play*][73]

Suppose you think in plays or suppose you do not.
Suppose you do not at all think in plays.

[*Byron a Play*][74]

If three characters are in the play is it in the way.

[*Listen to Me*][75]

Acts
Curtain

Characters
Characters
Curtain
Acts
There is no one and one
Nobody has met any one
Curtain can come.
CURTAIN

[*Listen to Me*][76]

How many acts are there in it. Acts are there in it.

[*Four Saints in Three Acts*][77]

I dont quite understand what I have done.

[*Mexico*][78]

One does not run around in a circle to make a circular play.
Do not run around in a circle to make a circular play.

[*A Circular Play*][79]

A lyrical opera not an announcement. Fairly well. Half begun is
well done.

[*A Lyrical Opera. Made by Two*][80]

As a play is a lane for a lion.
Who makes paws purr.
   An invitation to a space.

[*A Play a Lion. For Max Jacob*][81]

Converse with me. In a play you converse with me.

[*Saints and Singing*][82]

I have here a great many different signs of saintly singing

[*Saints and Singing*][83]

This is the way a play fades away.

[*A List*][84]

I do hate sentences.

[*Reread Another*][85]

Perhaps the most prominent example of attention to process lies in *Four Saints in Three Acts* (1927) in which Stein documents her attempts to realize the characters of St. Therese and St. Ignatius. It takes Stein nearly seven pages to even bring St. Therese on the stage. She begins her preparations for the saints:

> In narrative prepare for saints.
> Prepare for saints.
> Two saints.
> Four saints.
> Two saints prepare for saints it two saints prepare for saints in prepare for saints.
> A narrative of prepare for saints in narrative prepare for saints.[86]

then abandons it:

> Remain to narrate to prepare two saints for saints.[87]

and sidetracks into a separate narrative:

> What happened to-day, a narrative.
> We had intended if it were a pleasant day to go to the country it was a very beautiful day and we carried out our intention. We went to places that we had been when we were equally pleased and we found very nearly what we could find and returning saw and heard that after all they were rewarded and likewise This makes it necessary to go again.[88]

She documents her difficulty some three pages later:

> Come panic come.
> Come close.[89]

makes some progress soon after:

> My country tis of thee sweet land of liberty of thee I sing.
> Saint Therese something like that.
> Saint Therese something like that.
> Saint Therese would and would and would.
> Saint Therese something like that.
> Saint Therese.
> Saint Therese half in doors and half out of doors.[90]

and finally presents her:

> The garden inside and outside of the wall.
> Saint Therese about to be.
> The garden inside and outside outside and inside of the wall.

Nobody visits more than they do visits them.
Saint Therese. Nobody visits more than they do visits them Saint Therese.
As loud as that as allowed as that.
Saint Therese. Nobody visits more than they do visits them.
Who settles a private life.
Saint Therese. Who settles a private life.
Saint Therese. Who settles a private life.
Saint Therese. Who settles a private life.
Saint Therese. Who settles a private life.[91]

Introducing Saint Ignatius is a more difficult proposition still. Though she makes a valiant start, she immediately backs off:

Introducing Saint Ignatius.
Left to be.[92]

More problems are encountered later:

Saint Ignatius Loyola. A Saint to be met by and by by and by continue reading reading read read readily.[93]

Saint Ignatius.   Withdrew with with withdrew.
Saint Ignatius.   Occurred.
Saint Ignatius.   Occurred withdrew.
Saint Ignatius.   Withdrew Occurred.
Saint Ignatius.   Withdrew occurred.
    Saint Ignatius occurred Saint Ignatius withdrew occurred withdrew.[94]

And suddenly, he is revealed:

Saint Ignatius. Met to be to be to leave me be with him in partly left to find find with it call call with to them to them that have to be with it as when letting letting it announce announced complacently in change change having fallen two to one in restitution in their inability to leave. Leave left as lost. Might white. From the stand-point of white.
Saint Sulpice. A masterpiece.[95]

References to the outside world in the plays can be summarized by *Not Sightly* (1915) in which Stein breaks the fictional content to ask the following questions of Alice Toklas:

Explain looking. Explain looking again. Alice explain looking again.[96]

Why do I say blows noses
Alice why do I say blows noses. Alice I hear you.[97]

Many of the plays seem to be based on actual events occurring at the time of their composition and can be sorted out and understood if one reconstructs the events. *For the Country Entirely. A Play in Letters* appears to be just such a play, composed during a letter-writing session with the requisite letters and bantering that occurs between them recorded in the text. In a case such as this, it is difficult to determine the presence of interpolations dealing with external reality:

> Dear Mr. Lindo Webb.
> I understand why you are not better liked. A great many people expect you to teach them English. You do so and very well. You might be married and have a wife and son. With these helping you to teach you could teach many more people English.
> Then we can expect that you will change your place of residence.
> We do not expect you to change your coat. No Englishman does. We understand that.
> Young Bonnet.
> We have been very much annoyed by the impertinence of Mr. Alfred Bonnet.
> Little pieces of paper are suddenly burnt.
> In believing a shoe maker you believe his father.
> I do not believe his father.
> Why because he does not dress well.
> Dress well dress well.[98]

The passages after "young Bonnet" could very well refer to an external reaction to the Bonnet letter, but the persona attached to those passages is so veiled that it is impossible to tell.

Included in Smiley's discussion of traditional diction in a play are "clear," "interesting," and "appropriate" stage directions. He states that stage directions are for the artistic producers of the play and thus indirectly communicate with the audience.[99] From what we have seen in preceding chapters, Gertrude Stein avoids clarity in her texts at all costs since it "explains" rather than "makes plain" the thing in itself. She would prize it neither in dialogue nor stage directions. Her stage directions are often quite playful and inappropriate, quite obviously meant, in most cases, for the ears of the spectator and not for the exigencies of a producer. It was a perspective Stein wanted the spectator to experience for full apprehension and enjoyment of the theatre event.

Recognizable physical stage directions are evident in forty-one of Stein's plays. Rarely distinguished in any formal way from the surrounding text, they range from the simplest type (*"All together,"* White Wines)[100] to the most complicated and evasive (*"They do come together but some come more frequently than others and we like to see them all,"* Photograph).[101] Some are straightforward (*"in this act they count,"* A Play a Lion)[102] and some are playful (*"Play III in which Louise the wife,"* Play I–III[103]; *"Repeat First Act,"* Four Saints[104]; *"Reread Another. A Play. To be Played Indoors or Out. I Wish to be a School,"* Reread Another)[105]. Some are detailed (*"Philip Hall on one side and Kit Racoon on the other each carrying a battle axe come behind and listen," In a Garden*)[106], but only the plays from *In a Garden* (1943) to *The Mother of us All* (1945–1946) contain stage directions distinct and complete enough to ensure consistent production.

Extra-physical or psychological stage directions appear in twenty-one plays beginning with *Four Saints* in 1927:

> If it were possible to kill five thousand chinamen by pressing a button would it be done. Saint Therese not interested.[107]

> Saint Therese in a storm at Avila there can be rain and warm snow and warm that is the water is warm the river is not warm the sun is not warm and if to stay to cry. If to stay to if to stay if having to stay to if having to stay if to cry to stay if to cry stay to cry to stay.[108]

She operates more traditionally in *Doctor Faustus* (1936):

> Doctor Faustus says
> Little boy and dog can be killed by a viper but Marguerite Ida and Helena Annabel not very well no not very well
> (He bursts out)
> Leave me alone
> Let me be alone.[109]

and in *Yes is for a Very Young Man* (1944–1946):

> CONSTANCE.   (Startled) Of course he has gone to Germany.
> (Dreamily)
> He was going to be homesick for us all, us all, of course he has gone to Germany.[110]

Stein purged the author's perspective — save for conventional stage directions — from only four of her plays, *In a Garden* (1943), *Three Sisters who are not Sisters* (1943), *Look and Long* (1943), and *Yes is for a Very Young Man* (1944–1946). She used it solely in fourteen other plays from *What Happened* in 1913 to *Byron a Play* in 1933. The remaining fifty-nine plays reflect a multiple perspective that pulls the spectator to the surface of the theatre experience at intervals. Whether the technique calls attention to the process of composing or to the theatrical medium itself, it disrupts the flow of the play and any fiction Stein might be presenting, demanding that the spectator view his experience from a number of points of view at once. The process of the spectator's experience, like the process of her own writing experience, is Gertrude Stein's focal point. And it is that process which keeps the spectator's attention rooted to the dynamic-static moment of performance.

Format. The most concrete evidence for dynamic movement within the play as described by Stein's multiple perspective is found in text format, or the detailed lay-out of the text on the printed page. The format of the traditional play involves presentation of ideas, events, and conversations in dialogue form. Character name is most often placed against the left margin with a line to be spoken arranged to the right of the name, a format I have described in Appendix B as character-speech format. The voice of the author speaks through the character, as Smiley described, and every now and then appears in well-distinguished stage directions placed strategically throughout the script.

Stein's plays violate this standard format in a number of ways, conforming neither to the orthodox character-speech format nor to the strict confinement of narrative voice to distinguishable stage directions, as we have seen. Often they violate it to such a degree that it is impossible to determine structure at all. *White Wines* (1913), for example, could be said to be organized according to all three of the subcategories of format applied to the plays of Stein in Appendix B: character-speech; title-text, a segment of text headed by a title; and straight narrative, a succession of paragraphs, as in a story:

WHITE WINES

THREE ACTS

1. All together.
2. Witnesses.
3. House to house.
    (5 women)

ALL TOGETHER.
Cunning very cunning and cheap, at that rate a sale is a place to use type writing. Shall we go home.
Cunning, cunning, quite cunning, a block a strange block is filled with choking.
Not too cunning, not cunning enough for wit and a stroke and careless laughter, not cunning enough.
A pet, a winter pet and a summer pet and any kind of a pet, a whole waste of pets and no more hardly more than ever.
A touching spoon a real touching spoon is golden and show in that color. A really touching spoon is splendid, is splendid, and dark and is so nearly just right that there is no excuse. . . . [111]

The alternation of lines and the apparent presentation of character (5 women) at the start of this play would seem to suggest a character-speech format, though the play is literally set up according to title-text format and narrative, dealing in description as much as in character rendering. The hermeticism of the text adds to the confusion and makes all structures equally conceivable.

Fifty-nine of the plays from 1913 to 1945 are arranged according to character-speech format. That is, they seem to be composed in a series of speeches which alternate by character. This is not to say that they are set up with a character name at the left margin and a sentence to the right. Often no character name is even linked to the sentence, but one is left with the distinct impression that the name is merely unstated because the sentence reflects so conversational a tone that it could hardly represent narrative.

Whether these speeches are actual lines to be spoken by the characters or descriptions of characters is often open to question. In many instances the format is deliberately ambiguous, and the reader is continually reminded of the theatrical present. There is not much opportunity for identification with character in *A Bouquet. Their Wills* (1928):

> Pauline and Charles Daniel and Dolene Chorus of Baltimoreans
> Food fusses me as blowing wind fusses you.
> Chorus of Baltimoreans
> Have not had a habit of wills. Let us make wills. He and she hurried.[112]

Please do not Suffer (1916):

> (Mrs. Marchand.)   She does not know any of them. She knows Mr. Rothschild.
> (Genevieve.)   What is the use of being tranquil when this house is built for the winter. The winter here is warm.
> (Count Daisy Wrangel.)   He will not stay longer than November.[113]

Accents in Alsace (1919):

> Louisa.   They call me Lisela.
> Mrs. Zumsteg.   Are you going to hear me.
> Young Mr. Zumsteg.   I was looking at the snow.
> All of them.   Like Flowers. They like flowers.[114]

and *Play I-(III)* (1930):

> Louis de Kerstradt and Pierre Revel alone.
> It is in our reply that we have chosen. They will be wise in disappointment. They will there will be weddings.[115]

The alteration of speeches with description has a distancing effect for the reader. Some of the plays which rely on character-speech format are less ambiguous, however; *For the Country Entirely* (1916), *Every Afternoon* (1916), *Captain Walter Arnold* (1916), *I Like It to be a Play* (1916), *An*

Exercise in Analysis (1917), *Monday and Tuesday* (1919), *A List* (1923), *In a Garden* (1943), *Three Sisters who are not Sisters* (1943), *Look and Long* (1943), and *Yes is for a Very Young Man* (1944–1946) rely solely on dialogue or monologue structuring like the traditional play. But few of these eleven plays specify what lines are to be assigned to what characters, or indeed, who the characters are with any consistency. *For the Country Entirely. A Play in Letters* (1916) demonstrates it well:

> Almond trees on the hill. We saw them today.
> Dear Mrs. Steele.
> I like to ask you questions. Do you believe that it is necessary to worship individuality. We do.
> Mrs. Henry Watterson.
> Of course I have heard.
> Dear Sir. Of course I have heard.
> They didn't leave the book.
> Dear Sir.
> They didn't leave the book. Yes, yes.
> I know what I hear. Yes Sir.
> Dear Sir.
> I heard her hurrying.
> We all did
> Good night.
> Isabel Furness.
> I like their names
> Anthony Rosello.[116]

The later plays approach character-speech ordering more conventionally, exhibiting definite lines and not descriptions, and provide a definite link between particular characters and particular lines. A passage early in *Yes is for a Very Young Man* (1944–1946) reads like this:

> Constance. Denise is very lovely.
> Ferdinand. Yes.
> Constance. And Henry really loves her.
> Ferdinand. Yes.
> Constance. And she loves Henry.
> Ferdinand. Yes.
> Constance. And you, Ferdinand?
> Ferdinand. Yes.
> Constance. Yes can be said too often.[117]

Still other plays have characters connected with sentences which are clearly not lines, but descriptions, as in *Please do not Suffer* (1916). In performance, of course, the character could speak the lines, but it would give a distancing effect since the character refers to herself in the third person:

(Mrs. Marchand.) Where was she born and with whom did she go to school. Did she know the Marquise of Bowers then or did she not. Did she come to know her in Italy. Did she learn English in Morocco. She has never been to England nor did she go to school in Florence. She lived in the house with the friends of the Count Berny and as such she knew them and she knew him. She went to eat an Arab dinner.[118]

Plays which do not exhibit character-speech structuring exhibit title-text structuring which assumes narrative of some kind, or strict narrative structuring, as in a story composed of paragraphs. Pure title-text structuring is evident only in Stein's earlier plays, *What Happened* (1913), *One. Carl Van Vechten* (1913), *Old and Old* (1913), and *Simons a Bouquet* (1913), where she was consciously breaking away from her portraits, all of which were organized according to title. The third section of *Old and Old*, "Collecting Poles," reads, in part:

> Old mans and a cost in corsets and a grand guard and a good gold flour a good flour, a cold flower, a bad flavor, a certain decent and a request a request for a distant smell, a request for a smell, a request, a distant smell, a smell distant, a request, a smell, a smell distant, a smell, a distant smell.
> That is the end of a solid tree in a fog, that is the end in noon, that is the end of a chance to sit in change, that is the end spinach and an egg much more egg, much more green.[119]

Plays organized according to narrative (story format) include *A Curtain Raiser* (1913), *A Movie* (1920), *Objects Lie on a Table* (1922), *A Saint in Seven* (1922), *A Village* (1923), *Paiseau* (1928), *Film* (1929), *Parlor* (1930), *Scenery and George Washington* (1932), *Byron a Play* (1933), *A Play Called Not and Now* (1936), *Lucretia Borgia* (1938), *Lesson Sixteen* (1941), and *John Breon* (1946). *Byron a Play* proceeds in this fashion:

> He comes back bringing something. Of course he comes back and of course bringing something. Neither one of two. And therefore having left that behind he remains not to share to care or rather yes as he uses. Of course nothing need be used even at this distance.[120]

A Play Called Not and Now reflects this format too:

> Nobody is late, nobody who looks like anybody is late oh no they can not be left and they can not be late oh no.
> The one that was like Picasso was not late, the one that was like Dashiell Hammett was not late the one that was like Charlie Chaplin no he was not late and the one who was like Lord Berners was not late.[121]

Most of the plays, however, are a combination of character-speech, title-text and narrative format, and avoid the format of the traditional play:

fifty-two plays from 1913 to 1946 do not present themselves in a unified format. *Do Let Us Go Away* (1916) reads:

Jenny is sick.

(Jenny.)   I am sick.

(The lawyer.)   I went often to see you and every day I said I love you better I do love you better. That's it.

They were together and they said
John are you going. He said something.
They were altogether.
I often think about it.
Genevieve was patient. She was angry
because the water was another color.

She said. He is very good now.[122]

They Must. Be Wedded. To Their Wife (1931) reads:

Violet.   Oh will you. Ask him. To marry me.

Marcel.   He laughed.[123]

With the exception of eleven plays, then, written from 1916–1946, the plays of Gertrude Stein do not reflect the format of the traditional play, but combine character-speech format (lines and description) with title-text and narrative format. Of these eleven, only the last five, *A List, In a Garden, Three Sisters who are not Sisters, Look and Long,* and *Yes is for a Very Young Man* consistently reflect dialogue connected directly to a character name, though many previous plays inconsistently reflected such a format. *A List* is an interesting progression toward this conventional format, for while character name is always connected with a speech, it plays overtly with the character-speech set up:

Maryas

and   Nearly all of it has made nearly all of it.

Martha   Nearly all of it has made nearly all of it.

Maryas

and   Nearly all of it has made nearly all of it has

Martha   made nearly all of it has made nearly all of it.

Martha

and   Nearly all of it has made nearly all of it[124]

Maryas

The format is straightforward in the last four plays.

It is possible, of course, to deny Stein's disruption of conventional play format by presenting her plays in the theatre in pure dialogue form, ignoring the title-text structuring and transforming the narratives into unstated stage directions. Many productions, in fact, have been mounted in this fashion. To perform the plays in this way, however, is to limit the possibilities of her scripts and to short-circuit the complete realization of her aesthetic. The productions which are truest to the multiple possibilities in the scripts tend to dramatize every single line, as Virgil Thomson did in 1934 for *Four Saints in Three Acts.*

Hermeticism and non-logical expression.   The fictional aspect of the stage is also disrupted by Stein's use of hermetic language and non-logical expression. These are categories not explored by Smiley, who says that the traditional play "presents select and well-arranged words to communicate information to an audience."[125] As we have seen, Stein was little concerned with clarity and much concerned with "making plain" the thing in itself. Her language reflects directly this concern.

In approaching these categories, I established a level of hermeticism or clarity within sentence and paragraph, explored the type of expression from logical (sense) to non-logical (sound) characteristic of the play as a whole, and found that most of the plays are complex combinations of these, in the Stein tradition. The plays which are predominantly hermetic keep the spectator from referring consistently beyond the language itself and are the most complete fulfillments of her aesthetic of stillness and entity. It would be difficult, for example, to pierce the surface of *Old and Old* (1913), a play I have characterized as hermetic within and between sentences and dependent upon non-logical expression:

I. CONDITIONS

House plants.
Cousin to cousin the same is a brother.
Collected tumblers.
Pretty well so called, pretty careful and going all the detention.
Hopping.
Pretty well Charlie, pretty sour poison in pears, pretty well henny soon most soon bent.
Collect.
In do pot soon, in loud coal bust, in do pot soon, in chalk what.
In do pot soon in hold hot. In do pot soon, in due point, in die point.
In due point and most visible.
In vain, in vain, in a vein, in a vein. In do point that. Bay weight and balk and be wet.
Be wake and white and be wet, Be count and lunge and see wall, be how, be how but can than.[126]

The significance to be found in this play is in the sounds and textures of the words as they relate in a flat landscape and in the possibilities of their connection with each other and with the outside world. There is repetition, alliteration, rhyming, attention to patterns and rhythms of lines, but no clarity, and no apparent logical connections between words or phrases. The text does not connect itself to any thing or experience beyond the quality of the perceptive moment. It provides no fictional reality for the spectator's involvement but an opaque picture he cannot see beyond. When presented on stage it would remain so, on the whole, the language and its sounds and rhythms vocalized and made more concrete, more immediate. The perceptive moment experienced by Stein as she wrote would become the theatrical moment, full of textures, sounds and patterns, but no more.

Not Sightly (1915) is just as hermetic, but depends more upon logical than non-logical expression:

> Slightly painful and really more satisfactorily stinted and mentioned in long singling birthdays. Shall it seem strange.
> Not wintered my dear.
> Not wintered my dear.
> Not wintered my dear.
> . . . .
> I meant to wait and I was simple and I did say shelter god give him shelter. I did go away and I did not mutter I did not believe goats I was not delicate I was not careful to release more excellent tons of really sound apples. This was so painful. This was very painful. I meant to do the same yesterday.[127]

Relationships based on sound here are less important than those based on logic or the pretense of logic. There is less word play, less alliteration, less rhythmic variation, and a more conceptual approach. As a result, this play would appear to be more clear to a spectator as a type of expression, yet just as hermetic in reality. What, for instance, did the speaker mean to do yesterday and how could she release more tons of really sound apples? There is no telling, yet the opportunity to at least pose such questions arises in this play. Hermetic or not, it is based on logical expression. It speaks the language of the spectator, though the only concrete answers it can give are possibilities of connections, not the connections themselves.

It is clear after considering this aspect of Stein's technique that there is definite progression from hermeticism to clarity in her plays. It would seem that she used hermeticism originally to give the spectator no choice but to focus upon the moments as they occurred, but that she modified the extreme technique once she felt that the spectator could accept a clearer text and focus on the moment in the same fashion. *They Must. Be Wedded. To Their Wife* (1931) is a clear text which Stein breaks up in such a way as to force the spectator to retain a number of sentences at once if he wants to experience clarity. If the sentences are taken one by one, the text is as hermetic as any of her plays:

They see a river. Which. Runs through a marsh. One might think. That the mother
was unhappy. But not at all. She has hopes. For her future.
They have. Not forgotten. The sister. And daughter. Neither. Will they. Like it.
Marcelle. Who has known. When. He. Can smile.
                                                    All who remain. Come in.
He is. Sure. To dance. Well. If not. Now.
And so. The month. Of July. Opens. And closes.[128]

After *Not Sightly* in 1915, all of the plays reflect some amount of clarity, relying on varying degrees of logical and non-logical expression. Plays
which share complete clarity and complete logic would seem to come the
closest to transporting the spectator from the flat reality of the stage to a
fictional one. But interestingly enough all of these plays—*He Said It.
Monologue* (1915), *For the Country Entirely. A Play in Letters* (1916),
Every Afternoon. A Dialogue (1916), *Do Let Us Go Away* (1916), *Captain
Walter Arnold* (1916), *Please do not Suffer* (1916), *Turkey and Bones and
Eating and We Liked It* (1916), *Polybe in Port* (1916), *Mexico* (1916), *An
Exercise in Analysis* (1917), *A Movie* (1920), *Film* (1929), and *Listen to Me*
(1936)—contain enough self-reference and enough textual interpolation to
disrupt the alternate reality manifested through such clarity. In *Listen to
Me* the spectator is confronted with an indeterminate number of characters
who keep losing track of how many characters there are, and who are
obsessed with using one-syllable words. *Every Afternoon* does not so much
give him a conversation between characters as an exercise in dialogue, as
does *He Said It*, though Stein calls it a monologue. *An Exercise in Analysis*
is exactly that; *For the Country Entirely. A Play in Letters* is exactly that:
the others are so disrupted by character inconsistency and multiple
perspective that there is no consistent fiction, save for *A Movie* and *Film*
whose characters are consistent but spare indeed.

The plays possessing fictions a spectator could easily identify with are,
in fact, the later plays which are less self-referring, more consistent in character and perspective, completely clear, and combinations of logical and
sound expression. Sound expression is really not an obstacle to understanding and identification as long as it is at least in part rooted in logic.
Yes is for a Very Young Man is one such later play based as much on
logical expression as it is on sound:

DENISE. Oh dear I am so tired of working I wish I could be rich again, oh dear. I
want to be rich, anyway I never want to shell a pea or dig a potato or wash a dress. I
want all vegetables to grow in cans not in the ground. I want all clothes washed in a
laundry and I want all stockings bought new and thrown away. That is what I want, oh
dear. Ferdinand, when Henry and I were first married and he was in the army, oh it was
wonderful and now he just does nothing, for Heaven's sake can't you make him earn
something and help us. Ferdinand just don't stand there, take my side, make your

brother Henry do something, I love Henry. You know I love him, he is my husband but you can influence him. Ferdinand why don't you take my side, Ferdinand, why don't you take my side?

FERDINAND. Denise, I do take your side, I do, I do take your side, I take everybody's side. Don't keep at me, you make me cry, I know you're miserable. I take everybody's side, that is the way I am, I do take everybody's side.

DENISE. Don't cry, Ferdinand, no Ferdinand don't cry, no don't cry, but I am not everybody. I am just me, why don't you take my side.

FERDINAND. (*FERDINAND crosses away angrily*) My God, Denise, everybody's side, no you are right, Denise, I don't take anybody's side, of course I don't take anybody's side, of course I don't take anybody's side, of course I don't take everybody's side.[129]

The last nine plays of Stein's career, from *Doctor Faustus Lights the Lights* (1938) to *John Breon* (1946), display a similar combination, though *Lucretia Borgia, Doctor Faustus,* and *The Mother of Us All* are disrupted through multiple perspective, *Three Sisters who are not Sisters* is self-referring, and *Lesson Sixteen* and *John Breon* are straight narratives. *A Movie, Film, In a Garden, Look and Long,* and *Yes is for a Very Young Man,* then, emerge as the plays most likely to transport the spectator into the fictional reality Stein so assiduously avoided for most of her career.

The fact remains, however, that these last plays still exhibit the attention to the continuous present which emerged in 1911, though Stein modifies this somewhat by her attention to narrative. They do not progress smoothly, but stop and start at every moment, sacrificing development to stillness. Though they are characterized as containing a complete story from beginning to end, climactic events are always avoided, leaped over. As a result, they are jarring to a spectator, and repeatedly bring him back from fiction to the immediacy of the stage picture.

Subject Matter

Stein's plays are first and foremost attempts to call attention to the theatre experience. Forty-one of them refer often enough to themselves and to Stein's writing process to be considered metaplays, or plays about plays. Her inclusion of process as an integral part of her plays makes most of them self-referential at some point. *IIIIIIIIII* (1913) chronicles her difficulty in writing *IIIIIIIIII, He Said It. Monologue* (1915) reveals what is spoken between them, *For the Country Entirely. A Play in Letters* (1916) plays in letters, *Ladies' Voices* (1916) is a description of the pleasure to be had in ladies' voices. Repetition theory abounds in *Captain Walter Arnold* (1916) and *Saints and Singing* (1922); juxtaposition in *A List* (1923) and *A Village*

(1923). *Am I to Go* (1923) is a play in and on places, *Paiseau* (1928), an exercise in not reminiscing, and *At Present* (1930) experiments only with contemporaries. *They Must. Be Wedded. To Their Wife* (1931) explains why it deals with particular characters. *Short Sentences* (1932), *The Five Georges* (1931), *A Play Without Roses* (1931), and *A Manoir* (1932) play with names; *A Manoir* (1932) also chronicles what goes on in a manoir; *A Play a Lion* (1932) is "an invitation to a space"; *Short Sentences* (1932) is an exercise in short sentences, and *Listen to Me* (1936), in one syllable words. *Byron a Play* (1933) is an attempt to make the activities of Byron the dog a play. *Identity a Play* (1935) is an attempt to figure out identity through a series of "plays." *Listen to Me* (1936) has characters who are aware of themselves as characters. *Three Sisters who are not Sisters* (1943) exposes the whole theatre experience by exhibiting a play within a play:

SAMUEL: I have an idea a beautiful idea, a fine idea, let us play a play and let it be a murder.

JENNY:
HELEN: Oh yes let's.
ELLEN:[130]

The fictional aspect of the theatre is undermined by this self-reference. Once a play refers to itself as a play, the spectator acknowledges his presence in a theatre, and disengages from the fictional character of the proceedings. Contrary to traditional practice since the Renaissance, which posited the unreal (a flat painted in perspective) as the real (a town square), Stein posits the actual presence of actors and spectator as real.

Stein's plays are not pure attempts at metaplay, however. All of them have subject matter, however sketchy or disrupted. Fictional names, for instance, occur in sixty-eight plays, fictional locations in fifty-four, and a background or context in sixty. *A Curtain Raiser* (1913) has none of the above:

Six.
Twenty.
                    Outrageous.
Late,
Weak.
                    Forty.
More in any wetness.
Sixty three certainly.
Five.
Sixteen.
Seven.
Three.
More in orderly. Seventy-five.[131]

Though Stein preferred to think of her plays as events in themselves[132] forty-six of them chronicle some event, however short, and fifty-seven include short-term stories. In *Play I-(III)* (1930), for instance, Blanche Lavielle comes in calling and Pierre Revel has met a young man fencing.[133] In *The Mother of Us All* the characters gather for a debate between Susan B. and Daniel Webster: they meet later at the statue of Susan B. and her supporters at Congressional Hall, and Indiana Elliot gets married. In *Doctor Faustus* (1938) Faustus kicks Mephisto, in *Three Sisters* (1943) Jenny kicks Samuel, in *Look and Long* (1943) four characters undergo magical transformations, in *A Movie* (1920) there is an automobile crash and a duel, and in *Film* (1929) a package is dropped. Though these events may appear to be rudimentary in the extreme they are the only type to occur in Stein's plays, all of which avoid overt action at all costs. *Will He Come Back Better. Second Historic Drama. In the Country* (1930) is an example of this avoidance: while the play is organized according to movements made toward the country, in the country, near the county, back from the country, and so on, there is absolutely no evidence of actual movement. The play, an event in itself, contains no event within.

Short term stories abound in the plays, most of them being non-stories in the Stein tradition. Jo the Loiterer tells Chris the Citizen about his wife in *The Mother of Us All* (1945–1946):

Jo. I want to tell
Chris. Very well
Jo. I want to tell oh hell.
Chris. Oh very well.
Jo. I want to tell oh hell I want to tell about my wife.
Chris. And have you got one.
Jo. No not one.
Chris. Two then.
Jo. No not two.
Chris. How many then
Jo. I haven't got one. I want to tell oh hell about my wife I haven't got one.
Chris. Well.
Jo. My wife, she had a garden.
Chris. Yes.
Jo. And I bought one.
Chris. A wife.

No said Jo I was poor and I bought a garden. And then said Chris. She said, said Jo, she said my wife said one tree in my garden was her tree in her garden. And said Chris, Was it. Jo, we quarreled about it. And then said Chris. And then said Jo, we took a train and we went where we went. And then said Chris. She gave me a little package said Jo. And was it a tree said Chris. No it was money said Jo. And was she your wife said Chris, yes said Jo when she was funny, How funny said Chris. Very funny said Jo. Very funny said Jo. To be funny you have to take everything in the kitchen and put it on the floor, you

have to take all your money and all your jewels and put them near the door you
have to go to bed then and leave the door ajar. That is the way you do when
you are funny.

Chris.   Was she funny.

Jo.   Yes she was funny.[134]

Jo's elaborate story establishes, with the diligent prodding of Chris the
Citizen, that Jo has a wife, a conclusion reached only upon linking the
woman Jo talks about with being funny. The ridiculous character of this
storytelling in addition to Stein's presence as narrator halfway through the
conversation makes the passage as much about storytelling as it is a story
in itself. *Accents in Alsace* (1919) contains a more straightforward story
concerning a young man who runs from military service to join the foreign
legion. It, too, is disrupted by questions such as "And what happens to the
family," "and how did they escape by paying somebody money," and "so
then what happened," followed by an irrelevant passage. Stories are a
momentary diversion to Stein, never more important than the moment in
which they occur. Still, there are fairly conventional stories and events in
the later narrative plays and in *A Movie* and *Film*, though the totality of
those stories is never dramatized, as we have seen.

The presence of short-term events and stories, of names and places,
then, demonstrates the fictional aspect of these plays. Yet thirty-one plays
lack events of any kind other than the sheer theatrical event of the play's
performance, and twenty plays lack even short-term stories. Six plays, in
fact, lack fictional names and places, short-term events, and stories. The
only thing to disrupt in *What Happened* (1913), *One. Carl Van Vechten*
(1913), *Old and Old* (1913), *A Curtain Raiser* (1913), *Counting her Dresses*
(1917) and *A Play of Pounds* (1932) is the subject matter they exhibit aside
from these categories.

Before proceeding to specific subject matter, it is important to note
the distinct departure from traditional story evident in these plays. Though
Smiley is quick to point out that not every play needs to have a story, he
believes that such plays need a sustained view of a single occurrence or
quality, like Beckett's *Waiting for Godot,* for instance. Stein does not even
fulfill this requirement. As we have seen, she gives us segmented views of a
multitude of events and qualities. In Smiley's terms, she writes more than
one play in each of her plays, and makes those plays essential expressions—rather than explorations—of character and event.

Stein's plays can be said to reflect nine broad categories of subject
matter: identity, mystery, domestic life, conversation, war, movement,
nature, sex and love, and religion. Most of the plays, save the ones concerned with identity, should be considered less explorations of topics than
distillations of her life concerns.

Domestic life of some kind comprises the subject matter of forty-three plays from *White Wines* in 1913 to *The Mother of Us All* in 1946. Stein's overriding concern in these plays, most of which reflect her own household, was in capturing the essence of day to day living. Typical snippets of cozy domesticity are found in *Counting her Dresses* (1917):

PART VIII.

Act I.

Shall I wear my blue.

Act II.

Do.

PART IX

Act I.

Thank you for the cow.

Thank you for the cow.

Act II.

Thank you very much.

PART X.

Act I.

Collecting her dresses.

Act II.

Shall you be annoyed.

Act III

Not at all.

PART XI.

Act I.

Can you be thankful.

Act II.

For what.

Act III.

For me.

PART XII.

Act I.

I do not like this table.

Act II.

I can understand that.

Act III.

A feather

Act IV.

It weighs more than a feather.

PART XIII.

Act I.

It is not tiring to count dresses.[135]

In *He Said It* (1915):

We are going to have a picnic. With chicken not today today we are going to have eggs and salad and vegetables and brown bread and what else. False smuggled contraband tobacco. You mean by that that it isn't tobacco. No it's only leaves. I laugh.[136]

In *Bonne Année* (1916):

> We do not understand why they do not think this is a good market.
>
> We do understand our pleasure. Our pleasure is to do every day the work of that day, to cut our hair and not want blue eyes and to be reasonable and obedient. To obey and not split hairs. This is our duty and our pleasure.
>
> Every day we get up and say we are awake today. By this we mean that we are up early and we are up late. We eat our breakfast and smoke a cigar. That is not so because we call it by another name. We like the country and we are pressed people. Do not be upset by anything. No I wont be. Dear one.[137]

References, usually veiled, to love and sexuality are made in fourteen plays from *Old and Old* (1913) to *Yes is for a Very Young Man* (1944-1946). These generally take the form of descriptions of Stein's own relationship with Alice Toklas, and become quite explicit once it is understood that her euphemism for orgasm was "cow," and that Alice's nickname for her was "baby." In *The King or Something. The Public is Invited to Dance* (1917) we find the following:

> There was a little apple eat.
> By a little baby that is wet.
> Wet from kisses.
> There was a good big cow came out.
> Of a little baby which is called stout.
> Stout with kisses.
> There will be a good cow come out.
> Of a little baby I don't doubt.
> Neither does she covered with kisses.
> She is misses.
> That's it.[138]

A Lyrical Opera. Made by Two (1928) is more picturesque:

> Quietly installed and not used to wishing. Husband is so simply sleepy he does love his wife alway. Husband is so simply sleepy what does he what does he say.
>
> An interval of not seeing anybody.
>
> Meaning in a voice baby has a choice. Of me.
>
> She can see tenderly shining out of me for she. And so, tenderly if it is me for she it is me for she tenderly in a cow coming out now tenderly me for she tenderly as a cow coming out come out now by she for me tenderly as a she coming out of a cow out of from she for me tenderly.
>
> Another acting as she can makes it have come and fan the air with the sound of a poise from the end not a bend just come out out of a little she is a little not a very little tenderly out of she a cow comes out. My sweet dear hear.
>
> My sweet dear does hear her dear here saying little and big coming and true discern and firmly coming out softly shoving out singly coming out all of the cow that has been registered as around now. The cow can come out and it does and the cow is now now that it has come out is was.
>
> Navigation sub-marine of the cow come out of queen my queen. That is what the cow

does it sinks and a little it sinks so sweetly, my own cow out of my own queen is now seen.

My own queen, has a cow seen by my own queen and it is now a submarine.

Kiss my lips she did kiss my lips again she did kiss my lips over and over again she did.

Mrs. misses kisses Mrs. kisses most Mrs. misses kisses misses kisses most.[139]

She moves away from her own relationship in *Yes, In a Garden, Listen to Me, Civilization,* and *They Must. Be Wedded. To Their Wife,* though the majority of the plays in this category seem to evoke her own relationship with Alice.

Nature provides the subject matter for forty plays and ranges from oblique references to birds, animals, and landscapes to plays based entirely on nature imagery. *Lend a Hand or Four Religions* (1922) is one such play:

Fourth Religion   Are grasses grown and does she observe that the others remove them. Are grasses grown four times yearly. Does she see the grasses that are grown four times yearly. Does she very nearly remove them. Does she remove them and do they very nearly grow four times yearly. Does she as she sees some one does she advance and does he very nearly remove the green grasses that grow nearly four times yearly. In this country they do.
Third Religion   Does she very nearly or does she see the green grasses grow four times yearly. Does she remove them or does she know that they do grow four times yearly. Does she see some one as she advances or does she kneel there where the water is flowing or does she furnish a house as well. Does she nearly remove them.[140]

Four Saints in Three Acts (1927) displays a multitude of nature references:

It is very easy in winter to remember winter spring and summer it is very easy in winter to remember spring and winter and summer it is very easy in winter to remember summer spring and winter it is very easy in winter to remember spring and summer and winter.[141]

Ordinary pigeons and trees. This is a setting which is as soon which is as soon which is as soon ordinary setting which is as soon which is as soon and noon.
Ordinary pigeons and trees.[142]

And *A Lyrical Opera. Made by Two* does, too:

A cuckoo bird is sitting on a cuckoo tree singing to me oh singing to me.
A cuckoo bird is sitting on a cuckoo tree singing to me oh singing to me.
A rocky undulating road side small orchids growing not abundantly and some lavender. Two walking.
John Quilly John Quilly my babe baby is sweeter than even John Quillies are.[143]

Nature was obviously a source of delight and comfort to Stein, and forms the basis of what she termed her landscape plays, many of which are set in an actual nature landscape like the ones we have discussed here.

Stein's preoccupation with movement within a landscape finds expression in the subject matter of thirty-two plays. *Will He Come Back Better. Second Historic Drama. In the Country* (1930) expresses sheer movement, organized according to shifts away from and back to the country.

The country

Nuna. It is only that is only.

Amelia. It is only not that it is this not only

Ashley. They may more they may not more not only

Harry. May they own not only.

Humphrey. Should they not just not when felt that they should not jointly leave it to be not only but not for them.

Near the country.

Nuna. To be best known lean and leaving with it may they come.

Amelia. It is nearly with them nearly with them and with them they nearly come.

Ashley. Should they nearly be with them when they nearly come.

Harry. They may be nearly with them.

Humphrey. Should they be not with them when they come without them which is the way they do and can come.[144]

Three Sisters who are not Sisters depends upon shifts of position by the characters in the darkness to produce suggestions of murder when the lights come up:

The light goes out. When it comes up again, the policeman is gone and Ellen murdered is on the floor.[145]

Four Saints in Three Acts establishes the simple movement of the saints in the landscape of Avila and of Saint Therese and Saint Ignatius in and out of the play:

Saint Therese seated and not surrounded. There are a great many persons and places near together. Saint Therese not seated there are a great many persons and places near together.

Saint Therese not seated.

There are a great many persons and places near together.

Saint Therese not seated at once. There are a great many places and persons near together.

Saint Therese once seated. There are a great many places and persons near together. Saint Therese seated and not surrounded. There are a great many places and persons near together.

Saint Therese visited by very many as well as the others really visited before she was seated. There are a great many persons and places near together.[146]

A Play Called Not and Now, A Movie, Film, and *A Manoir* are all based almost entirely on movement. *A Saint in Seven* summarizes Stein's impulse to chart sheer movement in this group of plays:

No one knows how easily he can authorize him to go, how easily she can authorize her to go how easily they can authorize them to come and to go. I authorize you to come and go. I authorize you to go. I authorize you to go and come.[147]

Twenty-two plays, most of them occurring between 1915 and 1919, reflect Stein's preoccupation with conversation to such a degree that they can be considered metaplays. The number and variety of subjects combined with an overriding dialogue perspective makes these plays intensely conversational in tone:

Americans are very clever.
So are others.
Yes indeed.
And all men are brave.

[I Like It][148]

Ladies' voices give pleasure.
The acting two is easily led. Leading is not in winter. Here the winter is sunny.
Does that surprise you.
Ladies voices together and then she came in.
Very well good night.
Very well good night.
(Mrs. Cardillac.)
That's silver.
You mean the sound.
Yes the sound.

[Ladies' Voices][149]

Do I begin this.
Yes you began this.
Of course we did.
Yes indeed we did.
When will we speak of another.
Not today I assure you.
Yes certainly you mentioned it.
We mention everything.
To another.

[Every Afternoon][150]

Spoken.
In English.
Always spoken.
Between them.

[He Said It][151]

Am I to Go or I'll Say So (1923) reduces conversation to its skeletal form:

A conversation between them.
Actively rapidly.
Response.
Rapidly and actively.
Nor when.
Response.
Now and then.
Actively and more rapidly.
Response.
And when not more rapidly.
Now and then more actively.
Response.
Now and then not more than actively and rapidly.[152]

and shows Stein's awareness of it as a purely formal construct.

War is the subject matter of ten plays, the most integrated and consistent descriptions of life in wartime appearing in *Am I to Go or I'll Say So* (1928), *Please do not Suffer* (1916), *Accents in Alsace* (1919), *A Movie* (1920), and *Yes is for a Very Young Man* (1944–1946). *Please do not Suffer* chronicles the hardships of country people living in an occupied territory during World War I. Genevieve says:

This is my history. I worked at a cafe in Rennes. Before that I was instructed by a woman who knew knitting and everything. My mother and father worked at gardening. I was ruined by a butcher. I am not particularly fond of children. My child is a girl and still a little one. She is living in an invaded district but is now in Avignon. I had a coat made for her but it did not fit her very well and now I am sending the money so that it will be made at Verdun. I am not necessarily a very happy woman. Every one is willing. I like knitting and I like to buy provision. Yes I enjoy the capital. There is plenty of meat here. I do not care for the variety. I prefer veal to chicken. I prefer mutton. I understand that it is difficult to have anything.[153]

Accents in Alsace (1919) deals in part with a young man who avoids military service in his own country:

Brother brother go away and stay.
Sister brother believe me I say.
They will never get me as I run away.
He runs away and stays away and strange to say he passes the lines and goes all the way and they do not find him but hear that he is there in the foreign legion in distant Algier.
And what happens to the family.
The family manages to get along and then some one of his comrades in writing a letter which is gotten hold of by the Boche find he is a soldier whom they cannot touch, so what do they do they decide to embrew his mother and sister and father too. And how did they escape by paying somebody money.

That's what you did with the Boche. You always paid some money to some one it might be a colonel or it might be a sergeant but anyway you did it and it was necessary so then what happened.[154]

A Movie, as we have seen, deals with an American painter turned secret service agent who involves himself in wartime activities. *Yes* is the most complete depiction of life in wartime, the domestic situation of Denise and Henry, the love affair between Constance and Ferdinand, and the war itself sketched with a thoroughness not approached in most of her other writing. The play deals specifically with the activities of the French Resistance, for whom Henry and Ferdinand fight, and Marshal Petain's "toy" army, for whom Achille, Denise's brother, fights:

CONSTANCE.   My dear, American or not, I do know that Achille, he is nice, he is sweet, he is not much of a worker.

DENISE.   He brought down five airplanes all by himself.

HENRY.   Six

DENISE.   Six.

CONSTANCE.   Yes I know, of course and he is so modest he never mentions it and he does not wear his decorations, but everybody does know about those six planes.

DENISE.   You are horrid and American, American and horrid. Ferdinand, say something, you always understand, say something.

FERDINAND.   Yes, sure I understand you and Achille too, but I understand Henry too. Oh nonsense, there is no sense to it, I am not like some, I do think the Marshall has helped France by making his armistice, but an armistice is not peace, it is a truce and as long as there is no peace we are at war with Germany even if we are not fighting and an army is just silly, an army that is not supposed at any time to fight against Germany. It is just silly. No, Henry is right, he should not join a silly army like that.

HENRY.   (*Looking up*) And you might add, Ferdinand, to be an army under the Marshal who lets our two brothers rot in prison in Germany while he makes a toy army that can never fight for them. Oh, let everybody shut up, let everybody shut up, shut up, shut up.

DENISE.   (*Going to HENRY*) I won't shut up, I won't, Achille—

CONSTANCE.   Oh for Heaven's sake, quote your mother or your uncle or your father, if it has to be in the family but not always Achille, besides he is too modest to speak, of course he is.

DENISE.   Don't you dare talk like that, Constance. Well if you want that I quote my mother, she says well she does not say she wants Germany to win but she says Germany will win, and when they do a noble family like ours that has always owned land in France will once more rule over France and teach everybody what discipline is.

HENRY.   Yes, discipline, you can't do a day's work without making a fuss, always making a fuss, and all your ground gets less and less productive. Bah, aristocrats make me sick, everything makes me sick, everything.[155]

Religion is the subject matter for four plays: *Lend a Hand or Four Religions* (1922), which presents four religions (first through fourth) as personages in a nature landscape, and *Four Saints in Three Acts* (1927), *Saints and Singing* (1922), and *A Saint in Seven* (1922), all of which sketch the saintly life. Stein was interested in saints primarily because of their self-contained existence, their ability to simply be:

A saint a real saint never does anything, a martyr does something but a really good saint does nothing, and so I wanted to have Four Saints who did nothing and I wrote the Four Saints in Three Acts and they did nothing and that was everything.[156]

The use of saints emphasized her static art since she could render them most completely, she felt, by not showing them doing anything. In these three plays she displays them in various attitudes and positions and against different backgrounds but she never shows them acting. The static religious life seemed to lend a certain purity of subject matter to her stylistically pure art.

Seven of the plays are mysteries. In *Film* the spectator is compelled to put together a series of ambiguous occurrences having to do with a picture of white dogs, small packets, and two ladies in an automobile. In *Listen to Me* he faces the possibility of a missing fifth and second character. In *Not and Now* he must determine the relationship of people who look like Charlie Chaplin, Anita Loos, and so on, to their actual counterparts. In *Lucretia Borgia* Jenny kills the twin she herself created in the midst of entirely ambiguous circumstances. *Three Sisters who are not Sisters* is also a murder mystery, no one ever knowing who has killed whom. *Look and Long* presents a mysterious apparition who splits Oliver in two, makes Muriel so thin that she slips through a ring, turns Susie into an addled white egg, and Silly into Willy. *Yes is for a Very Young Man* deals with undercover operations of the French Resistance. In the last three the mysteries are resolved in some fashion; the first four remain ambiguous.

The mystery play is a prototype for all of Stein's plays, since she avoids presenting connections between events in all her plays in the few instances that events occur. Anyone who faces the plays and attempts an explanation spends much time reflecting upon what she so deliberately makes ambiguous and equivocal for the sake of her static art. The danger lies in positing meanings and connections for plays that depend on non-connections and non-significance for their very existence.

The subject matter explored most intensively in the plays is identity vs. entity, the overriding concern of her life and art. Does the essence of a person or thing depend upon its connections with extraneous things or upon a quality that issues from within? If the latter is the case how does one establish it? How does one really know who one is? *Identity a Play* (1935) is the first play to approach the question with any thoroughness. Written just three years after her first move into narrative (1932), it addresses directly the question of identity, and indirectly, perhaps, the question of her own integrity during this phase of her career. *Identity a Play* explores the ramifications of the deceptively simple Mother Goose rhyme "I am I because my little dog knows me." Her conclusion, reached after an anguished series of "plays" to discover the relationship between the dog and the figure, is as follows:

SCENE II

> I am I because my little dog knows me even if the little dog is a big one and yet a little dog knowing me does not really make me be I no not really because after all being I I am I really has nothing to do with the little dog knowing me, he is my audience, but an audience never does prove to you that you are you.[157]

A Play Called Not and Now (1936) follows up *Identity* by stating that the men and women who look like Dashiell Hammett, Pablo Picasso, Charlie Chaplin, Lord Berners, David Green, Anita Loos, Gertrude Atherton, Lady Diana Gray, Katharine Cornell, Daisy Fellowes, and Mrs. Andrew Greene can only be said to look like who they look like. They cannot be said positively to be who they look like, even if they are. Not even a dispassionate observer could establish it because he is only the little dog, and the little dog can never prove to you that you are you.

Doctor Faustus Lights the Lights considers the subject in a different way. Doctor Faustus has sold his soul for the knowledge of electric light, and doubts the wisdom of that move from the beginning of the play:

> What am I. I am Doctor Faustus who knows everything can do everything and you say it was through you but not at all, if I had not been in such a hurry and if I had taken my time I would have known how to make white electric light and day-light and night light and what did I do I saw you miserable devil I saw you and I was deceived and I believed miserable devil I thought I needed you, and I thought I was tempted by the devil and I know no temptation is tempting unless the devil tells you so....and I I who know everything I keep on having so much light that light is not bright and what after all is the use of light, you can see just as well without it, you can go around just as well without it you can get up and go to bed just as well without it, and I I wanted to make it and the devil take it....[158]

After bathing in it awhile, he wants simply to be left alone:

> Let me Alone
> Let me alone
> Oh let me alone.
> Dog and boy let me alone oh let me alone
> Leave me alone
> Let me be alone
> little boy and dog
> let let me alone[159]

In fact, he desires complete darkness after all the light he has seen:

> I sold my soul to make it bright with electric light and now no one not I not she not they
> not he are interested in that thing and I and I I cannot go to hell I have sold my soul to
> make a light and the light is bright but not interesting in my sight and I would oh yes I
> would I would rather go to hell be I with all my might and then go to hell oh yes
> alright.[160]

The parallels between the situation Faust finds himself in and Stein's own in the "identity" segment of her career—the time in which she exchanged the complete solitude of some twenty years of writing for recognition by an audience—are imperative to note. After writing her widely-disseminated *Autobiography of Alice B. Toklas,* and *Everybody's Autobiography* in the early thirties, she wrote often about the consequences of fame for a writer, wondering openly in plays and theoretical writings whether it was possible to retain any sense of self in the glare of publicity and with the ever-present awareness of audience expectation. She wrote in *Everybody's Autobiography*:

> Henry McBride always said that success spoils one and he always used to say to me
> that he hoped that I would not have any and now I was having some. He was very sweet
> about it and said it pleased him as much as it did me and it did not spoil me but even so
> it did change me.
>   The thing is like this, it is all the question of identity. It is all a question of the outside
> being outside and the inside being inside. As long as the outside does not put a value on
> you it remains outside but when it does put a value on you then it gets inside or rather if
> the outside puts a value on you then all your inside gets to be outside. I used to tell all
> the men who were being successful young how bad this was for them and then I who
> was no longer young was having it happen.[161]

After the notoriety brought by her identity writing of the 1930s, Stein never wrote so clearly again. To write well, as she stated from the beginning of her career, a writer must have as little sense of her audience as possible. In her later plays, as we have seen in chapter two, Stein sought to combine writing as it is written with writing according to someone else's point of view. She withdrew from her audience to a large extent to accomplish this, and regained, at least in part, a solitude from which she could write.

There is subject matter in every one of Stein's plays, no matter how skeletal or veiled. As she said of painting, "The minute painting gets abstract it gets pornographic. That is a fact."[162] Her plays always emerge from first hand contact with things or persons. Still, the subject matter seems to be simple indeed, except for the few plays which explore in detail philosophical questions relating to identity and war. In fact, it is so very simple and multifaceted (99 percent of the plays reflect combinations of subject matter) that it can hardly be said to distract to any great degree from the surface of the theatre experience. Fictional though the plays are, they present only fleeting fictions, brief evocations of topics for the spectator to take in as he moves on.

Stein's innovation lies in her disruption of the alternate reality of the stage through manipulations of form and subject matter, both of which she expresses in essence, moment by moment, and forces to relate spatially within the landscape of the theatre. Through techniques of juxtaposition, repetition, modification, rhyme, simple language, and monotonous sentence structure she is able to keep the focus of the spectator on the present moment of perception. Through her use of hermeticism, non-logical expression, multiple perspective, and multiple stories, she achieves movement within her plays and confines the attention of the spectator to his experience in the theatre. Only four of her plays, as we have seen, even risk transporting that attention to fictional stage reality, and those plays need to be considered departures from her general technique and aesthetic.

Daniel Webster. Eighteen in America. A Play, 1937.
Notebook cover of original manuscript, Volume 1.

UNION

[handwritten notations] ⌐separate folder. vol.9¹
512b

Cahier de *Daniel Webster*

à M *Alice Toklas*

demeurant *27 rue de Fleurus*

Etablissement *Stein*

Classe de *Premiere*
Vol. II

Daniel Webster. *Eighteen in America. A Play,* 1937.
Notebook cover of original manuscript, Volume II.

Daniel Webster. Eighteen in America. A Play, 1937.
First page of original manuscript, Volume I.

Dorothy Dow as Susan B. Anthony, *The Mother of Us All,*

Four Saints in Three Acts premiere, Hartford, Connecticut, 1934. (Photo: The Collection of American Literature, The Beinecke Rare Book and Manuscript Library, Yale University)

Judith Malina and Helen Jacobs in The Living Theatre's *Ladies'
Voices,* New York City, 1951.
(Photo: Estate of Carl Van Vechten by Joseph Solomon, Executor)

4

Theatrical Legacy

The work of a major artist is a highly perishable commodity, doomed to insignificance if not appreciated early enough to be valued and preserved for its effect and affect. In light of this fact, it has become all too clear that a valuation of Gertrude Stein's contribution to the theatre is a pressing need. Seminal as it is, her theatrical work has lain largely dormant and unrecognized in the seven decades since 1913.

This is not to say that production of her work is unheard of; twenty-three of her plays—and portions of more—have been produced, however rarely. (See Appendix C for detailed program information). The first of these was brought about through the efforts of Virgil Thomson, the American composer who had set to music her play *Capital Capitals,* and her portraits "Susie Asado," "Preciosilla," and "Portrait of F.B.," and who would compose music for Stein's later opera *The Mother of Us All.* Written at Thomson's prompting and tailored by Maurice Grosser into a scenario, *Four Saints in Three Acts* premiered in February 1934 at the Wadsworth Athenaeum in Hartford and moved to Broadway later that month. It was originally thought that Jean Cocteau might direct and that Christian Berard[1] or Pablo Picasso[2] might design, but John Houseman and Florine Stettheimer filled those functions. Under the sponsorship of the Friends and Enemies of Modern Music and A. Everett Austin, Jr., and part of a program inaugurating that museum which attracted art connoisseurs, intellectuals, and novelty seekers, the production became the social and artistic event of the year. Of the major productions of her works, this had the most fashionable success and the most historical impact on the American theatre. It was one of the earliest instances, for example, in which a major composer used an experimental text for an opera libretto. In 1934 the operatic norm was illustration of well-known and well-plotted stories, whether specifically intended for opera or not. Stein's libretto allowed Thomson to concentrate on the linguistic and semantic moment in an innovative way. According to him, her works possessed meanings already abstracted, or absent, or so multiplied that choice among them was impossible, there was no temptation toward tonal illustration, say of birdie babbling by the brook or heavy heavy hangs my heart.[3]

Up to this time, too, there had been few American operas that generated music of quality, and fewer that reflected the heritage of American culture. Gershwin, Blitzstein, and others would soon follow Thomson's lead, but *Four Saints, The Mother of Us All*, and *Porgy and Bess* remain the most significant American operas, even if they are not often performed.

Four Saints also marked one of the earliest productions in which blacks assumed roles for reasons other than color and appeared in such roles on the Broadway stage. As Houseman explained it, Thomson's reasons for specifying black singers was "simple and basic: quality of voice, clarity of speech, and an ability to move with dignity and grace."[4] Thomson later wrote:

Not only could they enunciate and sing; they seemed to understand because they sang...they took on their roles without self-consciousness as if they were the saints they said they were.[5]

Thomson had worked with black singers before in church choirs; they seemed a natural choice for *Four Saints*. Further, it made perfect sense to use an amateur cast unfamiliar with the existing operatic repertory, since Stein's libretto and Thomson's score would diverge so far from it. Still, it provided the occasion for some of the most patronizing — however well-intended — reviews of black performers in theatre history. The *Literary Digest* wrote:

The singers are all negroes. They do not know what the words mean and do not care.... The Negro has no intellectual barriers to break down; he is satisfied with the beauty of the words and doesn't worry about their meaning.[6]

The production's use of a major painter as set and costume designer was also a departure of note from existing practice. Florine Stettheimer was an esteemed though not renowned New York painter whose vivid sense of color, humor, and decoration for its own sake seemed to capture perfectly Stein's sense of the Spanish landscape with its static saints. She devised a sky-blue, tufted cellophane backdrop to be draped on the set, pink tarleton palm trees, and silk and velvet costumes of brilliant hue, all to be lit by white light only. The effect was one of celestial radiance and clarity.

Thomson's approach to this first production of a Stein play had enormous impact on subsequent productions of her works. There emerged a tendency — born of Thomson's ability to make a difficult text palatable to a wide audience through music—to conceive of Stein's plays as operas or musicals. Many would-be producers sensed that putting her words to music made them less static, and made word play and meanings more definite. And many felt that such non-logical language fit the conventions of opera or the musical better than it did the conventions of the existing theatre. The sung Stein line does not jar like the spoken one. To be sure, even the first production of *Four Saints* could not be considered earthshaking: though the music critics preferred the libretto to the score, and the drama critics preferred the score to the text, most agreed that the two complemented each other exceedingly well, and that the piece succeeded as an opera. Very few productions of her works have relied on other means to explore the space relationships within her texts—such as dance, incidental music, or props—which keep the moment more static. Thomson's use of a scenario conceived by Maurice Grosser, his reliance on character to convey text relationships, and his extensive internal cutting of *Four Saints* was influential, too. Though Thomson did set stage directions and other narrative interpolations to music along with characters' lines, the scenario and the cuts effectively made Stein's possibilities of stories and relationships certainties. Instead of illuminating the existing design—a series of disconnected presents—they imposed a story design.

The fashionable audience that greeted the first *Four Saints* remained with Stein's mainstream productions wherein her most extreme experiments were modified to their taste via song, scenario, or dance. Since *Four Saints* these have consisted of various of its revivals, all with Thomson's music and all following his concept; *The Mother of Us All,* her other opera set to music by Thomson, and its revivals; *A Wedding Bouquet*, a ballet version of *They Must. Be Wedded. To Their Wife,* now part of the Sadler's Wells repertory; and *Yes is for a Very Young Man,* her naturalistic war drama performed by the Pasadena Playhouse.

The Mother of Us All is one of the few texts that considers a single subject at some length. Though it spatializes events and poses as contemporaries such personages as John Quincy Adams and Lillian Russell, it reflects the clarity of the conventional play without sacrificing Stein's unique style. In addition, its theme of women's rights has become more and more relevant as years have passed. It is no wonder that the saga of Susan B.'s struggle to win the vote for women is the most often performed of her works since its premiere at Columbia University in 1947. As with *Four Saints,* Thomson's music and Maurice Grosser's scenario for the opera have become as much a part of the play as any part; there has been no attempt that I know of to compose new music, or to try a non-operatic approach.

Lord Gerald Berners and Frederick Ashton accomplished in the ballet world what Thomson did in opera when their ballet, *A Wedding Bouquet,* premiered at Sadler's Wells Theatre in 1937. Based on a text that is very much shorter and more traditionally structured than Stein's play, the production strengthened the impression given by *Four Saints* that Stein parodied theatrical convention to great and witty effect:

> The theme treated with irrepressibly frivolous mockery is a provincial wedding in France; no character is permitted to make an entrance unscathed by Gertrude Stein's disruptive lines.[7]

Yes is for a Very Young Man was Stein's first play to be performed without music. It is also Stein's most naturalistic play, lacking the pageant quality and scope of her other works, and depending more upon logic than play or poetry to fill the moment. At the same time, playfulness and poetry crop up regularly in the text, and make productions of the work problematic. The reaction of Tom Browne Henry, Lamont Johnson, and others associated with the 1946 Pasadena Playhouse production of *Yes* to this problem was to ask Stein to cut, rewrite, and rearrange portions of the play to make it more naturalistic, and to create a more compact story line. Existing reviews indicate that this was probably not the best tactic; neither the audience that came for the renowned Steinian language nor the one that expected an evening of traditional theatre was pleased. Subsequent productions have used the entire text as Stein wrote it to slightly better effect; still, the confinement of playful and poetic language to a context of naturalism ensures that the play never reaches the heights of poetry or pageantry typical of her other plays and reveals that Stein's talent did not lie in the naturalistic play.

Though these mainstream productions of Stein's plays were responsible for making her name and her art known to the theatre world, they largely altered the unique structure of her plays to serve the already-established conventions of specific media. There have been productions of Stein's works, however, that approach them expressly for the challenge they pose to traditional theatre, and for the alternative they represent. The Living Theatre's productions of *Ladies' Voices* at their West End Avenue apartment and *Dr. Faustus Lights the Lights* at the Cherry Lane Theatre, both in 1951, were the first of these. In its inaugural season, that pioneer American avant-garde theatre headed by Judith Malina and Julian Beck wished to

> encourage the modern poet by providing him with a stage where his plays may be produced and to bring interest and stimulation to an art medium which tends to become repetitive in its form rather than creative.[8]

The production of *Ladies' Voices* featured Judith Malina and Helen Jacobs, dressed in black, standing on each side of a dressmaker's dummy that held an assortment of scarves, necklaces, purses, glasses, gloves, shawls, and a calling card. The spare, formal set backed by a curtain and the relative staticity of the two performers as they took on various roles in the short play marked a breakthrough in productions of Stein's works. *Dr. Faustus* followed close on its heels. Aimee Scheff, writing in *Theatre Arts* Magazine found Julian Beck's single set

> strikingly ingenious and well attuned to Stein's unique dramatic idiom. Consisting of panels of light, rope, plaster, and wood, it was designed to express the structure of Faustus' brain. The other characters, Mephisto, who rationalizes everything, Marguerite Ida and Helena Annabel who wonders about and looks for her own identity, the Little Boy who represents Faustus' youth, and the dog, symbolizing social amenities, were all projections of Faustus illustrating his struggle.[9]

Productions of Stein's works from Thomson's through the Becks' and beyond would search for a means to represent the single consciousness of a narrator — present in Stein's works without exception — in addition to characters on the stage. Julian Beck's solution was as ingenious as Thomson's invention of a commere and compere in *Four Saints* to comment on the action, and less dependent on character; it foreshadows his set for *Frankenstein* during the Living Theatre's more political years.

The Judson Poets' Theatre was the next off-off Broadway group to take up Stein beginning with *What Happened* in 1963, and continuing through *Three Sisters who are not Sisters* and *Play I-III* in 1965, *In Circles* in 1967, *Listen to Me* in 1974, *A Manoir* in 1977, and *Dr. Faustus Lights the Lights* in 1979. Theirs has been the most extensive association with Stein's plays, if not the most innovative — always following the musical format — and has relied throughout on Al Carmines' music and Lawrence Kornfeld's direction. Their production of *What Happened* attracted attention from many corners, winning Kornfeld the 1964 directing Obie, and prompting Susan Sontag to describe the production in *Against Interpretation* as "the closest thing to theatre of cruelty that we have."[10] Sung by three men and danced by five women, it included actions such as skipping rope, chases, counting, cake slicing, hopscotch, falling down, and photographs, suggesting an illustration of Stein's text through physical action, and not necessarily an exploration of its spatial quality.

Judson's best-known Stein production was *In Circles* in 1967, which eventually moved from Judson Church to the Cherry Lane Theatre for 222 performances and to the Gramercy Arts Theatre for 56 performances. Jack Kroll captured the spirit of the production:

In Circles is a beautiful recapturing of that time early in the century when art seemed to be a Paris of the mind where all sensitive spirits could live in a universal communion of form, wit, and feeling.

Ten characters — five from each sex — inhabit this madly meaningful tea party which composer Al Carmines has turned into a gemlike operetta. Carmines' brilliant songs — which he leads from his interlocutory position at the piano — leap nimbly from fugues to rounds to tangoes to walzes, do-si-dos, gypsy airs and chorales. No one can set a tautology and a nonsequitur to music like Carmines — and he captures perfectly that quality which makes Gertrude Stein sound like a metaphysical Molly Goldberg. All this takes place in a Versailles-like setting — the gardens of the West before it blew itself up. The ten people, like guests of the Zeitgeist itself, are polite, bitchy, lecherous, tender, gay, petulant, debonair, boorish, clever, clumsy — swinging from a troubled melancholy to a mad euphoria, dancing like Valentino, riposting like Clifton Webb, brooding like Hamlet in a tennis blazer.

Over everything plays the prismatic mind of Stein who can create a verbal Matisse from a litany on the theme "the balcony is airy," or a hilarious choral cacophony on the word "Negro," or a miniature Henry James novel in the exchange "I have been deceived." "No, you have been refused."[11]

Judson's production in 1974 of *Listen to Me* gave quite a different picture of Stein and her plays, and emphasized that while consistent subject matter and depth of theme are not hallmarks of her plays, the atmosphere arising from relations between characters and between words and their meanings can have as great an impact. Michael Feingold writes:

"Listen to Me" is not a cute Steinian party-gossip jamboree from the '20s, nor an early play festooned with pretty Carmines tunes, like "In Circles" or "What Happened." It is a work of immaculate seriousness, that dates from the somber middle years of the 1930s, when Stein, having become rich and famous from "The Autobiography of Alice B. Toklas," was preoccupied with the nature of identity and how it altered as one's life changed.

"Sweet William had his genius and he looked for his Lillian." That is the argument of "Listen to Me," and its seeming stasis contains a deathtrap: when "the world is all covered with people, and no one knows who anyone looks like," it is impossible to find another person. The world is too confusing, too crowded, too alienated, too channeled; there are so many lights at night that "no dog barks at the moon."....

Lawrence Kornfeld's production, a painstaking lesson in weaving complexities out of simple statements...appears to be breathing with Stein...the big risks — like playing against Stein's words to bring out her feelings — are all successful. The use of space and groupings, which sometimes harks back to (Martha) Graham, and sometimes forward into some nameless sci-fi future, is always beautiful and to the point; so is the very daring and sensitive use of divided focus and repetition.

Carmines' music is not a be-all and end-all here, but an element of the whole, even a sinister one. Music is used to show the futility of having music; the phrases break off, the extended pieces come back in discredited form. Lillian's aria, "Dear Sweet William," palmed off on us as a straightforward love song in the first half, becomes a parody love song, in a parody play within a play in the second.[12]

The Judson productions of Stein have done much to make the true tenor of her playwriting known, and have inspired various non-professional revivals.

There are at least two productions of note that have approached Stein's plays in more experimental ways yet, relying less on the behavior of characters than these productions, and avoiding the urge to have the characters sing. James Lapine's Performance Group presented *Photograph* in 1977 at the Open Space Theatre in New York City, and Richard Eder described it:

> The Performance Group, directed by James Lapine, shares a roughly common theatrical territory with avant-garde groups such as Robert Wilson's, the Ontological-Hysterical Theatre of Richard Foreman and Mabou Mines. Although they differ somewhat in style, intention, and above all, mood, they all produce what might be called a theatre of the subconscious.
>
> They use music, rhythmic sounds and silences; they use mime and movements that have the discipline and expressiveness of ballet; they use lighting to enhance these movements and, just as frequently, to blur them and make them indistinct. They use disassociation as a cardinal principle: one image seems arbitrarily related to the next, as in dreams. Finally, they use a text; but this is as submerged, as disconnected as the other elements and only slightly more prominent. If it is more prominent, in fact, it is because words serve more clearly than anything else to mark the disconnections, and to nail down for use the distance between what is happening at one moment and what is happening at the next. "Alice is serving tea to John," a voice may say and we see John suddenly hoisted to the ceiling while Alice meditatively stacks a pile of books.
>
> The setting is a square, useful space with columns at each side. "Photograph" starts in blackness. Flash bulbs suggest rather than pick out the presence of the performers: five women, two men, and one child. The light comes up part way and we see the eight, their backs to us, each isolated in a kind of gray illumination.
>
> Suddenly a vivid color photograph is projected onto the back wall. It is momentarily more real than the real figures. "For a photograph we need a wall," the narrator says, reading the first line of the poem; and it is true. The figures standing there are homeless; only the slide projection seems comfortable.
>
> "Photograph" proceeds in this fashion. The actions do not so much follow its lines— some narrated, some spoken by the actors—as accompany and intersect them in the way that a river appears and reappears beside a railroad track.
>
> "And so we resist," says the narrator, and the actors heave and bunch up, effortfully and untidily. The child half turns at the end of the struggling group and voices a tiny "Wow." It is more description than explanation.[13]

The Independent Theatre of Rotterdam performed *A Circular Play* in the Fall of 1979 at La Mama E.T.C. in a style that differed markedly from earlier productions, too. The two performers did not impersonate characters, but worked simply and immediately with extensive properties and dance that illustrated the spatial qualities of the text and word play. Stemming from their wish to leave the Stein text unaltered and still make it clear to an audience, they exposed the seams of the theatre event existing between text, performers, and audience in ways that Stein might have appreciated: though they demonstrated the word games and semantics in Stein's text, they avoided reproducing her context, creating a performance context of their own. This struck a happy balance between performance art as might be observed in a Stuart Sherman spectacle and a representation of a finished text.

Production of the Stein play is still in its infancy. Though more than half the plays had been written by 1927, and though all 77 of them have existed since 1946, they have been quite obscure. Methods for producing them have emerged very slowly and have been advanced, ironically enough, by the high-profile methods of various avant-garde theatre artists inspired by her theories and writings. While it is possible to approach the plays of Stein in a variety of ways, as is obvious from their production history, a standard has emerged that begins with leaving the unique characteristics of the Stein play unaltered. Though there may be some amount of internal cutting of lines, there is no tampering with the key characteristics of staticity, multiple perspective, self-reference, and internal balancing. There is a recognition in this standard that the fullest and most innovative achievement of these characteristics in specifically theatrical terms is the test of Stein and that to alter the balance that exists in the Stein play between character, language, fiction and nonfiction, and spectacle is to skirt her challenge. While it is true that the best productions of orthodox plays achieve such balance between production elements, it is also true that the very detailed work on the fiction by actors and directors in rehearsal is generally conducted separately from the work on style and design, and is very often primary to it. Today's orthodox theatre is still very much a theatre of psychology and storytelling, utilizing these at the expense of other production elements. Gertrude Stein simply asked that directors see her plays, as she saw the world, all on one plane—that they consider no one aspect more important than any other.

In the Stein production the director's task is one of distribution—through the space that is the stage and through the fictional and actual components of the event. A director presented with *A List* (1923), for example, would notice that the text is composed of lines clearly connected to character names:

Martha. If four are sitting at a table and one of them is lying on it and there are pomegranates on it and one of the five is leaning on the table it does not make any difference.

Martha. It does not make any difference if four are seated at a table and one is leaning upon it.

Maryas.   If five are seated at a table and there is bread on it and there are pomegranates on it and one of the five is leaning on the table it does not make any
difference.

Martha.   If on a day that comes again and if we consider a day a week day it does
come again if on a day that comes again and we consider every day to be a day that
comes again it comes again then when accidentally when very accidentally every other
day and every other day every other day and every other day that comes again and every
other day comes again when accidentally every other day comes again, every other day
comes again and and every other and every day comes again and accidentally and every
day and it comes again, a day comes again and a day in that way comes again.

Maryas.   Accidentally in the morning and after that every evening and accidentally
every evening and after that every morning and after that accidentally every morning
and after that accidentally and after that every morning.

Maryas.   After that accidentally. Accidentally after that.

Maryas.   Accidentally after that. After that accidentally.

Maryas and Martha.   More Maryas and more Martha.

Maryas and Martha.   More Martha and more Maryas.[14]

The easiest and dullest solution to this scene is to present two static characters in conversation, a solution that hardly captures the play as Stein wrote
it. To begin with, the lines are not conversational, and do not necessarily
address either character. Rather, the lines are merely attached to a character name, and seem more like recitations — lectures, even — on possibilities
existing in a space that may be entirely distinct from the characters. In
addition, there is playfulness in Stein's assignment of the lines, many of
which are virtually identical, but spatially rearranged, and still assigned to
a different character. The playfulness extends to the lines themselves —
modified ever so slightly from the preceding line, and yet changed indeed —
and culminates in the last two lines which differ only in the fact that they
list the characters in opposite order. The content of the lines creates a
possible landscape consisting of a table, four or five people who may move
around it or on it, pomegranates, and bread. The lines convey through
their rhythms and conditional clauses a feeling of the great, slow tedium of
day-to-day living, deftly extending it into a theatrical tedium in the last two
lines. They also convey a comical effect in the pointing out of slight shades
of difference that are only differences in possibilities, after all. The
director will find the key to Stein in the investigation of the script for such
aspects, and above all, in the duplication of these aspects in theatrical
terms. To convey the self-referential twist at the end of the passage and to
convey the non-conversational quality of the lines, Maryas and Martha

might speak the names connected to the lines and deliver the lines with the idea that they are describing a separate landscape, emerging as narrators. The fatigue and tedium inherent in the text can ensue as much from the narrator's presentation of the description as from the landscape itself, which might deteriorate as time went on. In addition, the landscape devised by the director may work against the lines; it might make a difference if four are seated at a table and one is leaning upon it. It might be that Martha sees pomegranates where are there are none. In this way the two levels on the stage might feed each other. Though there is certainly no single solution to producing any of Stein's texts, this kind of meticulous sorting out of the spatial aspects and levels of her plays by directors can provide imaginative ones. The mix of perspectives, moments, fictions, realities, and characters with the dance of words is the Stein play.

The work of directors, actors, and designers upon the plays of Stein is among the most liberating in all of theatre. While there are few psychologies or unstated realities to explore there is the demand that artists confront the most rudimentary aspects of their craft to meet the challenge of her unorthodox use of language, character, and action and that they collaborate fully with others to decide questions already answered in the orthodox play such as what lines are to be assigned and to whom, whether they are to be conversation or narration, whether a landscape in the text is to be literal or conceptual, and whether the reality at any one moment is to be fictional or theatrical. They are theatre artists in the fullest sense, determining the character of the function as well as the fiction. Virgil Thomson's description of his singers was truly spoken: "they seemed to understand," he said, "because they sang." In the making plain through the act of performance lies the clarity of the Stein play.

The presence of Stein's theatre is not felt solely through productions of her works: its most significant impact so far, in fact, has been through theory and technique. The concepts we have isolated in relation to time and entity in her plays are common usage in today's theatrical avant-garde, and are effective means of analyzing its work. While departing in some ways from Stein's theatre, the work of Richard Foreman[15] and Robert Wilson[16] depends on the very techniques Stein pioneered in the theatre in 1913, and takes to practical ends a number of her theories. Other current American avant-gardists can be studied profitably with a Steinian apparatus, but the work of Foreman and Wilson actually owes debts to Stein, and can depict more accurately her impact.

Richard Foreman maintains that Stein's theoretical writings have been the primary influence on his writing method and style.[17] He shares Stein's aversion to the traditional theatre experience dependent upon progressive, crisis-centered action, and posits instead an "ontological-hysteric" theatre, one which shatters the hysteric (conflict) structure of traditional theatre and focuses upon its parts moment by moment. In breaking up time in this way, Foreman achieves the same staticity, the same finality that Stein does in her plays: the perceiver focuses upon a network of relations and connections that have final, physical significance. The reality of the theatre experience per se, as opposed to the alternate reality of the fiction, is Foreman's focal point as much as it is Stein's. In "How To Write A Play" he proposes:

make a kind of beauty that isn't an
ALTERNATIVE to a certain environment
(beauty, adventure, romance, dream, drama all
take you out of your real world and into their
own in the hope you'll return refreshed, wiser,
more compassionate, etc.)

but rather

makes GAPS in the non-beautiful, or looks carefully at the structure of the non-beautiful, whatever it is (and remember that structure is always a combination of the
THING
and the
PERCEIVING of it)
and see where there are small points, gaps, unarticulated or un-mapped places within it
(the non-beautiful)
which un-mapped places must be the very places where beauty CAN be planted in the midst of the heretofore unbeautiful.[18]

Stein's aesthetic stemmed from the simple perception that if the audience was not presented with the thing in itself, it would have difficulty seeing it. Though Foreman's seems to show a more broadly philosophical base, the ends of his theatre are quite similar to those of Stein since he depends upon the self-contained movement, a new concept of time, and the notion of entity inherent in Stein's plays.

Foreman attempts in his plays a deliberate creation of new relationships between heretofore unconnected things, which is Stein's juxtaposition. In Stein's plays this takes the form of substantive parts of speech, characters, occurrences, and perspectives which do not function as connectors as much as they force a fresh relationship between moments of the play. Though Foreman may use juxtaposition in some of these ways, he also pursues it in a very physical, painterly sense. A string will be attached from an orange to a chair, for example, creating juxtaposition in a Steinian way and forcing the spectator to view the objects as objects. He writes:

So let the chair that is for sitting have a string run from it to an orange, because if chair was just "chair for sitting" we would not "confront" as we not confront in kitsch because we are too close to the chair, its meaning is too much our meaning; but now chair-connected-to-orange is an "alien" chair that we must CONFRONT.[19]

Kitsch for Foreman implies hypnotism of the spectator, a function carried out, he believes, by the traditional theatre. If a spectator can directly contact a thing, he identifies with it and can't see it as a thing. If he sees it in a network of relationships with things that are startling in their conjunction, he can. Foreman attempts, in fact, the flatness and relationality that Stein brought about in language and theatrical conventions, and poses it in plastic terms. His chair-connected-to-orange is similar to Stein's flattened, "abused" noun, her static characters and essential action, her "mistaken" adverb, preposition, pronoun, and article, and her multiple perspective. Connecting objects in the same fashion as she connected word-objects and moments of plays, Foreman forces them to relate horizontally and demands that the spectator meet them actively or not at all. This, in Foreman's sense, is "art" and "awakedness."[20]

Self-contained movement as pioneered by Stein is expressive of other areas of Foreman's work as well. He injects, as she did, the narrative voice through stage directions and textual interpolations designed to pull the spectator to the surface of the theatre experience and make him aware of multiple perspective. Moreover, his voice is often present in the production itself:

> Before the rehearsal period begins, Foreman records all of the music, noises and most of the dialogue on tape. All of the lines spoken by the "Voice" and many of the "legends" are Foreman's own voice while the voices of individual characters are those of the performers designated for each role. During each performance, Foreman sits at a table, directly in front, or above and in back, of the audience seating section. From this table, he operates the various tape recorders and lighting instruments thereby "conducting" the performance since he controls all of the lighting and tape-recorded cues.[21]

The self reference, or entity, of Stein's theatre is also exhibited by Foreman's. Characters refer to themselves and to each other as characters, to Foreman as narrator/conductor, and to the process of the theatre experience. But they take it one step further at times by a complete reliance on staticity and a confrontation of the audience:

> Foreman uses picturization or tableaux, employing the traditional "picture-frame stage" viewing arrangement for the spectators. In staging, he presents almost all of the scenes as sequences of static pictures. The performers are relaxed yet posed and motionless, creating tableau compositions. They usually gaze steadily at or toward the audience. In so doing, the performers force the spectator to notice where he is by implying with their stare, "i am here, where are you."[22]

Though it is hard to say exactly what Stein intended for her own plays in production, in all probability she intended neither the absolute staticity nor the direct confrontation of audience and actor that Foreman employs. His motionless stage picture which allows the spectator's perception to create the movement is actually a violation of Stein's aesthetic. She desired above all that nothing transpire on stage or in the audience that did not occur in both places simultaneously. She wanted her plays to move within the still moment, like the seated spectator whose attention roams from momentary fiction to knowledge of the theatre experience in itself. To still the stage picture in Foreman's sense risks syncopation in reverse.

Foreman's language utilizes a Steinian simplicity and monotony which forces the spectator to apprehend the words as words and disengages him from an alternate reality. It does not, however, express the rampant playfulness, the rhythms and rhymes, the modifications, the repetitions, the complete self-reference, or the beauty and wit in language as language typical of Stein. Where Stein's plays are best perceived as playful pageants of words, characters, events, and perspectives "with a great deal of glitter in the light and a great deal of height in the air," Foreman's plays lack this aspect. Though not without humor, they are more austerely intellectual in rooting the spectator's perception to the surface of the theatre experience. In the undecorated theatre space, words, and connection of chair-to-orange lies Richard Foreman's Ontological-Hysteric Theatre. Through repetition and reiteration of theatrical points and through fictional investigations of consciousness the spectator is pushed to a perception of his own perception.

Robert Wilson does not adhere as strictly to Stein's aesthetic principles as Foreman does, but his theatre shares the circus or pageant quality typical of her theatre. Frantisek Deak's description of Act One of *The Life and Times of Joseph Stalin* captures the intention:

> The stage is covered with sand; there is a blue sky drop. A chair hangs from the flies. All movement is made along several planes parallel to the proscenium line. No one crosses in front of the Byrdwoman, a black woman in a black dress with a black stuffed bird. Among the many figures are runners who pass at irregular intervals throughout the act and, with some exceptions, throughout the entire performance. Three dancers, nude above the waist, execute a repeated series of seven simple movements. Bears and a turtle cross. A man, only his legs visible, walks a beam lowered from the flies. A man in a heavily padded suit wearing a black stocking over his head does a whirling dance across the sand. Freud and his daughter Anna pass. Forty black mammies, identically dressed in kerchiefs, long dresses and aprons dance to Strauss's "Blue Danube." At the end of the act, the Byrdwoman stands, places an Egyptian figure on a downstage table, looks out at the audience, and emits a long scream-like sound.[23]

Stein's theatre can be seen as the ultimate rescue of drama from the social, moral, and psychological concerns of the late nineteenth century—a challenge to the supremacy of significance. Wilson's, by contrast, is a glance back at imagism, surrealism, and symbolism, showing affinities with Mallarme or Tzara. His stage picture, though it exhibits a Steinian self-contained movement, creates all kinds of connections in the spectator's mind with social and historical constructs, psychology, and so on, reflecting identity, in Stein's terms, not entity. He creates a richness that transports the spectator from his experience in the theatre, even though he does it through a series of disconnected presents. Lest we think that Wilson confines himself to a non-verbal pictorial theatre, however, we need but look to a more verbal creation, *A Letter to Queen Victoria*. In this play Wilson utilizes the repetition and modification of Stein's language, keeping the spectator attuned to the present:

> Yeah
> Yeah the sundance was beautiful
> The sundance kid was beautiful
> Because he was beautiful
> Very beautiful
> The beautiful sundance kid
> The sundance kid was beautiful
> The sundance kid could dance around
> The sundance kid could dance around the room
> The sundance kid was beautiful because
> The sundance kid could dance around a lot
> Yeah the sundance kid was beautiful
> Yeah
> Beautiful
> So beautiful
> So very beautiful
> A little bit beautiful
> A beautiful dancer[24]

Though he only rarely uses non-referential language in Stein's sense, he now and then exceeds Stein's hermeticism:

> cosabi nhjgt bnhg vfcd cvfesw xcvf bgh nmkji mnhjuygthfrd vbnh bg v b bbnhj bgv per glos o chocolate[25]

He accomplishes in parts of this play what he did not in *Stalin*: a Steinian awareness of the word as object which keeps the spectator in the theatrical present.

Both of these plays reach a point of stillness similar to Stein's plays by breaking up the conflict basis of traditional theatre. They work for movement within stillness as Stein's did by reflecting multiplicity of subject matter and perspective. Though Wilson, as we have seen, often goes beyond the sheer moment by having it evoke extraneous subject matter, he insists upon its multiplicity. The atom bomb, imperialism, human interaction, the Civil War, ecology, ancient civilization, justice, murder, and pilots in a plane crash comprise the multiple focus in *Queen Victoria*. Multiple perspective can be seen to operate in a speech made by the Chinaman in Act IV, Section I:

> A person appears in a place for a length of time, interacting with others, and goes—nothing unusual in that...a person appears in another place for the exact same length of time, interacting identically with the same number of people down to the smallest details—who can know that one is part of the other?...who can recognize the same names, the same faces, the same course of events? Only one with a view of sufficient breadth and patience.[26]

The speech is a summary of the course of the play, intended for spectator attention. It works in the same way as Stein's and Foreman's textual interpolations, pulling the spectator back from identification to a perception of his perception.

Wilson's manipulation of time in his productions, while showing the influence of Stein's aesthetic, departs from it in various ways. He often distends or prolongs time, for example, so much so that a complete action may appear to be a series of discrete moments. The Byrdwoman, for example, takes 48 minutes to cross downstage and emit her scream. Wilson intends that the spectator focus on the apparent still moments within the larger movement so that he may notice the movement within them. This is very like Stein's self-contained movement, and it works against syncopation in Steinian fashion. It shares her intent—from William James—to capture transitive states and transform them into substantive ones, and shows the fleeting movements in daily life that occur too fast to be reckoned with. Though Wilson combines such slow-motion actions with other more rapid, multidirectional actions in the same stage picture, and though his productions are more likely perceived as a network of pace and action, his plays nevertheless prolong action rather than break it up. They can be said to exhibit action in Smiley's sense, for though the action is distended, it is there. Action in Stein's plays, as we have seen, is nearly always confined to the moment in itself.

This is not to say that Wilson's plays are traditional. Most of them employ simultaneous action which evokes the pageant quality of Stein's plays—especially *Four Saints in Three Acts, A Circular Play,* and *The Mother of Us All,* where most of the characters are onstage at once throughout the performance. Wilson's simultaneous actions, however, are more evocative of the Happening: each action is heterogeneous, each story element is a play in itself occurring in the same space. In Stein's plays moments are presented one at a time, not simultaneously, and focus shifts among aspects of that moment—character, costume, set, language, story, and movement.

Wilson's concepts of time and perspective are drawn from his model for modern consciousness, Christopher Knowles. An autistic who has performed in many of Wilson's plays, Knowles has come to represent for Wilson the modern consciousness that withdraws from reality to reach a new level of perception. It is a concept similar to Stein's human mind, and approaches the capability of the human mind to disengage from the flow of time and forge a new way of writing. Wilson has said:

> You might call autistic what Gertrude Stein did with language, with words, with sounds. It's the repetitiveness and the obsessiveness of it all.[27]

The difference between Stein's concept and the autistic mind to her would likely lay in the ability of the human mind to separate itself completely from human nature and the world to perceive them through the isolated instants of its attention. The autistic mind would seem to distend time, stretching it to see new things, and carry some knowledge of social self and the world along with it. The human mind approaches it moment by moment, assured.

Wilson and Foreman share Stein's uncompromising attitude. It is doubtful, for example, that their plays will ever be performed out of their presence. Their productions have so completely been processes of Wilson and Foreman at work that the value of production apart from the creators seems doubtful. Not even Stein worked herself into her plays to this degree, though it would be a neat realization of her aesthetic to have her there in production, dispensing stage directions and interpolations at will.

On the other hand, their plays do not display the formal coherence that binds Stein's plays to her aesthetic. In virtually all cases, for example, they possess sequential scenes and acts which provide a unity for the action (or non-action) within. They are set up according to character-speech format, and though this may be combined with narrative interpolation, these interpolations and stage directions are clear and well-distinguished. Stein's plays display more self-contained movement, more vitality, because perspectives of author and character can often not be distinguished. Wilson shares Stein's departure from the standard format more often, repeating in *Queen Victoria* whole scenes with a new set of actors or new sounds. But his directions for these repetitions are clear, not playful, and certainly inadequate, in Stein's sense, to the moment as it unfolds and to the final reality of the theatre event.

The major difference, of course, between Stein and these artists is that she operated as a writer outside the theatre who remained true to her aesthetic at all costs, confident that the theatre could realize that aesthetic most completely and concretely if the theatre would only do it. Free from confronting the enormity of its challenge, she made no concessions in her playwriting. Foreman and Wilson are artists of the theatre: because they function as playwrights, directors, designers, and actors, they conceive their work in terms of production.

The theatres of Foreman, Wilson, and Stein, despite their differences, address a common, fluctuating reality which they must capture through disengaged attention to the present. Through juxtaposition of text elements and images, horizontal time, repetition, modification, hermeticism, multiple perspective, textual interpolation, and monotony, they achieve a present reality which refers as much to itself as to any alternate reality.

Besides Foreman and Wilson, there are other artists functioning today who carry on the techniques and aesthetic pioneered by Stein. Contemporary dance artists such as Trisha Brown, Meredith Monk, and Lucinda Childs call attention to the process of theatre in their productions and operate according to a new conception of time which focuses upon the moment, whatever they conceive that moment to be. And that ubiquitous twentieth-century theatre form performance art as practised by performers like Stuart Sherman, Laurie Anderson, Spalding Gray, and Mel Andringa's Drawing Legion treads the space between real time and fiction, personality and character, disconnection and causality, and actuality and pretense. Together with Foreman and Wilson and such companies as the Wooster Group, James Lapine's Performance Group, Snake Theatre, Soon 3, Mabou Mines, and Nightfire, they sustain concepts that Gertrude Stein utilized when she wrote her first play in 1913.

It should be clear from this study that Gertrude Stein never attempted to create drama in the traditional sense. Though at first glance the plays may stun those accustomed to traditional methods of ordering and styling plays based on a consequential concept of time, it is soon clear that the plays operate according to a form and style of their own. We have seen how Stein's style emerged directly from the uncompromising aesthetic she posed in response to the changing reality of the twentieth century. It had no relation to orthodox ways of viewing the world because it was not addressed to the orthodox world. It suggested that the only way to observe the fluctuating universe was by disengaging the human mind from it to view it moment by moment. Such moments, once created, would have nothing to do with previous or subsequent moments, nothing to do with significance or meaning, nothing to do with traditional embellishment. Rather, they would live in and for themselves in a perfect present tense.

The style she evolved to capture these moments needed to be as absolute as the moments themselves. She tore language from traditional usage and flattened it. She favored words which could be "mistaken" and achieved vibration within that stillness. She avoided the comma, or anything which would serve to keep the perceiver from experiencing her work as actively as she experienced the thing in itself. Her style was a simple, direct attempt bordering on the impossible to capture a thing for her audience exactly as she saw it. It resulted in an absolute art which completely subsumed that all-important thing in the rendering.

Once this style evolved in non-dramatic writing, chiefly novels and portraits, Stein turned to the theatrical medium for its ability to convey, in performance, her absolute art in a vibrant present tense and in a finite space. She wrote seventy-seven plays in the course of her career as a composer for the stage, all of which are embodiments of her aesthetic and style as of 1911. Though virtually all scholars have dealt with these plays in the phases set forth by Stein in her critical writings, it is clear that—whether dealing with relational movement between persons and the essence of an occurrence, movement within a static landscape, or narrative treated as landscape—all the plays are attempts to achieve in the theatrical mode her immediate and self-contained art.

The detailed examination of her dramaturgical technique shows how the body of plays succeeds in achieving this in text. Stein strove to keep the spectator attuned to the present tense of his experience and to avoid "syncopation," through various devices of her invention. Rather than move away from the spectator at any point, as Stein believed traditional plays did, her plays move within themselves, allowing perception of a landscape from a distance.

This dynamic movement creates a lively experience for the spectator, and is accomplished through her use of multiple perspective, fanciful stage directions meant obviously to be an integral part of the text, and textual interpolations. By bringing the attention of the spectator to the surface of the theatre experience at intervals, Stein forces him to experience the process of her perception and his own during the course of the play. The plays are, as I have suggested, perspective continua wherein the process of the theatre event interacts with the fictions on the stage. It provides the spectator with a fresh view of his reality in the theatre.

Together with her use of hermeticism, non-logical expression, simple words, and monotonous sentence structure, these techniques keep the spectator's attention rooted to the theatrical experience in itself and avoid losing it to the alternate reality of fiction. They create an absolute theatre; one which posits its own being as its ultimate reality.

Gertrude Stein's attempt to render in the theatre medium the fluctuating reality of the twentieth century in a manner appropriate to it was com-

pletely unprecedented. Chekhov, Maeterlinck, Craig, Copeau, and Reinhardt had arrived at a new treatment of time in their work, Pirandello had
experimented with perspective, and Cocteau had achieved a new physicality in the theatre. But most of these artists created pieces that could be
integrated into the theatre virtually as it stood. These were, after all, men
who knew intimately the traditional theatre process; they cast their work in
accordance with it. To a lesser extent the same is true of Jarry, Tzara,
Marinetti, and the surrealists—including Witkiewicz, with his theatre of
"pure form" that avoids psychology and storytelling—whose experiments
were closer to Stein's than any others.

Stein's lack of knowledge and lack of reverence for established forms
freed her to create theatre on her own terms. But it is testament to her dedication to rendering the "complete actual present" in the theatre that she did
so, with no thought of gratification, for some twenty years. Still, her plays
were not meant to be closet dramas. "They are to be kept to be played," she
wrote peremptorily to Mabel Dodge in 1913. She knew they were plays; she
knew their ultimate realization lay in live performance. But she would wait
until 1934 to have a play of hers produced, and productions since then
have been few, far between, and variably adequate to the realization of her
aesthetic.

The lack of specificity and breadth which has characterized even the
best critical studies of Stein's plays, and the conventional approach to
many of them in production have obscured her art and have encouraged
the conception that it must be considered apart from—not integral with—
the vital theatrical forms of our day. But Gertrude Stein's work in the theatre was so far ahead of its time that we can only now begin to perceive
what she attempted in the medium. And the theatre itself, traditionally
behind the other arts in recognizing new ideas and forms since it is so col-
laborative an art and so rooted in social process, is just now beginning to
accommodate the world view emerging from Einstein, Faraday, Maxwell,
and Rutherford. It is now producing artists who can, paradoxically, clarify
our view of Stein in their very emulation of her. That these artists are by
and large confined to the murky realms of the avant-garde indicates well
the position Gertrude Stein might have if she were still writing for the
theatre.

But despite the fact that these artists display the influence of her technique in one way or another, directly or indirectly, not one of them has
approached her magical combination of moment-to-moment perception
and celebration of theatre as theatre. Foreman comes from the world of
philosophy and seems austere by comparison. Wilson comes from the
world of psychology and incorporates much of its imagistic baggage into
his lively, colorful productions. Gertrude Stein comes from the simple

world of her own experience. Divorced from extraneous concerns, occupied with knowledge and knowledge alone, she captures the thing as thing with precision and propels it to final form in the theatre. She creates out of great feeling and humor a resonant theatre born of the moment, a theatre of the absolute that a spectator can come to share.

Appendix A

Chronological List of Plays

This appendix lists by date of composition the 77 plays of Gertrude Stein discussed in Chapter 3. Titles are shown as they appear in the text of the published book rather than the table of contents, where alterations sometimes occur. The title of the book in which each play appears and the page number on which it begins follow the play title. Book titles are abbreviated as follows:

BTV	Bee Time Vine
FOUR	Four in America
G&P	Geography and Plays
GSFR	The Gertrude Stein First Reader and Three Plays
LO&P	Last Operas and Plays
O&P	Operas and Plays
P&P	Portraits and Prayers
REFL	Reflection on the Atomic Bomb (R. B. Haas, ed.)
UK	Useful Knowledge
WAM	What Are Masterpieces
YCAL	Yale Collection of American Literature, Gertrude Stein Collection

The play chronology is based on Richard Bridgman's list of Stein's canon in Appendix C of his study, *Gertrude Stein in Pieces*, which is derived from the Gallup and Haas list in the Yale Catalog, part 4 (completed with the assistance of Stein), and from Julian Sawyer's chronology for post-1940 works. The number within parentheses is that given the play by Bridgman and describes its position in the canon as a whole. The number at the left margin describes its position in the play canon.

1913

1.	(52)	What Happened. A Five Act Play.	G&P,205
2.	(53)	One. Carl Van Vechten.	G&P,199
3.	(55)	White Wines. Three Acts.	G&P,210
4.	(57)	IIIIIIIIII.	G&P,189
5.	(58)	Old And Old.	O&P,219
6.	(61)	A Curtain Raiser.	G&P,202
7.	(63)	Simons A Bouquet.	O&P,203

1915

8. (105) Not Sightly. A Play. G&P,290
9. (120) He Said It. Monologue. G&P,267

1916

10. (121) For The Country Entirely. A Play In Letters. G&P,227
11. (129) Ladies' Voices. G&P,203
12. (130) Every Afternoon. A Dialogue. G&P,254
13. (132) Do Let Us Go Away. A Play. G&P,215
14. (134) Bonne Annee. A Play. G&P,302
15. (136) Captain Walter Arnold. A Play. G&P,260
16. (138) Please Do Not Suffer. A Play. G&P,262
17. (139) I Like It To Be A Play. A Play. G&P,286
18. (141) Turkey And Bones And Eating And We Liked It. A Play. G&P,239
19. (143) Polybe In Port: A Curtain Raiser. [part of A Collection] G&P,23
20. (148) Mexico. A Play. G&P,304

1917

21. (154) The King Or Something. (The Public Is Invited To Dance). G&P,122
22. (156) Counting Her Dresses. A Play. G&P,275
23. (158) An Exercise In Analysis. A Play. LO&P,119

1919

24. (187) Monday And Tuesday. A Play. YCAL
25. (189) Accents In Alsace. A Reasonable Tragedy. G&P,409

1920

26. (210) A Movie. O&P,395
27. (222) Photograph. A Play In Five Acts. LO&P,152
28. (228) A Circular Play. A Play In Circles. LO&P,139

1921

29. (251) Capture Splinters. BTV,218
30. (257) Reread Another. A Play. To Be Played Indoors Or Out. I Wish To Be A
School. O&P,123

1922

31. (258) Objects Lie On A Table. A Play. O&P,105
32. (264) Saints And Singing. A Play. O&P,71
33. (268) A Saint In Seven. WAM,41
34. (269) Lend A Hand Or Four Religions. UK,170

1923

35.	(286)	A List. O&P,89
36.	(287)	Capital Capitals. O&P,61
37.	(290)	A Village. Are You Ready Yet Not Yet. A Play In Four Acts. [published separately]
38.	(293)	Am I To Go Or I'll Say So. O&P,113

1927

39.	(349)	Four Saints In Three Acts. An Opera To Be Sung. O&P,11

1928

40.	(367)	A Lyrical Opera Made By Two. To Be Sung. O&P,49
41.	(371)	Paiseau. A Play. A Work of Pure Imagination In Which No Reminiscences Intrude. LO&P,155
42.	(372)	A Bouquet. Their Wills. O&P,195

1929

43.	(382)	Film. Deux Soeurs Qui Ne Sont Pas Soeurs. O&P,399

1930

44.	(398)	Parlor. A Play. Between Parlor Of The Sisters. And Parlor Of The Earls. O&P,325
45.	(401)	At Present. A Play. Nothing But Contemporaries Allowed. O&P,315
46.	(416)	Madame Recamier. An Opera. O&P,355
47.	(417)	They Weighed Weighed-Layed. A Drama Of Aphorisms. O&P,231
48.	(419a)	An Historic Drama In Memory Of Winnie Elliot. LO&P,182
49.	(420)	Will He Come Back Better. Second Historic Drama. In The Country. LO&P,189
50.	(420a)	Third Historic Drama. LO&P,195
51.	(422)	Louis XI And Madame Giraud. O&P,345
52.	(423)	Play I–(III) LO&P,200

1931

53.	(425)	Say It With Flowers. O&P,331
54.	(426)	The Five Georges. O&P,293
55.	(436)	Lynn And The College De France. O&P,249
56.	(437)	They Must. Be Wedded. To Their Wife. A Play. LO&P,204
57.	(438)	Civilization. A Play. In Three Acts. O&P,131

1932

58.	(441)	A Play Without Roses. Portrait Of Eugene Jolas. P&P,200
59.	(442)	A Play Of Pounds. LO&P,239

60. (445)   A Manoir. An Historical Play In Which They Are Approached More Often. LO&P,277
61. (446)   A Play A Lion For Max Jacob. P&P,28
62. (447)   Short Sentences. LO&P,317
63. (453)   Scenery And George Washington. A Novel Or A Play. FOUR,161

1933

64. (455)   Byron A Play. But Which They Say Byron A Play. LO&P,333

1935

65. (486)   Identity A Poem. WAM,71

1936

66. (493)   Listen To Me. A Play. LO&P,387
67. (494)   A Play Called Not And Now. LO&P,422

1937

68. (508)   Daniel Webster. Eighteen In America: A Play. REFL,95

1938

69. (515)   Doctor Faustus Lights The Lights. LO&P,89
70. (517a)   Lucretia Borgia. A Play. REFL,118

1941

71. (537)   Lesson Sixteen. A Play. [part of First Reader] GSFR,42

1943

72. (543)   In A Garden. A Tragedy In One Act. GSFR,59
73. (544)   Three Sisters Who Are Not Sisters. A Melodrama. GSFR,63
74. (545)   Look And Long. A Play In Three Acts. GSFR,73

1944–1946

75. (533)   Yes Is For A Very Young Man. LO&P,1

1945–1946

76. (565)   The Mother Of Us All. LO&P,52

1946

77. (569)   John Breon A Novel Or A Play. YCAL

Appendix B

Play Traits

I. List of Play Traits

The forty-eight traits applied to the plays of Stein in Chapter Three appear in their respective categories of Form (1–30), Subject Matter (1–15), and Miscellaneous concerns (1–3) in the first section of Appendix B.

II. Play Trait Data

Section II tabulates the presence or absence of traits in the plays of Gertrude Stein as listed in Section I. Plays appear in their order of composition along the left margin; traits are listed according to the numbers assigned them in Section I (Form: 1–30; Subject Matter: 1–15; Miscellaneous: 1–3) along the top horizontal line. Plays which reflect a particular trait have a 1 in the corresponding position under that trait number. Plays which do not reflect that trait have a 0. An exception to this is trait 25 under Form which reflects five degrees from non-logical (0) to logical (4) expression. Using this tabular representation, a trait can be followed by isolating the trait at the top of the page and following it downward to see the extent to which Stein's plays reflect it from 1913–1946.

I. List of Play Traits

1. Form

1. Text divided into sections
2. Character-speech format
3. Title-text format
4. Narrator-description (story format)
5. Juxtaposition (lack of transition) within sentence and paragraph
6. Juxtaposition within paragraph only
7. Resulting images homogeneous
8. Resulting images heterogeneous
9. Spiral time
10. Horizontal time
11. Vertical (developmental) time
12. Act construction
13. Scene construction

14. Monologue construction
15. Dialogue construction
16. Narrator-description perspective
17. Author-character-speech perspective
18. Presence of named characters
19. Physical stage directions
20. Extra-physical stage directions
21. Text clear within sentence and paragraph
22. Text hermetic within paragraph
23. Text hermetic within sentence
24. Textual interpolation
25. Type of expression from logical (sense) to non-logical (sound)
26. Repetition as determinant of style
27. Modification of lines
28. Simple language (opposed to lyrical)
29. Monotonous sentence structure (opposed to varied)
30. Rhyme

2. *Subject Matter*

1. Names mentioned
2. Places mentioned
3. Background/context present
4. Events chronicled
5. Play as metaplay
6. Subject: identity
7. Subject: mystery
8. Subject: domestic life
9. Subject: conversation
10. Subject: war
11. Subject: movement
12. Subject: nature
13. Subject: sex/love
14. Story/stories present
15. Subject: religion

3. *Miscellaneous*

1. Play performed
2. Text described as play in text other than published version
3. Text labelled as play in published version

II. Play Trait Data

	PLAYS	YR	#	FORM 123456789012345678901234567890	CONTENT 123456789012345	MISC. 123
1	*WHAT HAPPENED	13	52	101110010101001100000110000100	000000001001000	111
2	ONE. CARL V.V.	13	53	101110100100000100000110011110	000001000000000	010
3	WHITE WINES	13	55	110101101010101010100110011111	100000010001000	010
4	IIIIIIIIII	13	57	111010010100000100000111000110	100010010001010	010
5	OLD AND OLD	13	58	101110010100000100000111011111	000000010001100	010
6	*A CURTAIN RAISER	13	61	000110010100000100000110000110	001000000000000	111
7	SIMONS A BOUQUET	13	63	101110010100100100100111011111	110100010000010	011
8	NOT SIGHTLY	15	105	111110010101010110000111301110	110010010001000	011
9	HE SAID IT	15	120	010101010100011110001001401110	111110011010010	011
10	FOR THE COUNTRY	16	121	110001010101111110010014 11100	111010011011010	011
11	*LADIES VOICES	16	129	110101010101001010110101401000	110100001010010	111
12	EVERY AFTERNOON	16	130	010001110100001111101001401110	111110011000000	011
13	DO LET US GO	16	132	111101010100011111101001401110	110100011011010.	011
14	BONNE ANNEE	16	134	010100100100011110001000211101	011100011000110	011
15	*CAPTAIN WALTER	16	136	000000010100111100010014 00110	100010011000000	111
16	PLEASE DO NOT	16	138	111011001000011111101000400110	111100011100010	011
17	*I LIKE IT TO BE	16	139	110001010100111110001011111100	011010011011110	111
18	TURKEY AND BONES	16	141	111101010101111111001000400110	111100011110010	011
19	POLYBE IN PORT	16	143	110101000100101110001000400110	110000000001010	011
20	MEXICO A PLAY	16	148	111010101011111110010014 11111	110100111110010	011
21	THE KING OR	17	154	111001010100011110001111111111	110100010001110	010
22	COUNTING HER DR	17	156	110101010101011110001001311111	001000011000100	011
23	*AN EXERCISE	17	158	110001010101011110001001411110	110000011100000	111
24	MONDAY & TUESDAY	19	187	111001010100011110001000211100	100000011000000	010
25	ACCENTS. ALSACE	19	189	111101110101111111001000111001	111100010100110	011
26	A MOVIE	20	210	000110100110011111001000400100	111100000110010	010
27	*PHOTOGRAPH	20	222	110111010101010110101011101001	110110000000000	101
28	*CIRCULAR PLAY	20	228	111010101010001111001111201001	111111011111010	111
29	CAPTURE SPLINTER	21	251	111101010100011110001001211110	100010010001000	000
30	REREAD ANOTHER	21	257	110111010100111111001111211011	100110010111010	011
31	OBJECTS LIE	22	258	000111010100000011000111211111	111010010000000	011
32	SAINTS & SINGING	22	264	110110101011111111001111111011	111110000000011	011
33	A SAINT IN 7	22	268	101111010100000111101110411011	101100000011011	000
34	*LEND A HAND	22	269	010111011100010111101001111011	111100000011011	100
35	A LIST	23	286	111011111100010111001111111111	111010000001010	010
36	*CAPITAL CAPITALS	23	287	111111111100010111001111111111	111010000011010	110
37	A VILLAGE	23	290	000111111100010101001111211111	111010010011010	011
38	AM I TO GO OR	23	293	111110110100010111101111111111	110100111110010	011
39	*FOUR SAINTS	27	349	110111111101111111111111111001	111110001011011	111
40	*A LYRICAL OPERA	28	367	110110110100110111101111111001	111110010001110	111
41	PAISEAU A PLAY	28	371	100110010101100101101111211110	111110010000110	011
42	A BOUQUET	28	372	110110010101100101111111311101	111111010001110	010
43	FILM. DEUX	29	382	000101100100000101111000400100	111101100000010	011
44	PARLOR A PLAY	30	398	100111110101100100100101401101	111111010000010	011
45	AT PRESENT	30	401	110111010101101111101111311101	101110010000000	011
46	MADAME RECAMIER	30	416	111110010101111111111111211111	111000010001010	011
47	THEY WEIGHED	30	417	110111010101110111101111201101	101100010001010	011
48	AN HIST. DRAMA	30	419	110110101010111111101200110	111100011010010	011
49	WILL HE COME	30	420	110110100100011111001110111110	111000001011000	011
50	THIRD HIST DR.	30	421	110110100100011111111110311110	111000000001010	011
51	LOUIS XI	30	422	110111010101110111101111301101	111000011011010	010
52	*PLAY I(-III)	30	423	111111010100011111101011011100	101110000010000	111
53	SAY IT W/ FL.	31	425	110111110101111111111111211100	111110000010010	011
54	THE FIVE GEORGES	31	426	110111110101110111111111111101	100111010011000	010
55	LYNN. COLLEGE	31	436	110111110101100111101011411101	111100000011010	010
56	*THEY MUST.WEDDED	31	437	110111110101110111111011411101	101110000001110	111

II. *Play Trait Data (continued)*

PLAYS	YR	#	FORM	CONTENT	MISC.
			1 2 3	1	
			12345678901234567890123 4567890	123456789012345	123
57 CIVILIZATION	31	438	110111110101010111001011411101	111110010011110	011
58 PLAY W.OUT ROSES	31	441	110110010100110111001111111111	100011010000010	011
59 PLAY OF LBS.	32	442	110110011101110110001111111111	001010010000000	011
60 *A MANOIR	32	445	110110010101110111111111411101	111110011011010	111
61 PLAY A LION	32	446	110110010101110111101111111101	101111000000000	011
62 SHORT SENTENCES	32	447	010110110100010111001111111111	100010000010000	010
63 SCENERY & G.W.	32	453	101111110100000101001111400101	111010000011010	011
64 BYRON A PLAY	33	455	100111110101100101111111411101	101111000001010	011
65 *IDENTITY A PLAY	35	486	110101110111110111001011401101	011111010001010	110
66 *LISTEN TO ME	36	493	110101101101111111111001411101	111111100001110	111
67 NOT & NOW	36	494	100101100101100111111010301100	101101100010010	011
68 DANIEL WEBSTER	37	508	110111110101101111111111401101	111110000011010	011
69 *DOCTOR FAUSTUS	38	515	110110100111111111111000211101	111101000000010	110
70 LUCRETIA BORGIA	38	517	100101100110001110100130110	111111100000010	011
71 LESSON 16	41	537	100100100110001111110003011	111101000001010	011
72 *IN A GARDEN	43	543	110000100111011011110003111	111101000000110	111
73 *THREE SISTERS	43	544	110000100111110111110003111	111101100010010	111
74 *LOOK & LONG	43	545	110000100111011011110012111	111101100001010	111
75 *YES IS FOR A	44-46	553	110011100111110111110002111	111101110100110	110
76 *MOTHER OF US	45-46	565	110111111111111111110012111	111111010000010	110
77 JOHN BREON	46	569	101111100110000111110002111	111101000000010	010
			1 2 3	1	
			12345678901234567890123 4567890	123456789012345	123

* = PRODUCED
1 = TRAIT PRESENT
0 = TRAIT NOT PRESENT

TRAIT 25 REFLECTS FIVE DEGREES FROM NON-LOGICAL (0)
TO LOGICAL (4) EXPRESSION

Appendix C

Chronological List of Productions

Productions of Plays

Key for Production Entries

Date	Entries are made according to the date of production opening. The number of performances, if known, follows the date and is designated "p".
Title	Abbreviated title of production + = partial works
Auspices	Production City Name of Theatre Performing Company Type of Production (if not Play) Producer Director Choreographer Composer Conductor Designers

Key for Play Titles

AM	Am I to Go or I'll Say So
ANAL	An Exercise in Analysis. A Play
CC	Capital Capitals (For 4 Male Voices & Piano; Score by Virgil Thomson)
CO	Counting her Dresses. A Play
CR	A Curtain Raiser
CWA	Captain Walter Arnold (Opera adapted by Stephen Hartke)
DF	Doctor Faustus Lights the Lights
DW	Daniel Webster. Eighteen in America. A Play
EV	Every Afternoon. A Dialogue
FCE	For The Country Entirely. A Play In Letters.

FR	The Gertrude Stein First Reader and Three Plays.
	(Lesson 16, In a Garden, Look and Long, Three Sisters Who are Not Sisters & other non-plays)
GA	In a Garden
HE	He Said It. Monologue
IC	In Circles (A Circular Play. A Play In Circles) (Score by Al Carmines)
ID	Identity a Poem
ILI	I Like It To Be A Play
LaH	Lend a Hand or Four Religions
L&L	Look And Long
LION	A Play a Lion. For Max Jacob
LIST	A List
LOUIS	Louis XI and Madame Giraud
LTM	Listen To Me
LV	Ladies' Voices
MAN	A Manoir. An Historical Play In Which They Are Approached More Often
MBT	A Lyrical Opera Made By Two
MO	The Mother of Us All (Score by Virgil Thomson, Scenario by Maurice Grosser)
NOT	A Play Called Not and Now
OLD	Old and Old
PH	Photograph. A Play In Five Acts.
PI-III	Play I(-III)
WED	They Must. Be Wedded. To Their Wife. A Play
WB	A Wedding Bouquet (They Must. Be Wedded. To Their Wife. A Play, ballet version.)
	(Score by Gerald Berners, Ballet Choreography by Frederick Ashton)
WH	What Happened
YES	Yes is for a Very Young Man
3S	Three Sisters Who Are Not Sisters
4S	Four Saints in Three Acts (Score by Virgil Thomson, Scenario by Maurice Grosser)

Date	*Title*	*Auspices*

1934

Feb. 8, 6p	4S	Hartford, CT.
		Wadsworth Athenaeum
		Opera
		Friends and Enemies of Modern Music and A. Everett Austin, Jr., producers
		John Houseman, director
		Virgil Thomson, musical director
		Frederick Ashton, choreographer
		Alexander Smallens, conductor
		Florine Stettheimer, set and costume designer
		Kate Lawson, set and costume construction
		Abe Feder, lighting designer

Date	*Title*	*Auspices*
Feb. 20, 32p	4S	New York City 44th Street Theatre Harry Moses, producer (see above)
16p	4S	Empire Theatre (transferrred, see above) Virgil Thomson, conductor
Nov. 7, 4p	4S	Chicago, IL. Sullivan Opera House Auditorium Theatre (see above)
Jul. 15, 4p	4S	New York City Ramapo Apts., Ft. Washington Ave. Monologue version with music Created and performed by Julian Sawyer

1936

Jul. 9, 1p	ID	Detroit, MI. Institute of Arts First American Puppetry Festival Puppet play Don Vestal and Associates, Chicago

1937

Apr. 27	WB	London, England Sadler's Wells Ballet Ballet Ninette Valois, director Constant Lambert, conductor Gerald Berners, designer

1941

Unknown	WB	England New Theatre (see April 27, 1937)

1943

Aug. 29	FR	Paris, France Pierre Balmain, director

1946

Mar. 13	YES	Pasadena, CA.

Date	*Title*	*Auspices*
		Pasadena Playhouse
		Gilmor Brown, producer
		Tom Browne Henry, director
		Donald Finlayson, set designer

1947

Fall	YES	ANTA Experimental Theatre

Apr. 15, 2p	WH	The Randall School

May 7	MO	New York City
		Brander Matthews Hall
		Columbia University
		Opera
		Columbia Theatre Associates and Department of Music,
		producers
		John Taras, choreographer
		Otto Luening, conductor
		Paul du Pont, set and costume designer

1948

May 16, 4p	YES	London, England
		48 Theatre
		Anglo-French Art Centre
		David Tutaev, producer

Jul. 26, 11p	YES	Princeton, NJ.
		Murray Theatre
		Princeton University
		University Players
		John Capsis, director

Summer	MO	Denver, CO.
		University of Denver
		Opera
		Roy White, director

Sep. 7	GA	Jan Hus House

Oct. 29	YES	Princeton, NJ.
		Theatre Intime
		Princeton University
		Dawin Curtis, producer
		(see Jul. 26, 1948)

1949

Feb. 17	WB	London, England

Date	*Title*	*Auspices*
		Covent Garden (see Apr. 27, 1937)
Feb. 18	MO	Cleveland, OH. Severance Hall Case Western Reserve University Opera Nadine Miles, director Karl Grossman, conductor Henry Kurth, designer
Oct. 25	WB	New York City Metropolitan Opera House Sadler's Wells Ballet (see Apr. 27, 1937)
Mar. 21, 5p	YES	Washington, D.C. Clendenen Hall American University Productions, Inc., producers Patricia Coates, director
Jun. 6	YES	New York City Cherry Lane Theatre Off-Broadway, Inc., producers Lamont Johnson, director Edwin Wittstein, set and lighting designer Marlin Maclintock, costume designer (see Mar. 13, 1946)
Dec. 29	GA	New York City Finch Jr. College After Dinner Opera Company Opera Richard Flusser, director

1950

Mar. 18, 8p	WH	Hartford, CT. Randall Playhouse Lindley Williams Hubbell, director
Apr.	YES	Moylan, PA. Hedgerow Theatre
Apr. 26	YES	Cambridge, MA. Brattle Hall Brattle Theatre Company

Date	Title	Auspices
Apr. 27, 5p	YES	Baltimore, MD. Dennis Dance Theatre Actor's Colony
May	WB	London, England Sadler's Wells Company (see Apr. 27, 1937)
Jun. 26	GA	New York City After Dinner Opera Company Opera Meyer Kupferman, composer
Sep. 21	WB	New York City Metropolitan Opera House Sadler's Wells Company (see Apr. 27, 1937)

1951

May	WB	London, England Covent Garden (see Apr. 27, 1937)
Jul. 20	YES	San Francisco, CA. San Francisco Interplayers Roy Franklyn, director
Unknown	YES	San Francisco, CA. Playhouse Repertory Company San Francisco Interplayers (see above)
Aug. 15	LV	New York City 789 West End Ave. The Living Theatre
Nov. 8, 2p	DF	Glenside, PA. The Play Shop in the Little Theatre Beaver College, Grey Towers campus Judith Elder, director
Dec. 2	DF	New York City Cherry Lane Theatre The Living Theatre Judith Malina, director Remy Charlip, choreographer Music by Richard Banks Julian Beck, designer

Date	Title	Auspices

1952

Feb. 21, 3p	DF	(see Nov. 8, 1951)
Feb. 25	DF	(see Nov. 8, 1951) Presented by Drama Committee of the Philadelphia Art Alliance
Mar. 2	LV	New York City Cherry Lane Theatre The Living Theatre
Mar. 4, 5p	YES	Evanston, IL. Northwestern University Edward Crowley, director
Apr. 16, 15p	4S	New York City Broadway Theatre Opera ANTA & Ethel Lindner, producers Virgil Thomson, artistic and musical director and conductor Book direction by Maurice Grosser William Dollar, choreographer William Morrison, designer Based on the original designs by Florine Stettheimer
May 30	4S	Paris, France Théâtre des Champs-Elysees Exposition: L'Art du Vingtieme Siecle (see above)
Jul. 16	YES	Evanston, IL. Northwestern University (see Mar. 4, 1952)

1953

Feb. 13, 5p	YES	Detroit, MI. Wayne State University Leonard Leone, director
Dec. 11	DF	Bronxville, NY. Ruisinger Auditorium Sarah Lawrence College Music by Meyer Kupferman

1954

Feb. 25	LV	Amherst, MA.

Date	Title	Auspices
	WH MO	Old Chapel University of Massachusetts
Jul. 27	YES	Provincetown, MA. Provincetown Playhouse

1955

May 6, 63p	GA 3S	New York City Tempo Playhouse Tempo Theatre Production Strowan Robertson, director Lester Hackett, designer

1956

Mar. 3	MO	Cambridge, MA. Sanders Theatre Harvard University Opera Victor Yellin, conductor
Apr. 5, 6p	YES	Berkeley, CA. Wheeler Auditorium University of California Theatre, producers Theodore L. Kazanoff, director
Apr. 16, 2p	MO	New York City Phoenix Theatre Opera Lincoln Kirstein, T. E. Hambleton and Norris Houghton, producers Bill Butler, director Virgil Thomson, conductor
Aug. 6	LV GA	Newton, CT. Little Theatre The Playshop Addison Metcalf, producer

1957

Mar. 1	YES	Plattsburgh, NY. Hawking Hall SUNY Teacher's College Footlight Organization, producers Harvey Whetstone, director

Date	Title	Auspices
Apr. 1	GA	New York City Phoenix Theatre Opera Lawrence Kornfeld, director Meyer Kupferman, composer
Apr. 8	DF	New York City Rooftop Theatre Dance Adaptation Paul Sanasardo, designer & director Music by Charles Wuorinen
Jun. 8	DF	Stockbridge, MA. Stockbridge School William McCue, director

1958

Jan. 18	DF	New York City Chapter Hall of Carnegie Hall Staged Reading with Music Adapted by Marvin Goldstein, Bernice Loren, & Bennes Mardenn Marvin Goldstein, director Music by Charles Wuorinen Laurence Siegel, conductor

1959

Mar.	WH LaH YES+ CR	Cedar Rapids, IA. Coe College Bruce Kellner, director
Dec. 16	GA	New Haven, CT. Yale School of Music Opera Ronald Byrnside, conductor

1960

May	YES	Purdue, IN. Purdue University Purdue Playshop

1962

Mar.	YES	Omaha, NE.

Date	Title	Auspices
		Red Lion Inn
		Repertory Players
Apr. 11	YES	Ames, IA.
		Shuttuck Theatre
		Iowa State University
		M. B. Drexler, director
Summer	4S	Hollywood, CA.
		Hollywood High School
		Opera

1963

Mar. 4, 1p	YES	New York City
		Players Theatre
		Stuart Duncan & Isabel M. Halliburton, producers
		Philip Minor, director
		David Moon, set and lighting designer
Sep. 26, 12p	WH	New York City
		Judson Memorial Church
		Judson Poets' Theatre
		Dance Drama
		Lawrence Kornfeld, director
		Al Carmines, composer
		Larry Siegel, set designer

1964

Unknown	PH	New York City
		American Theatre for Poets
Nov. 24	WB	London, England
		Covent Garden
		Robert Helpman, narrator
		(see Apr. 27, 1937)

1965

May	MO	Los Angeles, CA.
		Schoenberg Hall
		University of California
		Opera
		Jan Popper, conductor
		David Hilberman, designer
Jun. 5, 12p	3S	New York City

Date	*Title*	*Auspices*
		Judson Memorial Church
		Judson Poets' Theatre
		Musical
		Michael Smith, director
		Music by John Herbert McDowell
Jun. 25	LV	Paris, France
	YES +	Centre Culturel Americain
	FR	(Homage a Gertrude Stein)
		Nancy Cole and Guy Jacquet, producers
		Christian Bagot, director
		Pablo Picasso, designer
Dec.	PI-III	New York City
		Judson Memorial Church
		Judson Poets' Theatre
		Lawrence Kornfeld, director
	YES	Boston, MA.
		Theatre Company of Boston
		David Wheeler, director

1966

Mar.-Apr.	YES	Chicago, IL.
		Wright College

1967

Jan. 27	MO	Minneapolis, MN.
		Guthrie Theatre
		City Center Opera
		Opera
		Staged by H. Wesley Balk
		Thomas Nee, conductor
		Robert Indiana, designer
May 4, 2p	CR	Oneonta, NY.
	LaH	Hartwick Chapel
	ANAL +	Hartwick College Concert Choir & Cardboard Alley
	WH	Players
	LV	Illustrated Lecture
	4S	Conceived and directed by Bruce Kellner
Mar. 30, 3p	YES	Chicago, IL.
		Wright College
		Robert Cowan, director

Date	Title	Auspices
Aug. 1	MO	Vienna, VA. Wolf Trap Farm (see Jan. 27, 1967) (tour)
Aug. 7	MO	Ambler, PA. Temple University Music Festival (see Jan. 27, 1967) (tour)
Oct. 14, 10p	IC	New York City Judson Memorial Church Judson Poets' Theatre Musical Lawrence Kornfeld, director Al Carmines, composer Roland Turner, set designer Jay Poswolsky, lighting designer
Nov. 5, 222p	IC	New York City Cherry Lane Theatre Judson Poets' Theatre Franklin de Boer, producer Roland Turner and Johnnie Jones, set designers Eric Gutner, lighting designer (see Oct. 14, 1967)

1968

Date	Title	Auspices
Apr. 26, 36p	PH	Baltimore, MD. Center Stage Music by Richard Skapdik
Jun. 25, 56p	IC	New York City Gramercy Arts Theatre Judson Poets' Theatre Dina & Alexander E. Racolin and Samuel J. Friedman, producers Barry Arnold, lighting designer (see Nov. 5, 1967)
Oct. 20	ILI	New Haven, CT. Dining Hall Yale University Ezra Stiles Dramat

1969

Date	Title	Auspices
Unknown	FR	Long Island, NY. Artists Theatre Festival

Date	Title	Auspices
		Southampton College Herbert Machiz, artistic director John Bernard Myers, artistic consultant
Apr. 25, 3p	CWA	New Haven, CT. Dining Hall Yale University Ezra Stiles Dramat
Dec. 15, 40p	FR	New York City Astor Place Theatre Musical Revue Conceived by Herbert Machiz John Bernard Myers and Bob Cato, producers Herbert Machiz, director Musical adaptation by Ann Sternberg Kendall Shaw, set designer Patrika Brown, lighting designer (see FR, 1969)

1970

Date	Title	Auspices
Aug. 15, 2p	4S	San Francisco, CA. Paul Masson Vineyards Merola Opera Company Opera Dennis Rosa, director Charles Wilson, conductor
Nov.	4S	Washington, D.C. Opera Society Opera
Dec. 28, 4p	FR	New York City Auditorium Museum of Modern Art John Bernard Myers and the Jr. Council, producers (see Dec. 15, 1969)

1971

Date	Title	Auspices
Fall	4S +	Cleveland, OH. Eldred Theatre Case Western Reserve University Dance Theatre of Kathryn Karipedes and Henry Kurth Dance Henry Kurth, designer

Date	*Title*	*Auspices*
Jul. 24	3S	Philadelphia, PA.
		Temple University
		Student Opera Workshop
		Opera
		Henry Butler, director
		Ned Rorem, composer
Jul. 27	3S	Lake Placid, NY.
		Signal Hill Playhouse
		After Dinner Opera Company
		Opera
		Richard Flusser, director
		Ned Rorem, composer
Jul. 31	GA	Westport, CT.
	3S	White Barn Theatre
	L&L	After Dinner Opera Company
	PH	Opera
	LV	Richard Flusser, director
		Cynthia Auerback, music director
		Composers: Meyer Kupferman (GA), Ned Rorem (3S), Florence Wickham & Marvin Schwartz (L&L), Marvin Kalmanoff (PH), Vernon Martin (LV)
		Beth Flusser, set designer
		Elissa Larrauri, costume designer
Jul. 31, 2p	MO+	New York City
		Hunter College Auditorium
		City Center Opera of Minneapolis
		Opera (condensed version)
		Philip Brunelle, conductor
		(see Jan. 27, 1967)
Nov. 14, 3p	4S	Bridgeport, CT.
		University of Bridgeport
Nov. 25, 3p	MO	New York City
		St. Peter's Church
		Opera
		Richard Magpiong, producer
		William Vorenberg, director
		John Doepp, set designer
		Audrey Arnsdorf, costume designer
		Marjorie Brewster, conductor

1972

Jan. 15, 2p	4S	Stratford, CT.
		Shakespeare Festival Theatre

Date	*Title*	*Auspices*
		University of Bridgeport Opera Music Department, producer
May	DF	New York City Cafe La Mama Boston University La Mama Maxine Klein, director
July, 5p	MO	Lenox, MA. Munt Inn Lenox Arts Center Musical (see Nov. 26, 1972)
Oct. 4	GA 3S L&L PH LV	New York City Eisner & Lubin Auditorium Loeb Student Center of NYU (see July 31, 1971)
Nov. 26, 17p	MO	New York City Guggenheim Museum Theatre Musical Lyn Austin, Orin Lehman, Hale Matthews, and Oliver Smith, producers Virgil Thomson, artistic director Elizabeth Keen & Roland Gagnon, directors Roland Gagnon, musical director Oliver Smith, set designer Patricia Zipprodt, costume designer Richard Nelson, lighting designer (see July, 1972)

1973

Date	Title	Auspices
Feb. 22	4S	New York City Vivian Beaumont Theatre Metropolitan Opera's Forum Mini-Opera Alvin Ailey, director and choreographer Roland Gagnon, conductor Ming Cho Lee, set designer Jane Greenwood, costume designer Shirley Prendergast, lighting designer

1974

Date	Title	Auspices
Oct. 18, 12p	LTM	New York City

Date	Title	Auspices
		Judson Memorial Church
		Judson Poets' Theatre
		Musical
		Al Carmines, composer
		Lawrence Kornfeld, director
		Ed Lazansky, set designer
		Edward M. Greenberg, lighting designer

1975

Date	Title	Auspices
May 24	MO	Brooklyn, NY.
		Long Island University
		C.W. Post College Theatre Co.
		Encompass Theatre
		Musical
		Nancy Rhodes, adapter & director
Dec. 10, 4p	MO	New York City
		Colden Theatre
		Queens College
		Opera
		John Olon-Scrymgeour, director
		Hugo Weisgall, conductor
		Jane Thurn, set designer
		Rhonda Seidman, costume designer

1976

Date	Title	Auspices
Mar. 20	MO	New York City
		Greenwich Village Theatre
		Encompass Theatre
		Musical
		Nancy Rhodes, director
		William Boswell, musical director
		Simplified score by Virgil Thomson
		Christina Weppner, set designer
		T. Winberry, lighting designer
		Mim Maxmen, costume designer
		(see May 24, 1975)
	MO	Good Shepherd Faith Church
		(transferred)
Aug. 7	MO	Santa Fe, NM.
		Santa Fe Opera
		Opera
		Peter Wood, director
		Raymond Leppard, conductor

Date	Title	Auspices

Robert Indiana, designer
Jo Schreiber, lighting designer

1977

Jan. 21, 4p   PH

New Haven, CT.
Educational Center for the Arts
Asante Scott, producer
James Lapine, director
Maureen Connor, costume designer
Andrew Kufta, lighting designer

Feb. 24, 6p   MO

Amherst, MA.
Rand Theatre
Opera
University of Massachusetts
Vincent Brann, director

Apr. 22, 15p   MAN

New York City
Judson Memorial Church
Judson Poets' Theatre
Musical
Lawrence Kornfeld, director
Al Carmines, composer
Edward Lazansky, set designer
Theo Barnes, costume designer
Gary Weathersbee, lighting designer

Apr. 30   MO

Sacramento, CA.
Hiram Johnson Auditorium
Largely Volunteer Camellia Symphony
River City Choral Society
Ted Puffer, director
Daniel Kingman, conductor

Sep. 15, 18p   PH

New York City
Open Space Theatre
Lynn Michaels, artistic director
Performance Group
James Lapine, director
Music by Dwight Andrews
Maureen Connor, designer
Paul Gallo, lighting designer
Narration by Walt Jones
(see Jan. 21, 1977)

Nov. 10, 2p   4S

New York City
Beacon Theatre

Date	Title	Auspices
Dec. 15, 3p	CR LV LTM+ FCE WH	Urbana, IL. Armory Free Theatre University of Illinois Betsy Ryan, director

1978

May 23–24	MO	Baltimore, MD. Opera Virgil Thomson, conductor
Jun. 15	DF	New York City St. Peter's Church Craig Lowy, director
Fall	WB	New York City Joffrey Ballet Ballet

1979

Mar. 8	MBT	Pittsburgh, PA. Theatre Express William Turner, artistic director
May 1, 6p	MBT	New Haven, CT. Long Wharf Theatre, Stage II Theatre Express (see Mar. 8)
Oct. 26– Nov. 19	DF	New York City Judson Memorial Church Judson Poets' Theatre Musical Lawrence Kornfeld, director Al Carmines, composer
Nov.	IC	New York City Independent Theatre of Rotterdam Amy Gale and Gerritt Timmers, creators Amy Gale, choreographer

1980

Feb. 5, 8p	LTM	Purchase, NY. SUNY-Purchase Performing Arts Center Lawrence Kornfeld, director Richard Cameron, composer

Date	Title	Auspices
May 5, 1p	LION + AM + NOT + HE + LOUIS + LIST + FCE + WED + OLD + YES + WH + DW + ID + MO + PI-III + CO + EV + LV +	Iowa City, IA. MacLean Theatre University of Iowa Betsy Ryan, director Darrah Cloud, designer

1981

April	MO	New York City Saint Clement's Church Music Theatre Group Lenox Arts Center Opera Stanley Silverman, director Richard Cordova, musical director Power Boothe, set designer Lawrence Casey, costume designer

1982

Sept. 22, 3p	DF	Berlin Freie Volksbuhne Marie-Claire Pasquier, translator Ontological-Hysteric Theatre, Berliner Festpiele, Theatre de Gennevilliers, and Festival D'Automne à Paris, producers Richard Foreman, director
Oct. 5–24	DF	Paris Theatre de Gennevilliers (see above)

Concerts of Plays

1927

June	CC	Paris, France

Date	*Title*	*Auspices*
		Duchess de Clermont-Tonnerre, Costume Ball Virgil Thomson, conductor

1928

May 30	CC	Paris, France Salle d'Orgue, Vieux Conservatoire Virgil Thomson, conductor

1929

Feb. 24	CC	New York City Copland-Sessions Concert Series Virgil Thomson, conducting the Ionian Quartet
Jun. 17	CC	Cambridge, MA. Harvard Glee Club Virgil Thomson, conductor
Oct. 2	CC	Barre Opera House Barre Women's Club, producers Virgil Thomson, conducting the Ionian Quartet

1931

Jan. 10	SO	Paris, France Marthe-Marthine, soloist Virgil Thomson, conductor
Dec. 16	CC	London, England Aeolian Hall Tudor Singers British Contemporary Music Society and Aaron Copland, producers Virgil Thomson, conductor

1934

Nov. 16	4S	New York City Ritz Tower Musicale Luncheon Mme. Eva Gauthier, producer Virgil Thomson, conductor (see Feb. 20, 1934, Prods. of Plays)

1941

May 27	4S	New York City

Date	*Title*	*Auspices*
		Museum of Modern Art Virgil Thomson, conductor
	4S	Town Hall Louise Crane, producer Alexander Smallens, conductor

1942

Unknown	4S	Station WOR Alfred Wallenstein, conductor

1947

Unknown	4S	CBS: Philharmonic Hour Original Cast trained by Leonard de Paur Virgil Thomson, conductor
May	MO	WNYC Broadcast

1953

Jul. 26	4S+	New York City Lewisohn Stadium 40-minute Concert Virgil Thomson, conductor
Aug. 20	4S+	Yokohama, Japan Octagon Theatre Yokohama Symphony Orchestra Prologue and Act One Kojiro Kobune, director

1954

Oct. 1	DF	San Francisco, CA. Little Theatre on Hyde Street Playhouse Repertory Concert Reading Sydney Walker, director Space sculpture by Tom Hall

1960

Apr. 29	DF+	New York City Carnegie Recital Hall 2 arias: "I Am A Dog," "I Am The Only She" Meyer Kupferman, composer

Date	Title	Auspices

1964

Mar. 31	MO	New York City
		Carnegie Hall
		American Opera Society, producers

1972

Mar. 5	4S	St. Paul, MN.
		O'Shaughnessy Auditorium
		College of St. Catherine
		Center Opera Co. of Minneapolis with The St. Paul Chamber Orchestra
		Philip Brunelle, conductor

1981

Nov. 14	4S	New York City
		Carnegie Hall
		Orchestra of Our Times
		Joel Thome, conductor

Productions of Non-Dramatic Works

Key for Non-Dramatic Work Titles

B&W	Brewsie and Willie (adapted by Ellen Violett and Lisabeth Blake from Stein's Novel)
COM	Completed Portrait of Picasso
EV	Everything's the Same and Everything's Different, (Selections from Woolf, Beckett, and Stein)
GERT	Gertrude (Collage of GS Memorabilia written by Wilford Leach)
GS	Gertrude Stein's Gertrude Stein (created by Nancy Cole)
GSGS	GS/GS/GS (A One Character Play by Marty Martin)
HM	Storyette: HM
LCA	Lucy Church Amiably (adapted by Scott Fields)
MAT	Matisse
MOA	The Making Of Americans (adapted by Leon Katz from Stein's Novel and Notebooks)
PF	Paris, France
PLAY	Play
REY	Mrs. Reynolds (adapted by Philip Hansom)
RMOA	The (Re)Making of Americans (adapted by Linda Mussman from Stein's Novel)
SAT	Eric Satie

SUSIE	Susie Asado	
THREE	Three, Two, One (Not Much Limping, Monuments, May and December: Selections from Stein, Diana de Prima, and James Waring)	
VERY	A Very Valentine (from A Valentine to Sherwood Anderson)	
19	Lesson 19	
20	Lesson 20	
3H	If You Had Three Husbands	
SO	Songs of Gertrude Stein (score by Virgil Thomson)	

Date	*Title*	*Auspices*
1952		
Jul. 12, 2p	B&W	Westport, CT. White Barn Theatre Touring Players
1953		
Apr. 18	B&W	New York City Theatre de Lys ANTA and Touring Players, producers Performed by Touring Players (see Jul. 12, 1952)
1954		
Nov. 17	B&W	CBS Television "Omnibus" Robert Saudek, producer Seymour Robbie, director Staged by John Stix
1956		
May 14	B&W	New York City Neighborhood Playhouse School of Theatre Sanford Meisner, director
Aug. 6	PF 19 MOA 20	Newtown, CT. Little Theatre The Playshop Addison Metcalf, producer
1967		
May 4	SUSIE COM+	(see May 4, 1967, Prods. of Plays)

Date	Title	Auspices
1969		
Jan. 26	THREE	New York City Mannhardt Theatre Foundations
	GS	France & England Tour Performed by Nancy Cole
Apr. 21	REY	New York City New York Public Library
1970		
Nov.	GERT	New York City La Mama E.T.C. James Cuomo, musical director Music by Ben Johnston Masks and Props by Richard Laws William Weldenbacher and Peter Murketty, set designers Nancy Reeder, costume designer Beverly Emmons, lighting designer
1971		
Fall	COM MAT	Cleveland, OH. Dance (see 1971, Prods. of Plays)
1972		
Jan. 9	GERT	(see Nov. 12, 1970)
Jun. 4	LCA	New York City Washington Square Church
Nov. 10	MOA	New York City Judson Memorial Church Judson Poets' Theatre Musical Lawrence Kornfeld, director Leon Katz, librettist Al Carmines, composer Ed Lazansky, scene designer Roger Morgan, lighting designer Reve Richards, costume designer

Date	*Title*	*Auspices*
1975		
April	EV	New York City Time and Space, Ltd. Linda Mussman, director
1977		
Dec. 15, 3p	PLAY SAT VERY SUSIE HM	Urbana, IL. Armory Free Theatre Betsy Ryan, director
1979		
Feb.	3H	New York City Soho Repertory
Mar. 1	RMOA	New York City Time and Space, Ltd. Linda Mussman, adapter & director
Spring	GSGS	New York City (Tour) Herbert Barrett Management Pat Carroll, performer Milton Moss, director

Appendix D

Production Reviews

Brewsie And Willie

Clurman, Harold. "Theatre." *The Nation,* April 25, 1953, pp. 353–354.
Metcalf, Addison, Carl Van Vechten, Jessie Royce Landis, and Norris Houghton. "Drama Mailbag." *The New York Times,* April 12, 1953, p. 3.

Doctor Faustus Lights The Lights

Clement, Catherine. "Faust ou la fête electrique." *Le Matin,* October 6, 1982, p. 29.
Gauville, Herve. "Foreman et la Mère Stein." *Liberation,* October 9 and 10, 1982.
"Gertrude Stein Writes A 'Faust' And Makes It Very Different." *The New York Herald Tribune,* 1938. New Haven: Yale University, Stein Newspaper Clipping Collection.
J.P.S. "From the High Board." *The New York Times,* December 3, 1951, p. 23.
Sarpetta, Guy. "Richard Foreman: gertrude stein et les toboggans." *Art Presse,* October 1982, pp. 16–17.
Sucher, C. Bernd. "Und der Hund sagt danke schon." *Suddeutsche Zeitung,* September 25 and 26, 1982.
The New York Post, December 3, 1951. New Haven: Yale University, Stein Newspaper Clipping Collection.
The New York Times, September 8, 1951. New Haven: Yale University, Stein Newspaper Clipping Collection.
Russell, Bill. "Looking for America on Way To Hell." *Boston After Dark,* May 23, 1972, p. 7.
Scheff, Aimee. "Theatre Off-Broadway." *Theatre Arts,* February, 1952, p. 96.
V. R. "Gertrude That Is Stein." *The New York Post,* December 3, 1951. New York: New York Public Library at Lincoln Center, Theatre Review Collection.

Four Saints In Three Acts

Alsop, Joseph W., Jr. " Four Saints In Three Acts." *The New York Herald Tribune,* February 8, 1934, p. 18.
The American Magazine of Art, Volume 27, January 1934. New Haven: Yale University, Stein Newspaper Clipping Collection.
Anderson, John. " 'Four Saints In Three Acts'." *The New York Evening Journal,* February 21, 1934, p. 14.

Anderson, John. " 'Four Saints In Three Acts'." *The New York Journal American,* February 21, 1934. New Haven: Yale University, Stein Newspaper Clipping Collection.

Atkinson, Brooks. " 'Four Saints In Three Acts' Restaged by A.N.T.A. at the Broadway Theatre." *The New York Times,* April 17, 1952, p. 35.

Beebe, Lucius. "Smart Art and Miss Stein Overwhelm Hartford." *The New York Herald Tribune,* February 11, 1934, Section V, p. 2.

Bloomfield, Arthur. " 'Four Saints' Fine Nonsense." *The San Francisco Examiner,* August 17, 1970, p. 26.

Boston Transcript, January 30, 1934. New Haven: Yale University, Stein Newspaper Clipping Collection.

Brown, John Mason. "The Play." *New York Evening Post,* February 21, 1934. New Haven: Yale University, Stein Newspaper Clipping Collection.

The Catholic World, June 1952, p. 228.

Chicago, Illinois Music Education Journal, December 1934. New Haven: Yale University, Stein Newspaper Clipping Collection.

Coleman, Robert. " 'Four Saints In Three Acts' is for Limited Audience." *New York Daily Mirror,* April 17, 1952. In *New York Theatre Critics' Reviews,* 1952, p. 313.

The Commonweal, February 23, 1934, p. 453.

Downes, Olin. "The Stein-Thomson Concoction." *The New York Times,* February 25, 1934, p. 6.

———. "Broadway Greets New Kind of Opera." *The New York Times,* February 21, 1934, p. 22.

———. " 'Four Saints' Sung in the Town Hall." *The New York Times,* May 28, 1941, p. 32.

———. "Thomson's Opera in Paris Premiere." *The New York Times,* May 31, 1952, p. 13.

"The Drama." *The Catholic World,* April 1934, pp. 87–88.

"Dressmakers for Art." *The Saturday Review of Literature,* March 24, 1934, p. 572.

Ericson, Raymond. "Four Saints to Take New Trip." *The New York Times,* April 26, 1970, p. 19.

Field, Mrs. Henry. " 'the social whirl'....." *Chicago Herald and Examiner,* November 8 1934, p. 11.

Field, Mrs. Henry. " 'the social whirl'....." *Chicago Herald and Examiner,* November 9, 1934, p. 17.

Fleming, Shirley, et al. "Debuts and Reappearances." *High Fidelity/ musical america,* March 1978, MA 23–24.

"Four Innovations in 3 Acts." *The Stage,* April 1934, p. 22.

"Four Saints." *The New York Times,* November 6, 1977, p. 1.

" 'Four Saints' Acts is Acts in 30 Acts." *The New York Times,* February 8, 1934, p. 22.

" 'Four Saints' Cheered at Avery Hall." *Hartford Daily Courant,* February 8, 1934, pp. 1, 4.

"Four Saints In Three Acts." *Variety,* February 27, 1934. New Haven: Yale University, Stein Newspaper Clipping Collection.

"Four Saints In Three Acts One Of Many." *The New York Sun,* November 17, 1934. New Haven: Yale University, Stein Newspaper Clipping Collection.

" '4 Saints' and the 'ABC'." *The Wall Street Journal,* March 13, 1934, p. 5.

Fowler, Thomas L. "Drama Mailbag." *The New York Times,* May 4, 1952, Section 2, p. 3.

Garland, Robert. " 'Four Saints In Three Acts' Takes a Bow on Broadway." *New York World-Telegram,* February 21, 1934, p. 20.

Gent, George. "Mini-Operas Ready To Take Met Role." *The New York Times,* February 15, 1973, p. 50.

"Gertrude Stein Comes to Broadway." *The Literary Digest,* March 10, 1934, p. 22.

"Gertrude Stein Foresees Her Opera Opening New Era." *New York Herald* (Paris), February 16, 1934. New Haven: Yale University, Stein Newspaper Clipping Collection.

"Gertrude Stein Turns Smiles to Tributes in Loop City." *South Bend Indiana News-Times,* November 11, 1934. New Haven: Yale University, Stein Newspaper Clipping Collection.

Gilman, Lawrence. "Music." *New York Music Tribune,* February 21, 1934. New Haven: Yale University, Stein Newspaper Clipping Collection.

Grilli, Marcel. "Speaking of Music." *Nippon Times,* August 20, 1953. New Haven: Yale University, Stein Newspaper Clipping Collection.

Haggin, B. H. "Music." *The Nation,* May 3, 1952, pp. 437–438.

Hartford Daily Times, January 6, 1934. New Haven: Yale University, Stein Newspaper Clipping Collection.

Harvey, John H. "Center Opera's 'Four Saints In Three Acts'." *Hi Fidelity/musical america,* June 1972, MA 20.

Hawkes, William. " 'Four Saints In Three Acts Takes Curtain Call." *The New York World Telegram and The Sun,* April 17, 1952. In *New York Theatre Critics' Reviews,* 1952, p. 315.

Henderson, W. J. "American Opera Keeps Struggling." *The American Mercury,* May 1934, pp. 104–105.

Henderson, W. J. " 'Four Saints In Three Acts'." *The New York Sun,* February 21, 1934, p. 11.

Henderson, W. J. "Music and Musicians." *The New York Sun,* February 24, 1934. New Haven: Yale University, Stein Newspaper Clipping Collection.

Hughes, Allen. "Opera: Modern Touch." *The New York Times,* January 16, 1972, p. 65.

Kansas City Star, November 18, 1934. New Haven: Yale University, Stein Newspaper Clipping Collection.

Kastendieck, Miles. "A Unique Experience; A Handsome Show." *The New York Journal American,* April 17, 1952. In *New York Theatre Critics' Reviews,* 1952, p. 313.

Kerr, Harrison. "Three New Operas." *The American Magazine of Art,* April 1934, pp. 211–212.

Kerr, Walter. " 'Four Saints In Three Acts'." *The New York Herald Tribune,* April 17, 1952, p. 22.

Kerr, Walter. "Four Saints In Three Acts." *The Commonweal,* May 9, 1952, p. 116.

Kolodin, Irving. "Music To My Ears." *Saturday Review,* May 3, 1952, p. 33.

Krutch, Joseph Wood. "A Prepare for Saints." *The Nation,* April 4, 1934.

"La Stein's Little Joke-or-Pigeons on the Grass-Alas-" *Chicago, Illinois Music News,* November 15, 1934. New Haven: Yale University, Stein Newspaper Clipping Collection.

Lieberson, Goddard. "Strange Stein Song Startles Sophisticates." *Rochester, New York Sunday American,* February 18, 1934. New Haven: Yale University, Stein Newspaper Clipping Collection.

Liebling, Leonard. *New York American,* February 21, 1934, p. 14.

The Literary Digest, February 3, 1934. New Haven: Yale University, Stein Newspaper Clipping Collection.

Martin, John. "The Dance: 'Four Saints.' " *The New York Times,* 1934. New Haven: Yale University, Stein Newspaper Clipping Collection.

Moffett, India. "Audience Eyes a Simple Gown at Stein Opera." *Chicago Tribune,* November 8, 1934, p. 19.

Murray, Marian. " 'Four Saints' Cheered at World Premiere." *Hartford Daily Times,* February 9, 1934, p. 1.

Musical America, August 1952, p. 28.

Nathan, George Jean. "musicalized fog." *Theatre Arts,* June 1952, p. 19.

Nathan, George Jean. "The Theatre." *Vanity Fair,* May 1934, p. 49.

Newsweek, February 17, 1934, p. 38.

The New York Times, International Edition, April 6, 1952, p. 14.

The New Yorker, February 17, 1934. New Haven: Yale University, Stein Newspaper Clipping Collection.

"Not Four-Thirty Six." *Newsweek,* April 18, 1952, p. 52.

"Old Pigeons." *Time,* April 28, 1952, p. 42.

Parker, T. H. "Stein Opera is Elegant Performance." *Hartford Daily Courant,* February 9, 1934, pp. 1, 16.

"Paris." *Musical America,* July 1952, pp. 5, 20, 25.

Perkins, Francis D. " 'Four Saints' is Presented in Oratorio Form." *The New York Herald Tribune,* May 28, 1941, p. 18.

"Purpose in Paris." *Newsweek,* May 12, 1952, p. 84.

Rich, Alan. "Four Saints-Humanity Is the Key Word." *High Fidelity Magazine,* February 1965, pp. 70–71.

Rosenfeld, Paul. "Prepare for Saints." *The New Republic,* February 21, 1934, p. 48.

"Saints in Cellophane." *Time,* February 19, 1934, p. 35.

Sanborn, Pitts. "Hartford Hears Premiere of Stein-Thomson Opera." *New York World-Telegram,* February 9, 1934.

Saunders, Mrs. Faxon. "Chicago: Gertrude Stein is Fine; Opera, Fun; Brief Run." *The Kansas City Star,* November 18, 1934, p. 20.

Schonberg, Harold C. "Opera: Minimet's Playful 'Four Saints'." *The New York Times,* February 24, 1973, p. 17.

Seldes, Gilbert. "Delight in the Theatre." *Modern Music,* March–April 1934, pp. 138–141.

Skinner, Richard Dana. "The Play." *The Commonweal,* March 9, 1934, p. 525.

Sloper, L. A. "Opera Stein Picasso Museum." *The Christian Science Monitor,* February 10, 1934, p. 6.

Smith, Cecil. "Thomson's Four Saints Live Again on Broadway." *Musical America,* May 1952, p. 7.

Sobel, Bernard. "Four Saints or Maybe Thirty at 44th Street." *New York Daily Mirror,* February 21, 1934, p. 22.

The Stage, March 1934, p. 9.

"Stein Ballet Opens Tonight." *The New York Sun,* April 27, 1937, p. 19.

Stevens, Ashton, "Ashton Stevens." *Chicago American,* November 8, 1934, p. 16.

Stevens, George. "Syllabus of Syllables." *Saturday Review of Literature,* March 3, 1934, p. 519.

Stinson, Eugene. "Music Views." *Chicago Daily News,* November 8, 1934, p. 29.

Sylvester, Robert. " 'Four Saints In Three Acts' Again Musical, Mystical and Very Funny." *New York Daily News,* April 17, 1952. In *New York Theatre Critics' Reviews,* 1952, p. 134.

Theatre Arts, August 1942, p. 516.

Theatre Arts, August 1941, p. 599.

Tucker, Marilyn. "Pop Art for an Opera." *San Francisco Chronicle,* August 14, 1970, p. 45.

Tune In, September 9, 1945. New Haven: Yale University, Stein Newspaper Clipping Collection.

Van Vechten, Carl. "In the Drama Editor's Mail." *The New York Times,* February 18, 1934, Drama Section, p. 2.

Watt, Douglas. "Musical Events." *The New Yorker,* April 26, 1952, pp. 123–124.

Watts, Richard, Jr. " '4 Saints' Get New Praise at Public Opening." *The New York Herald Tribune,* February 9, 1934, p. 12.

———. "Revival of an Enchanting Opera." *The New York Post,* April 17, 1952. In *New York Theatre Critics' Reviews,* 1952, p. 312.

———. "Sight and Sound." *The New York Herald Tribune,* March 4, 1934, Section V., p. 4.

Young, Stark. "Might It Be Mountains?" *The New Republic,* April 11, 1934, p. 246.

———. "One Moment Alit." *The New Republic,* March 7, 1934, p. 105.

Zatkin, Nathan. " 'Four Saints' Analyzed." *New York Evening Post,* March 3, 1934, p. 11.

Zolotow, Sam. " 'Four Saints In Three Acts' Will Open Tonight." *The New York Times,* April 16, 1952, p. 30.

Gertrude

Gussow, Mel. " 'Gertrude' at LaMama Happily Fantastic." *The New York Times,* November 13, 1970, p. 29.

The Gertrude Stein First Reader

Barnes, Clive. "Theater: Stein Singers Do Wrong By Our Gertrude." *The New York Times,* December 16, 1969, p. 56.

Bunce, Alan. "And now 'Gertrude Stein's First Reader'." *The Christian Science Monitor,* December 29, 1969, p. 4.

Cooke, Richard P. *The Wall Street Journal,* December 18, 1969, p. 14.

Davis, James. " 'First Reader' Reaches for Phantom Age Group." *New York Daily News,* December 16, 1969, p. 69.

" 'First Reader' Sets Stein To Music." *Park East,* (New York) January 1, 1970, p. 8.

Gunner, Marjorie. "On and Off Broadway." *Bronx Home News,* January 2, 1970, p. 7.

Kraft, Daphne. " 'Gertrude Stein' Off Broadway." *Newark Evening News,* December 16, 1969, p. 58.

Kruger, Helen. "Gertrude Stein on Music." *Chelsea Clinton News,* January 1, 1970, p. 2.

Mishkin, Leo. " 'First Reader' Not A Children's Primer." *New York Morning Telegraph,* December 17, 1969, p. 3.

"Off Broadway Reviews: Gertrude Stein's First Reader." *Variety,* December 24, 1969, p. 48.

Oliver, Edith. "Off-Broadway." *The New Yorker,* December 27, 1969, p. 39.

Oppenheimer, George. "Gertrude Stein is Set to Music." *Newsday,* December 16, 1969. New York: New York Public Library at Lincoln Center, Theatre Review Collection.

Washburn, Martin. "Theatre: Gertrude Stein's First Reader." *The Village Voice,* December 25, 1969, p. 49.

Watts, Richard, Jr. "An Evening With Gertrude Stein." *The New York Post,* December 16, 1969, p. 68.

I Am I Because My Little Dog Knows Me

McLauchlin, Russell. "I Am I Because My Little Dog Knows Me." *The Detroit News,* July 10, 1936. New Haven: Yale University, Stein Newspaper Clipping Collection.

In Circles

Barnes, Clive. "Theatre: Gertrude Stein Words at the Judson Theatre." *The New York Times,* October 14, 1967, p. 12.

"The Best of the 1967-1968 Theatre Season." *Saturday Review,* June 1, 1968, p. 13.

Clurman, Harold. "Theatre." *The Nation,* November 27, 1967, pp. 572-573.

Feingold, Michael. "A Circular Play: Three Concentric Criticisms." *Yale Theatre,* Volume I, Spring 1968, pp. 112-113.

Kroll, Jack. "Stein Songs." *Newsweek,* November 27, 1967, p. 105.

Oliver, Edith. "Off-Broadway: Perfect Circles." *The New Yorker,* November 18, 1967, pp. 131-133.

Sullivan, Dan. "Another Delightful Look at 'In Circles,' a Drama of Obfuscation." *The New York Times,* June 28, 1968.

Wilson, Lanford. "In Circles: an appreciation." *After Dark,* May 1968, p. 13.

In A Garden

Fleming, Shirley. "When This You See..." *High Fidelity/musical america,* November 11, 1971, MA 10, 11.

Hughes, Allen. "The Opera: Reminiscences of Gertrude Stein." *The New York Times,* October 6, 1972, p. 35.

Time, June 26, 1950, pp. 76-79.

Ladies' Voices

Fleming, Shirley. "When This You See..." *High Fidelity/musical america,* November 11, 1971, MA 10, 11.

Hughes, Allen. "The Opera: Reminiscences of Gertrude Stein." *The New York Times,* October 6, 1972, p. 35.

Listen To Me

Feingold, Michael. "Triumph, the Stein Way." *The Village Voice,* October 24, 1974, p. 85.

Gussow, Mel. "Theater: Gertrude Stein, With Music." *The New York Times,* October 29, 1974, p. 31.

Labelle, Dale. " 'Listen To Me' at Judson." *The Villager,* October 2, 1974, p. 5.

Oliver, Edith. "Theatre." *The New Yorker,* November 4, 1974, p. 124.

Oltarsh, Martin. "Disappointing Carmines." *Show Business,* October 24, 1974, p. 10.

Rich, Alan. *New York,* November 11, 1974, p. 117.

Silverman, Jill. "College at Purchase Staging Stein Play." *The New York Times,* January 18, 1981, p. 8.

Look And Long

Fleming, Shirley. "When This You See..." *High Fidelity/musical america,* November 11, 1971, MA 10, 11.

Hughes, Allen. "The Opera: Reminiscences of Gertrude Stein." *The New York Times,* October 6, 1972, p. 35.

A Lyrical Opera Made By Two

Anderson, George. "Theater Express Will Take Stein Work To Connecticut Festival." *Pittsburgh Post Gazette,* March 9, 1979.

The Making Of Americans

Brukenfeld, Dick. "A bore is a bore is a..." *The Village Voice,* November 23, 1972, p. 66.

Feingold, Michael. *The Village Voice,* December 14, 1972, p. 74.

Gussow, Mel. "Theater: A Stein Tribute at Judson." *The New York Times,* November 29, 1972, p. 34.

Hayes, Richard. "The Making Of Americans." *The Commonweal,* September 28, 1956, pp. 634–35.

Oliver, Edith. "Off-Broadway." *The New Yorker,* December 2, 1972, p. 126.

Whitlock, Margay. "The Making of Americans." *Show Business,* November 30, 1972, p. 13.

A Manoir

Davis, Peter G. " 'A Manoir' is a Thin 'Opera' but Entertaining." *The New York Times,* May 23, 1977, p. 22.

"A Manoir." Judson Poets' Theatre Programme, April 1977. New York: New York Public Library at Lincoln Center, Theatre Program Collection.

The Mother Of Us All

Altman, Peter. " 'Mother' Has Broad Comic Touches." *Minneapolis Star,* January 28, 1967, p. 4A.

Barnes, Clive. "Theater: 'Mother Of Us All' Revived." *The New York Times,* November 27, 1972, p. 43.

Bookspan, Martin. "The Mother Of Us All." *TV Channel 11,* November 20, 1972. New York: New York Public Library at Lincoln Center, Theatre Review Collection.

Clurman, Harold. "Theatre." *The Nation,* December 18, 1972, pp. 636–37.

Downs, Joan. "An American Momma." *Time,* August 23, 1976, p. 37.

Eyer, Ron. "Queens' 'Mother.'" *The New York News,* December 15, 1975, p. 49.

———. "Thomson Opera Revived At Phoenix." *Musical America,* May 1956, p. 23.

Feingold, Michael. "Theatre: Men Govern and Women Know." *The Village Voice,* April 12, 1976, p. 121.

Frankenstein, Alfred. "An Explosive Santa Fe Opera Display." *San Francisco Examiner and Chronicle,* August 29, 1976, This World Section, p. 27.

———. " 'The Mother Of Us All' — A Brilliant Exhibition." *High Fidelity/musical america,* December 1976, MA 21-23.

———. "Nimble Virgil's Steinesque Triumph." *San Francisco Sunday Chronicle,* May 30, 1965, This World Section, p. 23.

Giffin, Glenn. "Reports: U.S." *Opera News,* November 1976, p. 88.

Glover, William. *Associated Press,* November 11, 1972. New Haven: Yale University, Stein Newspaper Clipping Collection.

Haggin, B. H. "Music." *The Nation,* May 31, 1947, p. 667.

Hague, Robert A. "A Pleasant Evening With Gertrude S. and Virgil T." *PM,* May 9, 1947, p. 15.

Hastings, Baird. "at long last! The Mother of Us All" *American Record Guide,* August 1977, p. 30-31.

Henahan, Donal. "Opera: Thomson and Stein in Revival." *The New York Times,* August 21, 1971, p. 21.

Hughes, Allen. "Lenox 'The Mother Of Us All' Lacks Nothing But Seats for the Crowd." *The New York Times,* July 3, 1972, p. 7.

————. " 'The Mother Of Us All' Pays Tribute to Thomson at 75." *The New York Times,* November 28, 1971.

————. "Opera: The Mother Of Us All Returns." *The New York Times,* April 18, 1976, p. 35.

J. W. F. "Return of Susan B." *Opera News,* May 2, 1964, pp. 2–28.

Lang, Paul Henry. "The Mother Of Us All." *The New York Herald Tribune,* April 17, 1956, p. 17.

Levitan, Alan. *Boston After Dark,* July 18, 1972, p. 12.

"The Mother Of Us All." *The New York Times,* July 25, 1967, p. 15.

"The Mother Of Us All." *Voice of Reserve,* January–February 1949, pp. 3–5.

"The Mother Of Us All." *Variety,* May 21, 1947.

"The Mother Of Us All." *The New York Times,* December 14, 1975, p. 73.

Perkins, Francis D. "Gertrude Stein-Virgil Thomson Opera, 'The Mother Of Us All.'" *The New York Herald Tribune,* May 8, 1947, p. 21.

Phelan, Kappo. "The Mother Of Us All." *The Commonweal,* May 30, 1947, p. 167.

Porter, Andrew. "Musical Events." *The New Yorker,* April 11, 1983, p. 117.

Schonberg, Harold C. "Opera: First Season in Minneapolis." *The New York Times,* January 29, 1967, p. 67.

Smith, Cecil. "Gertrude S., Virgil T. and Susan B." *Theatre Arts,* July 1947, pp. 17–18.

Smith, Cecil. "Sounds of Spring." *The New Republic,* June 2, 1947.

Smith, Patrick J. "The Mother Of Us All." *High Fidelity/musical america,* November 1971, MA 10.

" 'Susan B.' in Three Acts." *Newsweek,* May 19, 1947, p. 94.

Taubman, Howard. "Opera: The Aging 'Mother Of Us All'." *The New York Times,* April 17, 1956, p. 27.

"Thomson Opera To Be Staged On Wednesday." *The New York Herald Tribune,* May 4, 1947, Section 5, p. 6.

Thomson, Virgil. "Denver Delight." *The New York Herald Tribune,* August 1, 1948, Section V., p. 4.

Thomson, Virgil. "How 'The Mother of us All' Was Created." *The New York Times,* April 15, 1956, Section 2, p. 7.

Tircuit, Heuell. "An Extraordinary Fantasy Opera." *The San Francisco Chronicle,* May 2, 1977.

Wilson, John S. "Stein-Thomson Opera To Bow." *PM,* May 6, 1947, p. 15.

Photograph

Eder, Richard. "Stage: The Imagery of Gertrude Stein." *The New York Times,* September 22, 1977.

Fleming, Shirley. "When This You See..." *High Fidelity/musical america,* November 11, 1971, MA 10, 11.

Hughes, Allen. "The Opera: Reminiscences Of Gertrude Stein." *The New York Times,* October 6, 1972, p. 35.

"Stein Play Opens at Open Space." *Show Business,* September 8, 1977, p. 3.

"Theatre." *The Village Voice,* October 3, 1977, p. 55.

Play I(–III)

Tallmer, Jerry. "Across the Footlights, Within the Within." *The New York Post,* December 14, 1965, p. 54.

Three Sisters Who Are Not Sisters

Fleming, Shirley. "When This You See..." *High Fidelity/musical america,* November 11, 1971, MA 10,11.

Hughes, Allen. "The Opera: Reminiscences of Gertrude Stein." *The New York Times,* October 6, 1972, p. 35.

Lester, Elenore. "Theatre: Three at Judson." *The Village Voice.* June 10, 1965, p. 12.

A Wedding Bouquet

Croce, Arlene. "The Spoken Word." *The New Yorker,* November 6, 1978, pp. 179–181.

"Lord Berners and Gertrude Stein – Ballet Collaborators." *The Bystander,* May 5, 1937. New Haven: Yale University, Gertrude Stein Newspaper Clipping Collection.

Martin, John. " 'Bouquet' Offered by Sadler's Wells." *The New York Times,* September 22, 1950, p. 35.

————. "Own Works Given by Sadler's Wells." *The New York Times,* October 26, 1949, p. 32.

"Nonsense Ballet is Good Fun." *London Daily Herald,* April 28, 1937, p. 11.

"Stein Ballet Opens Tonight." *The New York Sun,* April 27, 1937, p. 19.

" 'A Wedding Bouquet' The Berners-Stein-Ashton Ballet at Sadler's Wells." *The Bystander,* May 12, 1937. New Haven: Yale University, Stein Newspaper Clipping Collection.

What Happened

Croce, Arlene. "The Spoken Word." *The New Yorker,* November 6, 1978, pp. 179–181.

Gilman, Richard. "A Hit and A Success." *The Commonweal,* November 15, 1963, p. 227.

"Judson Poets Do Weiners, Stein." *The Village Voice,* September 26, 1963, p. 10.

Tallmer, Jerry. "Theatre in the Church Stages Two Short Plays." *The New York Post,* October 6, 1963, p. 14.

"Theatre: Judson Poets." *The Village Voice,* October 3, 1963, p. 11.

" 'What Happened' Held Over." *The New York Post,* October 18, 1963. New York: New York Public Library at Lincoln Center, Theatre Review Collection.

When This You See, Remember Me

Fleming, Shirley. "When This You See..." *High Fidelity/musical america,* November 11, 1971, MA 10,11.

Hughes, Allen. "The Opera: Reminiscences of Gertrude Stein." *The New York Times,* October 6, 1972, p. 35.

Yes Is For A Very Young Man

Atkinson, Brooks. "Gertrude Stein's 'Yes' Put On At Cherry Lane Playhouse." *The New York Times,* June 7, 1949, p. 27.

Barnes, Howard. "Gertrude Stein's Last: A Resistance Epilogue." *The New York Herald Tribune,* June 12, 1949, Section 5, p. 1.

Daily Variety (Hollywood), March 14, 1946. New Haven: Yale University, Stein Newspaper Clipping Collection.

"The Drama." *The Catholic World,* August 1949, pp. 388–389.

Foote, Robert O. "Gertrude Stein's 'Yes Is For A Very Young Man' Triumph Over Skeptical Public." *Pasadena Star News,* March 14, 1946, Section 2, p. 13.

"The Forty-Eight: Yes Is For A Very Young Man." *London Stage,* June 10, 1948, p. 8.

Garland, Robert. "Princeton Players Give Fine Portrayal." *The New York Journal American,* July 27, 1948, p. 8.

———. "'Yes is for a Very Young Man' A Sturdy Document." *The New York Journal American,* June 7, 1949, p. 10.

"Gertrude Says Yes In Simple Language In Her War Play." The Washington, D.C. *Evening Star,* March 23, 1949, Section A, p. 22.

"Gertrude Stein Play Brings Warm Response at Cape Tip." *Cape Cod Standard Times,* July 28, 1954. New Haven: Yale University, Stein Newspaper Clipping Collection.

Hanna, David. " 'Yes Is For A Very Young Man'." *Los Angeles Daily News,* March 15, 1946, p. 21.

Hawkins, William. "Stein Play Given Fine Presentation." *New York World-Telegram,* June 7, 1949, p. 16.

Herridge, Frances. "Stein Play Revived Off-Broadway." *The New York Post,* March 5, 1963, p. 14.

Hollywood Reporter, March 15, 1946. New Haven: Yale University, Stein Newspaper Clipping Collection.

Los Angeles Times, March 14, 1946. New Haven: Yale University, Stein Newspaper Clipping Collection.

"Miss Stein's Play To Be Put On Here." *The New York Times,* July 25, 1946, p. 17.

Taubman, Howard. "Drama of Wartime Fails To Come To Life." *The New York Times,* March 6, 1963, 7:5.

Phelan, Kappo. "Yes Is For A Very Young Man." *The Commonweal,* June 24, 1949, p. 271.

Philadelphia Evening Bulletin, March 15, 1946. New Haven: Yale University, Stein Newspaper Clipping Collection.

Pihodna, Joe. "Theatre News: Experimental Plays To Start in November." *The New York Herald Tribune,* September 7, 1947.

Rosenberg, Ben. "Gertrude Stein's New Play Will Open Here In October." *The New York Post,* July 25, 1946.

Schmidt, Sandra. "Theatre Post-Mortem: Yes Is For A Very Young Man." *The Village Voice,* March 7, 1963. New York: New York Public Library at Lincoln Center, Theatre Review Collection.

Sloan, Lloyd L. "New Gertrude Stein Play Not Author's Best Work." *Hollywood Citizen News,* March 14, 1946, p. 18.

Stage, March 1946. New Haven: Yale University, Stein Newspaper Clipping Collection.

Sykes, Barbara M. Cready. "Gertrude Stein As Done By Murray Group is Charming and Unusual Entertainment." *Princeton Herald,* July 28, 1949. New Haven: Yale University, Stein Newspaper Clipping Collection.

Theatre Arts, July 1946, p. 372.

Time, January 28, 1946. New Haven: Yale University, Stein Newspaper Clipping Collection.

Vickers, John. "Theatre." *San Francisco Argonaut,* August 3, 1951. New Haven: Yale University, Stein Newspaper Clipping Collection.

Watts, Richard, Jr. "Gertrude Stein Drama Presented Downtown." *The New York Post Home News,* June 7, 1949, p. 32.

"Yes and No." *Time,* March 25, 1946, p. 67.

Notes

Introduction

1. See Howard Greenfeld, *Gertrude Stein: A Biography* (New York: Crown Publishers, 1973), p. 74.

2. Lamont Johnson, Interview with the Author (Greencastle, Indiana: De Pauw University, May 5, 1978).

3. Burns Mantle, *Best Plays of 1945-1946* (New York: Dodd, Mead, 1946), p. 26.

4. Richard Bridgman, *Gertrude Stein in Pieces* (New York: Oxford University Press, 1970), p. 335.

5. John Malcom Brinnin, ed., *Selected Operas and Plays of Gertrude Stein* (Pittsburgh: University of Pittsburgh Press, 1970), p. xvi.

6. Ibid., p. xvii.

7. Eugene Ionesco and N. F. Simpson, Letters to the Author (October 11, 1977 and April 1978).

8. Quoted by Wilford Leach, "Gertrude Stein and the Modern Theatre," Ph.D. Dissertation (University of Illinois, 1956), p. 2.

9. Quoted by Carl Van Vechten, ed., *Last Operas and Plays,* p. viii.

Chapter One

1. Gertrude Stein, "How Writing is Written," in *How Writing Is Written,* ed. Robert Bartlett Haas (Los Angeles: Black Sparrow Press, 1974), p. 151.

2. Gertrude Stein, *Geography and Plays* (Boston: Four Seas Company, 1922), p. 211.

3. Gertrude Stein, *Last Operas and Plays* (New York: Rinehart and Company, 1949), p. 139.

4. Ibid., pp. 467-468.

5. Gertrude Stein, "Composition as Explanation," in *Selected Writings of Gertrude Stein,* ed. Carl Van Vechten, (New York: Random House, 1962), p. 513.

6. Gertrude Stein, *Gertrude Stein on Picasso,* ed. Edward Burns, (New York: Liveright Press, 1970), p. 72.

7. "Composition as Explanation," p. 521.

8. *Gertrude Stein on Picasso,* p. 76.

9. Milic Capek, *Philosophical Impact of Contemporary Physics* (Princeton: Van Nostrand, 1961), p. 248.

10. Gary Zukav, *The Dancing Wu Li Masters* (New York: William Morrow and Company, 1979), pp. 171-172.

11. George Santayana, *Realms of Being* (New York: Charles Scribner's Sons, 1937), p. 47.

12. William James, *Selections from his Writings on Psychology* (London: Whitefriars Press, Ltd., 1950), p. 101.

13. Gertrude Stein, *The Geographical History of America, or the Relation of Human Nature to the Human Mind* (U.S.A.: Random House, 1936), pp. 46-47.

14. Ibid., p. 69.

15. Gertrude Stein, *How To Write,* with an introduction by Patricia Meyerowitz (New York: Dover Publications, Inc., 1975), p. xi.

16. Gertrude Stein, *Four In America* (New Haven: Yale University Press, 1947), p. 119.

17. Gertrude Stein, *Everybody's Autobiography* (New York: Random House, 1937), p. 298.

18. *Geographical History,* p. 81.

19. Ibid., p. 27.

20. Gertrude Stein, *Narration* (Chicago: University of Chicago Press, 1935), p. 39.

21. Ibid., p. 20.

22. *Four In America,* p. 122.

23. *Narration,* pp. 37-38.

24. *Four In America,* p. 120.

25. *Narration,* pp. 51-52.

26. Gertrude Stein, *Lectures In America* (Boston: Beacon Press, 1957), p. 32.

27. Ibid., p. 24.

28. James Mellow, *Charmed Circle* (New York: Praeger, 1974), p. 326.

29. *Four In America,* p. vii.

30. Mellow, p. 326.

31. Virgil Thomson, *Virgil Thomson* (New York: Knopf, 1966), p. 124.

32. *Geographical History,* p. 194.

33. *Narration,* p. 39.

34. "How Writing Is Written," pp. 152-153.

35. Ibid., pp. 157-158.

36. *Geography and Plays,* p. 222.

37. *Geographical History,* p. 158.

38. Ibid., pp. 146–147.

39. Ibid., p. 147.

40. Wylie Sypher, *Rococo to Cubism in Art and Literature* (New York: Random House, 1960), p. 267.

41. "Composition As Explanation," pp. 517–518.

42. Bruce Kawin, *Telling it Again and Again. Repetition in Literature and Film* (Ithaca and London: Cornell University Press, 1972), pp. 129–130.

43. Donald Sutherland, "Gertrude Stein and the Twentieth Century," in *A Primer for the Gradual Understanding of Gertrude Stein,* ed. Robert Bartlett Haas (Los Angeles: Black Sparrow Press, 1973), pp. 146–147.

44. *Lectures,* p. 176.

45. Roger Shattuck, *The Banquet Years* (New York: Harcourt, Brace and Company, 1958 [1955]), p. 257.

46. James, *Selections,* p. 86.

47. Ibid., p. 162.

48. William James, *The Principles of Psychology, Volume 1* (New York: Dover Publishing Company, Inc., 1950), pp. 643–644.

49. *Last Operas and Plays,* p. 476.

50. Ibid., p. 295.

51. *Lectures,* p. 183.

52. Ibid., pp. 194–195.

53. Ibid., pp. 199–200.

54. *Last Operas and Plays,* p. 153.

55. *Lectures,* p. 30.

56. Ibid., p. 220.

57. Ibid., pp. 211–214.

58. Ibid., p. 192.

59. *How To Write,* p. 23.

60. *Narration,* p. 23.

61. Ibid., p. 20.

62. Ibid., p. 18.

63. *Lectures,* p. 224.

64. Ibid., p. 225.

65. Gertrude Stein, *Operas and Plays* (Paris: Plain Edition, 27 Rue de Fleurus, 1932), p. 222.

66. *How To Write,* p. 25.

67. Ibid., p. 27.

68. Ibid., p. 29.

69. *Lectures,* p. 228.

70. Ibid., p. 231.

71. *Four In America,* p. vi.

72. "Tender Buttons," in *Selected Writings,* p. 480.

73. *Lectures,* p. 204.

74. Quoted by Donald Sutherland, "Gertrude Stein and the Twentieth Century," p. 143.

75. *Geographical History,* p. 61.

76. Ibid., p. 54.

77. Ibid., p. 80.

78. "A Transatlantic Interview," pp. 15–16.

79. *Everybody's Autobiography,* p. 116.

80. Sypher, p. 273.

81. James, *Principles,* pp. 258–259.

82. "A Transatlantic Interview," p. 25.

83. *Lectures,* p. 170.

84. Henri Bergson, *An Introduction to Metaphysics* (New York: The Bobbs-Merrill Co., Inc., 1955), p. 23.

85. Ibid., p. 36.

86. *Narration,* p. 20.

87. *Lectures,* p. 140.

88. Ibid., p. 152.

89. Ibid., p. 199.

90. Ibid., pp. 172–173.

91. "A Transatlantic Interview," p. 16.

92. *Lectures,* p. 237.

93. Ibid.

94. *Lectures,* pp. 191–192.

95. *Gertrude Stein On Picasso,* p. 114.

96. "Tender Buttons," in *Selected Writings,* p. 462.

97. Gertrude Stein, "The Autobiography Of Alice B. Toklas," in *Selected Writings Of Gertrude Stein,* p. 198.

98. Sypher, p. 298.

99. *Lectures,* p. 87.

100. Ibid., pp. 67–68.

101. Ibid., pp. 76–77.

102. Ibid., pp. 60–61.

103. Ibid., p. 157.

104. Gertrude Stein, "Answers to the Partisan Review," in *How Writing Is Written,* p. 55.

105. "Autobiography," p. 198.

106. "A Transatlantic Interview," p. 30.

107. *Four In America,* p. 128.

108. *Everybody's Autobiography,* p. 10.

109. Fritjof Capra, *The Tao of Physics* (Toronto, New York, London: Bantam Books, 1977 [1976]), p. 66.

110. Quoted by Carl Van Vechten, "A Stein Song," in *Selected Writings of Gertrude Stein,* p. xxiii.

111. *Everybody's Autobiography,* pp. 171–172.

112. *Lectures,* p. 220.

113. Ibid., p. 221.

114. John Dewey, *Art As Experience* (New York: Minton, Batch and Company, 1934), p. 54.

115. *Narration,* p. 60.

Chapter Two

1. *Lectures,* p. 111.

2. Gertrude Stein, "Coal and Wood," in *Painted Lace* (New Haven: Yale University Press, 1955), p. 6.

3. *Everybody's Autobiography,* p. 317.

4. "A Transatlantic Interview," p. 30.

5. Designers Pavlik Tchelitchev, Christian Berard, Eugene Berman, and Dior; set designers for the Ballets Russes Pablo Picasso, Henri Matisse, Juan Gris, Marie Laurencin, and Georges Braque; playwrights Jean Cocteau, Roger Vitrac, Thornton Wilder, Avery Hopwood, Guillaume Apollinaire, and Tristan Tzara.

6. Virgil Thomson, Interview with the Author (New York: Chelsea Hotel, October 2, 1977), p. 3.

7. Ibid., p. 2.

8. *Virgil Thomson,* p. 89.

9. Virgil Thomson, *Interview,* p. 8.

10. *Lectures,* p. 59.

11. "Autobiography," p. 72.

12. *Last Operas and Plays,* p. 336.

13. Gertrude Stein to Virgil Thomson, 25 June 1935 (New Haven: Yale University, Gertrude Stein Collection).

14. *Last Operas and Plays,* p. xiv.

15. Gertrude Stein to Lamont Johnson et al., 13 March 1946 (New Haven: Yale University, Gertrude Stein Collection).

16. Jean Cocteau, "Preface to *The Eiffel Tower Wedding Party,*" in *The Infernal Machine* (New York: New Directions, 1963), p. 154.

17. *Lectures,* pp. 198–199.

18. Ibid., p. 181.

19. Ibid., p. 188.

20. Ibid., p. 170.

21. Ibid., pp. 174–175.

22. Ibid., p. 188.

23. Ibid., pp. 198, 199.

24. Donald Sutherland, *Gertrude Stein: A Biography of her Work* (New Haven: Yale University Press, 1951), p. 100.

25. *Last Operas and Plays,* pp. 153–154.

26. *Lectures,* p. 199.

27. Tom Driver, *Romantic Quest and Modern Query* (New York: Delacorte Press, 1962), p. 361.

28. *Geographical History,* p. 202.

29. John A. Henderson, *The First Avant-Garde, 1887–1894. Sources of the Modern French Theatre* (London: George G. Harrap and Co., 1971), pp. 5–6.

30. Cocteau, p. 156.

31. Robert Brustein, "Why American Plays Are Not Literature," in Downer, Alan, *American Drama And Its Critics* (Chicago and London: University of Chicago Press, 1965), p. 250.

32. Stark Young, *The Theater* (New York: George H. Doran Company, 1927), p. 68.

33. *Everybody's Autobiography,* pp. 195–196.

34. *Gertrude Stein on Picasso,* p. 29.

35. *Four in America,* p. 131.

36. *Last Operas and Plays,* p. 336.

37. *Everybody's Autobiography,* p. 193.

38. *Last Operas and Plays,* p. 351.

39. Mellow, p. 175.

40. Nathan Zatkin, Press Release, *Four Saints in Three Acts,* 1934 (New Haven: Yale University, Gertrude Stein Collection), p. 3.

41. *Lectures,* pp. 118–119.

42. *Everybody's Autobiography,* p. 194.

43. "How Writing," p. 159.

44. *Lectures,* p. 181.

45. Ibid., p. 119.

46. *Geographical History,* p. 202.

47. Maurice Maeterlinck, "The Tragical In Daily Life," in *The Treasure of the Humble,* Alfred Suto, transl. (New York: Dodd, Mead, 1916), p. 103.

48. Martin Esslin, *An Anatomy of Drama* (New York: Hill and Wang, 1976), p. 116.

49. Calvin Tomkins, "Time to Think," *The New Yorker* (January 13, 1978), p. 61.

50. *Lectures,* p. 176.

51. Ibid., p. 104.

52. Ibid., p. 118.

53. Ibid., p. 122.

54. Ibid., p. 177.

55. Ibid., p. 171.

56. Robert Edmond Jones, *The Dramatic Imagination,* p. 181.

57. *Everybody's Autobiography,* p. 283.

58. *Lectures,* p. 199.

59. Ibid., pp. 172–173.

60. Ibid., p. 119.

61. *Last Operas and Plays,* p. 335.

62. Sutherland, p. 103.

63. *Lectures,* p. 93.

64. Ibid., p. 95.

65. Ibid., p. 96.

66. Ibid., p. 98.

67. Ibid.

68. Ibid., p. 109.

69. Ibid., p. 94.

70. Ibid., pp. 114–115.

71. Ibid., p. 112.

72. Ibid., p. 115–116.

73. Ibid., p. 116.

74. Ibid.

75. Ibid., p. 117.

76. Ibid., p. 118.

77. *Everybody's Autobiography,* p. 316.

78. See "Autobiography," p. 197 and *Everybody's Autobiography,* p. 118.

79. *Lectures,* p. 119.

80. Ibid.

81. Ibid., p. 121.

82. Ibid., p. 118.

83. "Autobiography," p. 125.

84. *Selected Writings,* p. 557.

85. *Geography and Plays,* p. 202.

86. *Selected Writings,* pp. 555–556.

87. *Geography and Plays,* p. 254.

88. Ibid., p. 286.

89. Ibid., p. 189.

90. Ibid.

91. *Operas and Plays,* p. 395.

92. *Lectures,* p. 119.

93. "Autobiography," pp. 196–197.

94. *Lectures,* p. 122.

95. *Operas and Plays,* pp. 92–93.

96. Ibid., pp. 105–106.

97. *Lectures,* p. 125.

98. Gertrude Stein, *Portraits and Prayers* (New York: Random House, 1934), p. 28.

99. *Operas and Plays,* p. 106.

100. *Lectures,* p. 131.

101. "Autobiography," pp. 211–212.

102. Ibid., p. 212.

103. *Operas and Plays,* p. 331.

104. Leach, p. 151.

105. Carl Van Vechten, "How Many Acts Are There In It?," Introduction to *Last Operas and Plays,* p. xvii.

106. *Four In America,* p. 122.

107. *Narration,* pp. 37-38, 51-52.

108. *Lectures,* p. 32.

109. "A Transatlantic Interview," p. 19.

110. Ibid.

111. Ibid.

112. Ibid.

113. Ibid., p. 20.

114. *Last Operas and Plays,* pp. 94-95.

115. Ibid., pp. 89-90.

116. Ibid., pp. 102-103.

117. Ibid., p. 78.

118. Ibid., pp. 79-80.

119. "Autobiography," pp. 196-197.

120. *Operas and Plays,* p. 230.

121. *Geography and Plays,* p. 293.

122. "Autobiography," pp. 124-125.

123. Ibid., p. 155.

124. *Lectures,* p. 122.

125. "Autobiography," p. 196.

126. "A Transatlantic Interview," p. 19.

127. Ibid.

128. Ibid., p. 20.

129. *Lectures,* p. 118.

130. *Four In America,* p. 165.

131. Ibid., pp. 163-164.

132. *Last Operas and Plays,* pp. 423-424.

133. *Primer,* p. 122.

Chapter Three

1. Herbert Marcuse, *The Aesthetic Dimension: Toward a Critique of Marxist Aesthetics* (Boston: Beacon Press, 1978), pp. xii–xiii.

2. Bernard Beckerman, *Dynamics of Drama: Theory and Method of Analysis* (New York: Alfred A. Knopf, 1970), p. 210.

3. Sam Smiley, *Playwriting: The Structure of Action* (Englewood Cliffs: Prentice Hall, 1971), p. 42.

4. Ibid., p. 52.

5. Ibid., p. 73.

6. Ibid.

7. *Selected Writings,* p. 558.

8. Ibid.

9. *Last Operas and Plays,* p. 89.

10. Ibid., p. 139.

11. *Geography and Plays,* p. 267.

12. Ibid., p. 263.

13. Ibid., p. 302.

14. Gertrude Stein, *The Gertrude Stein First Reader and Three Plays* (Dublin: Maurice Fridberg, 1946), p. 42.

15. Ibid., p. 66.

16. *Operas and Plays,* p. 396.

17. Ibid., pp. 66–67.

18. *Last Operas and Plays,* p. 70.

19. Smiley, p. 73.

20. Gertrude Stein, *Useful Knowledge,* pp. 170–171.

21. *Operas and Plays,* p. 117.

22. Ibid., p. 97.

23. *Geography and Plays,* p. 260.

24. *Last Operas and Plays,* p. 461.

25. Ibid., pp. 467–468.

26. Ibid., p. 53.

27. *Operas and Plays,* p. 118.

28. *Last Operas and Plays,* p. 476.

29. *Geography and Plays,* p. 410.

30. *Last Operas and Plays,* p. 279.

31. Ibid., p. 385.

32. *Geography and Plays*, p. 210.

33. *Selected Writings*, p. 555.

34. *Last Operas and Plays*, p. 350.

35. *Geographical History*, p. 197.

36. Smiley, p. 129.

37. *Operas and Plays*, p. 248.

38. Ibid., p. 83.

39. Ibid., p. 368.

40. *Last Operas and Plays*, p. 80.

41. Ibid., p. 88.

42. Smiley, p. 128.

43. Ibid., p. 161.

44. Ibid., p. 158.

45. *Last Operas and Plays*, p. 317.

46. *Geography and Plays*, p. 272.

47. Ibid., p. 288.

48. *Operas and Plays*, p. 76.

49. Ibid., p. 125.

50. *Last Operas and Plays*, p. 166.

51. *Operas and Plays*, pp. 113-114.

52. Ibid., pp. 120-121.

53. *Last Operas and Plays*, p. 139.

54. Ibid., pp. 140-141.

55. *Geography and Plays*, pp. 122-123.

56. *Last Operas and Plays*, p. 202.

57. Robert Bartlett Haas, ed., *Reflection on the Atomic Bomb* (Los Angeles: Black Sparrow Press, 1973), p. 98.

58. *Primer*, p. 117.

59. *Last Operas and Plays*, p. 156.

60. *First Reader*, p. 60.

61. *Primer*, p. 78.

62. Gertrude Stein, *Monday and Tuesday. A Play*, Typescript Copy (New Haven: Yale University, Gertrude Stein Collection), p. 1.

63. *Geography and Plays*, p. 260.

64. *Last Operas and Plays,* p. 387.
65. *Geography and Plays,* p. 227.
66. *Last Operas and Plays,* p. 402.
67. Ibid., p. 55.
68. Ibid., p. 75.
69. *Geography and Plays,* p. 215.
70. *Last Operas and Plays,* p. 52.
71. Ibid., p. 51.
72. Ibid., p. 358.
73. Ibid., p. 333.
74. Ibid., p. 334.
75. Ibid., p. 387.
76. Ibid., p. 421.
77. Ibid., p. 478.
78. *Geography and Plays,* p. 325.
79. *Last Operas and Plays,* p. 144.
80. *Operas and Plays,* p. 58.
81. *Portraits and Prayers,* p. 28.
82. *Operas and Plays,* p. 83.
83. Ibid., p. 84.
84. Ibid., p. 101.
85. Ibid., p. 124.
86. *Last Operas and Plays,* p. 440.
87. Ibid.
88. Ibid.
89. Ibid., p. 443.
90. Ibid., p. 444.
91. Ibid., p. 446.
92. Ibid.
93. Ibid., p. 459.
94. Ibid., pp. 464–465.
95. Ibid., pp. 468–469.
96. *Geography and Plays,* p. 290.
97. Ibid., p. 294.

98. Ibid., p. 230.

99. Smiley, p. 161.

100. *Geography and Plays,* p. 210.

101. *Last Operas and Plays,* p. 153.

102. *Portraits and Prayers,* p. 31.

103. *Last Operas and Plays,* p. 202.

104. Ibid., p. 445.

105. *Operas and Plays,* p. 123.

106. *First Reader,* p. 60.

107. *Last Operas and Plays,* p. 445.

108. Ibid., pp. 444–445.

109. Ibid., pp. 99–100.

110. Ibid., p. 28.

111. *Geography and Plays,* p. 210.

112. *Operas and Plays,* p. 196.

113. Ibid., p. 264.

114. *Geography and Plays,* p. 412.

115. *Last Operas and Plays,* p. 200.

116. *Geography and Plays,* p. 227.

117. *Last Operas and Plays,* pp. 8–9.

118. *Geography and Plays,* p. 262.

119. *Operas and Plays,* p. 221.

120. *Last Operas and Plays,* p. 351.

121. Ibid., p. 433.

122. *Geography and Plays,* p. 217.

123. *Last Operas and Plays,* p. 205.

124. *Operas and Plays,* p. 91.

125. Smiley, p. 161.

126. *Operas and Plays,* p. 221.

127. *Geography and Plays,* pp. 290–292.

128. *Last Operas and Plays,* p. 205.

129. Ibid., p. 3.

130. *First Reader,* p. 64.

131. *Geography and Plays,* p. 202.

132. *Four In America,* p. 165.

133. *Last Operas and Plays,* p. 200.

134. Ibid., pp. 54–55.

135. *Geography and Plays,* pp. 277–278.

136. Ibid., p. 274.

137. Ibid., p. 302.

138. Ibid., pp. 124–125.

139. *Operas and Plays,* p. 51.

140. *Useful Knowledge,* pp. 173–174.

141. *Last Operas and Plays,* p. 442.

142. Ibid., p. 474.

143. *Operas and Plays,* p. 49.

144. *Last Operas and Plays,* p. 192.

145. *First Reader,* p. 68.

146. *Last Operas and Plays,* p. 445.

147. *Primer,* p. 80.

148. *Geography and Plays,* p. 286.

149. *Selected Writings,* p. 555.

150. *Geography and Plays,* p. 254.

151. Ibid., p. 267.

152. *Operas and Plays,* p. 115.

153. *Geography and Plays,* p. 262.

154. Ibid., p. 409.

155. *Last Operas and Plays,* pp. 7–8.

156. *Everybody's Autobiography,* p. 109.

157. *Primer,* p. 122.

158. *Last Operas and Plays,* pp. 89–90.

159. Ibid., p. 93.

160. Ibid., p. 115.

161. *Everybody's Autobiography,* p. 47.

162. Ibid., p. 127.

Chapter Four

1. Gertrude Stein to Henry McBride, August 1927 (New Haven: Gertrude Stein Collection).

2. Virgil Thomson, p. 97.

3. Mellow, p. 307.

4. John Houseman, *Run-Thru: A Memoir* (New York: Simon and Schuster, 1972), p. 105.

5. Virgil Thomson, p. 239.

6. *Literary Digest* (February 3, 1934, New Haven: Yale University, Gertrude Stein Newspaper Clipping Collection).

7. "Lord Berners and Gertrude Stein-Ballet Collaborators," *The Bystander,* May 5, 1937 (New Haven: Yale University, Gertrude Stein Newspaper Clipping Collection).

8. "Doctor Faustus Lights the Lights," Program of the Living Theatre Production (1951, New York: New York Public Library at Lincoln Center, Theatre Program Collection).

9. Aimee Scheff, "Theatre Off-Broadway," *Theatre Arts* (February 1952), p. 96.

10. Susan Sontag, *Against Interpretation and other Essays* (New York: Dell Publishing Co., 1966 [1961]), pp. 171-172.

11. Jack Kroll, "Stein Songs," *Newsweek* (November 27, 1967), p. 105.

12. Michael Feingold, "Triumph, the Stein Way," *The Village Voice* (October 24, 1974), p. 85.

13. Richard Eder, "Stage: the Imagery of Gertrude Stein," *The New York Times* (September 22, 1977).

14. *Operas and Plays,* pp. 92-93.

15. See Kate Davy, *Richard Foreman: Plays and Manifestos* (New York: New York University Press, 1976), pp. ix-xvi.

16. See John Gruen, "Is It A Play? An Opera? No, It's A Wilson," *The New York Times* (March 16, 1975), p. 7; and Robert Wilson, "Robert Wilson," in *Intermedia,* Hans Breder and Stephen C. Foster, eds. (Iowa City: Publication of School of Art and Art History, The University of Iowa, 1979), pp. 165-166.

17. Kate Davy, *Richard Foreman and the Ontological-Hysteric Theatre* (Ann Arbor: UMI Research Press, 1981 [1979]), p. 19.

18. Richard Foreman, "How To Write A Play," *Performing Arts Journal* (Fall 1976), pp. 84, 86, 87.

19. Ibid., pp. 88-89.

20. Ibid., p. 89.

21. Davy, p. xiii.

22. Ibid., p. xv.

23. Frantisek Deak, "The Life and Times of Joseph Stalin," in Michael Kirby, ed., *The New Theatre* (New York: New York University Press, 1974), p. 182.

24. Quoted by Bonnie Marranca, ed., *The Theatre Of Images* (New York: New York University Press, 1978), p. 68.

25. Ibid., p. 70.

26. Ibid, p. 93.

27. John Gruen, p. 7.

Bibliography

Works By or About Gertrude Stein

Books

Berners, Gerald and Gertrude Stein. *A Wedding Bouquet: Piano Score.* London: J. & W. Chester, Ltd., 1938.

Blum, Daniel, ed. *Daniel Blum's Theatre World,* New York: Crown, 1955.

Bridgman, Richard. *Gertrude Stein in Pieces.* New York: Oxford University Press, 1970.

Brinnin, John Malcom, ed. *Selected Operas and Plays of Gertrude Stein.* Pittsburgh: University of Pittsburgh Press, 1970.

————. *The Third Rose: Gertrude Stein and Her World.* Boston, Toronto: Little, Brown, and Company, 1959.

Burns, Edward and Leon Katz. "They Walk in the Light." In *Gertrude Stein On Picasso.* Edited by Edward Burns. New York: Liveright Press, 1970.

Copeland, Carolyn Faunce. *Language and Time and Gertrude Stein.* Iowa City: University of Iowa Press, 1975.

Gallup, Donald, ed. *The Flowers of Friendship. Letters Written to Gertrude Stein.* New York: Alfred A. Knopf, 1953.

Greenfeld, Howard. *Gertrude Stein: A Biography.* New York: Crown Publishers, 1973.

Guernsey, Otis L., Jr., ed. *Best Plays 1967-1968.* New York: Dodd, Mead, 1968.

————. *Best Plays 1968-1969.* New York: Dodd, Mead, 1969.

————. *Best Plays 1969-1970.* New York: Dodd, Mead, 1970.

————. *Best Plays 1971-1972.* New York: Dodd, Mead, 1972.

————. *Best Plays 1972-1973.* New York: Dodd, Mead, 1973.

————. *Best Plays 1975-1976.* New York: Dodd, Mead, 1976.

Haas, Robert B. and Donald C. Gallup. *A Catalogue of the Published and Unpublished Writings of Gertrude Stein.* New Haven: Yale University Library, 1941.

Haas, Robert B., ed. *A Primer For The Gradual Understanding of Gertrude Stein.* Los Angeles: Black Sparrow Press, 1973.

————, ed. *Reflection on the Atomic Bomb.* Los Angeles: Black Sparrow Press, 1973.

Hewes, Henry, ed. *Best Plays 1963-1964.* New York: Dodd, Mead, 1964.

Hoffman, Frederick J. "The Color and Shape of the Thing Seen: Gertrude Stein." In *The Twenties,* pp. 186-196. New York: The Viking Press, 1955.

Hoffman, Michael J. *The Development of Abstractionism in the Writings of Gertrude Stein.* Philadelphia: University of Pennsylvania Press, 1965.

————. *Gertrude Stein.* Boston: Twayne Publishers, London: George Prior Publishers, 1976.

Katz, Leon. *The Making of Americans.* An Opera and a Play from the Novel by Gertrude Stein. Barton, Browington, Berlin: Something Else Press, Inc., 1973.

Kawin, Bruce F. *Telling It Again and Again. Repetition in Literature and Film.* Ithaca and London: Cornell University Press, 1972.

Kazin, Alfred. "The Mysteries of Gertrude Stein (1960)." In *Contemporaries.* Boston, Toronto: Little, Brown and Company, 1962.

Kupferman, Meyer and Gertrude Stein. *In a Garden, an Opera in One Act.* Vocal Score. New York: Mercury Music Company, 1951.

Martin, Vernon and Gertrude Stein. *Ladies' Voices. A Chamber Opera.* New York: Independent Music Publishers, 1955.

Marx, Robert. "Thomson, Stein, and *The Mother Of Us All.*" Liner Notes for Santa Fe Opera Recording. New World Records, 1976.

Mayorga, Margaret, ed. *Best Short Plays 1954-1955.* New York: Dodd, Mead and Company, 1955.

Mellow, James. *Charmed Circle: Gertrude Stein and Company.* New York, Praeger, 1974.

Perloff, Marjorie. "Poetry as Word-System: The Art of Gertrude Stein," in *The Poetics of Indeterminacy,* pp. 67–108. Princeton, NJ: Princeton University Press, 1981.

Porter, Katherine Anne. "The Wooden Umbrella (1947)." In *The Days Before,* pp. 42–60. New York: Harcourt, Brace and Company, 1952.

Preston, John Hyde. "A Conversation with Gertrude Stein." In *The Creative Process,* pp. 159–168. Edited by Brewster Ghiselin. New York: New American Library, 1952.

Rorem, Ned and Gertrude Stein. *Three Sisters who are not Sisters.* Vocal Score. New York: Boosey and Hawkes, 1974.

Stein, Gertrude. *Bee Time Vine and Other Pieces.* New Haven: Yale University Press, 1953.

———. *Everybody's Autobiography.* New York: Random House, 1937.

———. *Four in America.* New Haven: Yale University Press, 1947.

———. *The Geographical History of America, or the Relation of Human Nature to the Human Mind.* U.S.A.: Random House, 1936.

———. *Geography and Plays.* Boston: Four Seas Company, 1922.

———. *The Gertrude Stein First Reader and Three Plays.* Dublin, London: Maurice Fridberg, 1946.

———. *Gertrude Stein on Picasso.* Edited by Edward Burns. New York: Liveright Press, 1970.

———. *How to Write.* Introduction by Patricia Meyerowitz. New York: Dover Publications, Inc., 1975(1931).

———. *How Writing is Written.* Edited by Robert Bartlett Haas. Los Angeles: Black Sparrow Press, 1974.

———. *Last Operas and Plays.* Edited and Introduced by Carl Van Vechten. New York: Rinehart and Company, 1949.

———. *Lectures in America.* Boston: Beacon Press, 1957(1935).

———. *Narration.* Chicago: University of Chicago Press, 1935.

———. *Operas and Plays.* Paris: Plain Edition, 27 Rue de Fleurus, 1932.

———. *Painted Lace.* New Haven: Yale University Press, 1955.

———. *Portraits and Prayers.* New York: Random House, 1934.

———. *Selected Writings of Gertrude Stein.* Edited by Carl Van Vechten. New York: Random House, 1962(1945).

———. *Useful Knowledge.* New York: Payson and Clark, Ltd., 1928.

———. *A Village. Are You Ready Yet Not Yet. A Play in Four Acts.* Paris: La Galerie Simon, 1928.

———. *Wars I Have Seen.* New York: Random House, 1945.

————. *What are Masterpieces*. Los Angeles: Conference Press, 1940.

Steiner, Wendy. *Exact Resemblance to Exact Resemblance: The Literary Portraiture of Gertrude Stein*. New Haven, London: Yale University Press, 1978.

Sutherland, Donald. *Gertrude Stein: A Biography of her Work*. New Haven: Yale University Press, 1951.

Thomson, Virgil and Gertrude Stein. *Capital Capitals. For Four Male Voices and Piano*. Musical Score. New York: Boosey and Hawkes, 1968(1947).

————. *Four Saints in Three Acts*. Complete Vocal Score, with Scenario by Maurice Grosser. New York: Music Press, Inc. and Arrow Music Press, Inc., 1948.

Thomson, Virgil and Gertrude Stein. *The Mother Of Us All*, together with the Scenario by Maurice Grosser. New York: Music Press, Inc., 1947.

Toklas, Alice. *Staying on Alone*. Edited by Edward Burns. New York: Liveright Press, 1973.

Van Vechten, Carl. "How to Read Gertrude Stein." In Gertrude Stein: A Composite Portrait. Edited by Linda Simon. New York: Avon Books, 1974.

————. "A Few Notes About Four Saints in Three Acts." In *Four Saints in Three Acts*, pp. 5-10. New York: Random House, 1934.

Violett, Ellen and Elizabeth Blake. *Brewsie and Willie*, an adaptation of the novel by Gertrude Stein. In *Best Short Plays 1954-1955*, p. 72. Edited by Margaret Mayorga. New York: Dodd, Mead and Company, 1955.

Weinstein, Norman. *Gertrude Stein and the Literature of Modern Consciousness*. New York: Frederick Ungar Publishing Company, 1970.

Willis, John, ed. *Theatre World 1967-1968*. New York: Crown Publishers, 1968.

Yalden-Thomson, D. C. "Obscurity, Exhibitionism, and Gertrude Stein." *The Virginia Quarterly Review*, Winter 1958, pp. 133-137.

Periodicals/Newspapers

Bernstein, Leonard. "Music and Miss Stein." *The New York Times*, May 22, 1949, pp. 4, 22.

Davies, James. "Gertrude Stein's Vocabulary in Unclassified New Volume Astounds and Amazes Critic." *Minneapolis Tribune*, September 23, 1923.

"Editorials." *The Nation*, July 27, 1932, p. 67.

Fitz, L. T. "Gertrude Stein and Picasso: The Language of Surfaces." *American Literature*, May 1973, pp. 228-237.

Gallup, Donald. "Always Gertrude Stein." *Southwest Review*, Summer 1949, pp. 254-258.

————. "The Weaving of a Pattern: Marsden Hartley and Gertrude Stein." *Magazine of Art*, November 1948, pp. 256-261.

Gass, W. H. "Gertrude Stein: Her Escape From Protective Language." *Accent*, Autumn 1958, pp. 233-244.

Hall, Donald. "Gertrude Stein and Her Fords." *Ford Times*, June 1978, pp. 50-51.

Hoffman, Frederick J. "Gertrude Stein." *The University of Minnesota Pamphlets on American Writers*, No. 10, 1961.

Levinson, Ronald B. "Gertrude Stein, William James, and Grammar." *The American Journal of Psychology*, January 1941, pp. 124-128.

Rago, Henry. "Gertrude Stein." *Poetry*, November 1946, pp. 93-97.

Redman, Ben Ray. *Saturday Review*, April 2, 1949.

Roda, Roda and Gertrude Stein. "My Debt to Books." *Books Abroad*, Summer 1939, p. 307.

Rogers, W. G. "Gertrude Stein Hovering." *The New York Herald Tribune*, April 3, 1949.

Rudikoff, Sonya. "The Mama of Dada." *Commentary*, May 1974, pp. 80-85.

Van Vechten, Carl. "Medals for Miss Stein." *New York Tribune*, May 13, 1923.

Wilcox, Wendell. "A Note On Stein and Abstraction." *Poetry: A Magazine of Verse,* February 1940, pp. 254–257.

Wilson, Edmund. "A Guide to Gertrude Stein. The Evolution of a Master of Fiction into a Painter of Cubist Still-Life in Prose." *Vanity Fair,* September 1923, pp. 60, 80.

Wright, George T. "Gertrude Stein and Her Ethic of Self-Containment." *Tennessee Studies in Literature,* Volume 8, 1963, pp. 17–23.

Zinnes, Harriet. "Lively Syndicate of Modernism." *The Nation,* May 18, 1974, p. 631.

Secondary Works

Books

Apollinaire, Guillaume. "Preface to 'Les Mamelles de Tiresias.' " *Oeuvres Poetiques.* Paris: Pleiade, 1956, pp. 865–866.

Artaud, Antonin. *The Theatre and its Double.* Translated by Mary Caroline Richards. New York: Grove Press, Inc., 1958.

Beckerman, Bernard. *Dynamics of Drama: Theory and Method of Analysis.* New York: Alfred A. Knopf, 1970.

Bergson, Henri. *An Introduction To Metaphysics.* Translated by T. E. Hulme. New York: The Bobbs-Merrill Co., Inc., 1955(1903).

Blewett, John. *John Dewey: His Thought and Influence.* New York: Fordham University Press, 1960.

Brustein, Robert. "Why American Plays are not Literature." In *American Drama and its Critics,* pp. 250–254. Edited by Alan Downer. Chicago, London: University of Chicago Press, 1965.

Capek, Milic. *Philosophical Impact of Contemporary Physics.* Princeton: Van Nostrand, 1961.

Capra, Fritjof. *The Tao of Physics.* Toronto, New York, London: Bantam Books, 1977 (1976).

Cocteau, Jean. *The Infernal Machine and Other Plays.* New York: New Directions, 1963.

Coe, Richard N. *Samuel Beckett.* Revised edition. New York: Grove Press, Inc., 1968(1964).

Davy, Kate, ed. *Richard Foreman: Plays and Manifestos.* New York: New York University Press, 1976.

Davy, Kate. *Richard Foreman and the Ontological-Hysterical Theatre.* Ann Arbor: UMI Research Press, 1981(1979).

Dewey, John. *Art as Experience.* New York: Minton, Batch and Company, 1934.

Driver, Tom. *Romantic Quest and Modern Query.* New York: Delacorte Press, 1962.

Dukore, Bernard F. and Daniel C. Gerould, eds. *Avant-Garde Drama. A Casebook, 1918–1939.* New York: Thomas Y. Crowell Company, 1976.

Dukore, Bernard F., ed. *Dramatic Theory and Criticism.* New York: Holt, Rinehart and Winston, Inc., 1974.

Esslin, Martin. *An Anatomy of Drama.* New York: Hill and Wang, 1976.

———. *The Theatre of the Absurd.* Revised Updated Edition. Woodstock, New York: The Overlook Press, 1973(1961).

Fergusson, Francis. "James's Idea of Dramatic Form." In *American Drama and its Critics,* pp. 177–187. Edited by Alan Downer. Chicago, London: University of Chicago Press, 1965.

Gass, W. H. *The World Within the Word.* New York: Alfred A. Knopf, 1978.

Gibson, Walker, ed. *The Limits of Language.* New York: Hill and Wang, 1962.

Henderson, John A. *The First Avant-Garde, 1887–1894. Sources of the Modern French Theatre.* London, Toronto, Wellington, Sydney: George G. Harrap and Company, Ltd., 1971.

Houseman, John. *Run-Thru; A Memoir.* New York: Simon and Schuster, 1972.

Huizinga, Johan. "Nature and Significance of Play as a Cultural Phenomenon." In *Ritual, Play, and Performance,* pp. 46–66. Edited by Richard Schechner and Mady Schuman. New York: Seabury Press, 1976.

Ionesco, Eugene. *Notes and Counter-Notes.* New York: Grove Press, 1964.

James, William. *Collected Essays and Reviews.* New York, London: Longmans, Green and Company, 1920.

———. *Essays in Radical Empiricism.* New York: Longmans, Green and Company, 1922.

———. *The Principles of Psychology, Volume 1.* New York: Dover Publishing Company, Inc., 1950.

———. *A Selection From His Writings On Psychology.* Edited by Margaret Knight. London: Whitefriars Press, Ltd., 1950.

Kierkegaard, Soren Aabye. *Repetition; an Essay in Experimental Psychology.* Translated and Introduced by Walter Lowrie. Princeton: Princeton University Press, 1941.

Kirby, Michael. *The Art of Time.* New York: E. P. Dutton and Company, Inc., 1969.

Kirby, Michael. *The New Theatre.* New York: New York University Press, 1974.

Langer, Susanne. "The Dramatic Illusion." In *The Modern Theatre: Readings and Documents,* pp. 74–90. Edited by Daniel Seltzer. Boston: Little, Brown and Company, 1967.

———. *Philosophy in a New Key.* New York: New American Library, 1948.

Marcuse, Herbert. *The Aesthetic Dimension: Toward a Critique of Marxist Aesthetics.* Boston: Beacon Press, 1978.

Marranca, Bonnie, ed. *The Theatre of Images.* New York: New York University Press, 1978.

Pirsig, Robert M. *Zen and the Art of Motorcycle Maintenance.* Toronto, New York, London: Bantam Books, 1976(1974).

Pronko, Leonard Cabell. *Avant-Garde: The Experimental Theatre in France.* Berkeley and Los Angeles: University of California Press, 1963.

Raymond, Marcel. *from baudelaire to surrealism.* New York: Wittenborn, Schultz, Inc., 1950

Santayana, George. *Realms of Being.* New York: Charles Scribner's Sons, 1937(1936).

Sapir, Edward. *Language.* Cited in *Language, Thought and Reality,* p. 134. By Benjamin Lee Whorf. Cambridge, Mass.: M.I.T. Press, 1964.

Schechner, Richard. *Essays on Performance Theory. 1970–1976.* New York: Drama Book Specialists (Publishers), 1977.

Schlossberg, Edwin. *Einstein and Beckett. A Record of an Imaginary Discussion with Albert Einstein and Samuel Beckett.* New York, London: Links Books, 1973.

Shattuck, Roger. *The Banquet Years.* New York: Harcourt, Brace and Company, 1958(1955).

Simon, Linda. *The Biography of Alice B. Toklas.* New York, Garden City: Doubleday, Inc., 1977.

Simpson, N. F. *The Hole and Other Plays and Sketches.* London: Faber and Faber, 1964.

Smiley, Sam. *Playwriting: The Structure of Action.* Englewood Cliffs: Prentice Hall, 1971.

Sontag, Susan. *Against Interpretation and other Essays.* New York: Dell Publishing Company, 1966(1961).

Sypher, Wylie. *Rococo to Cubism in Art and Literature.* New York: Random House, 1960.

Szathmary, Albert. *The Aesthetic Theory of Henri Bergson.* Cambridge: Harvard University Press, 1937.

Tardieu, Jean. *The Underground Lovers.* Translated and Introduced by Colin Duckworth. London: George Allen and Unwin, Ltd., 1968.

Thomson, Virgil. *Virgil Thomson.* New York: Knopf, 1966.

Wilson, Robert. "Robert Wilson." In *Intermedia,* pp. 165–166. Edited by Hans Breder and Stephen C. Foster. Iowa City: Publication of School of Art and Art History, The University of Iowa, 1979.

Witkiewicz, Stanislaw Ignacy. "the analogy with painting." From *Introduction to the Theory of Pure Form in the Theatre.* (1920) In *Avant-Garde Drama. A Casebook, 1918–1939*, pp. 487–493. Edited by Bernard Dukore and Daniel C. Gerould. Translated by Daniel C. and Eleanor S. Gerould. New York: Thomas Y. Crowell Company, 1976.

———. *On A New Type of Play.* In *Dramatic Theory and Criticism*, pp. 973–978. Edited by Bernard F. Dukore. New York: Holt, Rinehart and Winston, Inc., 1974.

———. "theoretical introduction to tumor brainard." (1920). In *Avant-Garde Drama. A Casebook, 1918–1939*, pp. 483–485. Edited by Bernard Dukore and Daniel Gerould, Translated by Daniel and Eleanor Gerould. New York: Thomas Y. Crowell Company, 1976.

Woodbury, Lael J. *Mosaic Theatre. The Creative Use of Theatrical Constructs.* Provo, Utah: Brigham Young University Press, 1976.

Young, Stark. *The Theater.* New York: George H. Doran Company, 1927.

Zedler, Beatrice H. "Dewey's Theory of Knowledge." In *John Dewey: His Thought and Influence*, p. 59. Edited by John Blewett. New York: Fordham University Press, 1960.

Zukav, Gary. *The Dancing Wu Li Masters.* New York: William Morrow and Company, Inc., 1979.

Periodicals/Newspapers

"American Experimental Theatre: Then and Now." *Performing Arts Journal*, Fall 1977, pp. 13–24.

Barnes, Clive. "Theater: Or Is It Theater? Have No Preconceptions." *The New York Times*, March 24, 1975, p. 40.

Brustein, Robert. "Drama in the Age of Einstein." *The New York Times*, August 7, 1977, Section 2, pp. 1, 22.

Chapin, Louis. "Al Carmines and the Profundity of Pop." *The Christian Century*, August 21, 1974, pp. 802–804.

Donoghue, Denis. "Counterstatements." *The New York Times Book Review*, July 9, 1978, pp. 7, 39.

Dunning, Jennifer. "Men's Company to Bow at Judson Church." *The New York Times*, February 5, 1978, Section D, p. 17.

Evans, Calvin. "Temporal Aesthetics and the Dramaturgy of Jean Tardieu." *Drama Survey*, Winter 1963, pp. 305–321.

Foreman, Richard. "How To Write A Play." *Performing Arts Journal*, Fall 1976, pp. 84–92.

Gruen, John. "Is It A Play? An Opera? No, It's A Wilson." *The New York Times*, March 16, 1975, p. 7.

Kornfeld, Laurence. "From a Director's Notebook." *Performing Arts Journal*, Spring 1976, pp. 33–39.

Leverett, James. "Richard Foreman and Some Uses of Cinema." *Theatre*, Spring 1979, pp. 10–14.

Olf, Julian. "The Man/Marionette Debate in Modern Theatre." *Educational Theatre Journal*, December 1974, pp. 488–494.

Rader, Dotson. "Can the Reverend Al Carmines Save the Theatre?" *Esquire*, December 1974, pp. 126–127+.

Rockwell, John. "Robert Wilson After 'Einstein'." *The New York Times*, November 26, 1978, pp. 5, 35.

———. "The Magic Theatre of Richard Foreman." *The New York Times*, February 8, 1976, pp. 1, 5.

———. "Today's Blank Art Explores the Space Behind The Obvious. *The New York Times*, July 17, 1977, Section D, pp. 1, 14.

Tomkins, Calvin. "Time to Think." *The New Yorker*, January 13, 1978, p. 61+.

Unpublished Materials

Anthony, Susan B. to Alice B. Toklas, May 11, 1947. New Haven: Yale University, Gertrude Stein Collection.

Atkinson, Brooks. Letter to the Author, August 11, 1977.

Austin, Arthur Everett to Gertrude Stein, November 16, 1933. New Haven: Yale University, Gertrude Stein Collection.

Berners, Gerald to Gertrude Stein, 1936–1939. New Haven: Yale University, Gertrude Stein Collection.

Bradley, William Aspenwall to Gertrude Stein, 1933–1934. New Haven: Yale University, Gertrude Stein Collection.

Brinnin, John Malcom. Letter to the Author, March 1978.

"A Circular Play," Program of the Independent Theatre of Rotterdam Production, 1979. Author's Program Collection.

"Doctor Faustus Lights the Lights," Program of the Playhouse Repertory Company Production, 1954. New Haven: Yale University, Stein Program Collection.

"Doctor Faustus Lights the Lights," Program of The Living Theatre Production, 1951. New York: New York Public Library at Lincoln Center, Theatre Program Collection.

Foreman, Richard. Letter to the Author, July 1977.

"Four Saints in Three Acts," 1934. New Haven: Yale University, Stein Program Collection.

"Four Saints in Three Acts," by Julian Sawyer, 1934. New Haven: Yale University, Stein Program Collection.

Houseman, John. Letter to the Author, August 1977.

Ionesco, Eugene. Letter to the Author, October 11, 1977.

Johnson, Lamont. Personal Interview. Greencastle, Indiana: De Pauw University, May 5, 1978.

Johnson, Lamont to Gertrude Stein, November 1945–July 1946. New Haven: Yale University, Gertrude Stein Collection.

Johnson, Lamont to Alice B. Toklas, July 1946–July 1949. New Haven: Yale University, Gertrude Stein Collection.

Kaufman, Lilian to Gertrude Stein, May–August, 1938. New Haven: Yale University, Gertrude Stein Collection.

Kerr, Walter. Letter to the Author, September 14, 1977.

Leach, Wilford. "Gertrude Stein and the Modern Theatre." Ph.D. Dissertation, University of Illinois, 1956.

Lloyd, Alan. Letter to the Author (Re: Robert Wilson), August 17, 1977.

"Listen To Me," The Judson Poets' Theatre, 1974. New Haven: Yale University, Stein Program Collection.

Malina, Judith and Julian Beck. *Doctor Faustus Lights The Lights.* Scenario. As performed at The Cherry Lane Theatre, New York City, 1951. New York: New York Public Library at Lincoln Center, Theatre Program Collection.

Marsden Hartley. Marsden Hartley Exhibition. Little Gallery of Photo-Secession, January 5–February 5, 1914. New Haven: Yale University, Stein Program Collection.

Simpson, N. F. Letter to the Author, April 1978.

Stein, Gertrude to William A. Bradley, April–May, 1934. New Haven: Yale University, Gertrude Stein Collection.

———— to Lamont Johnson et al., January–March 1946. New Haven: Yale University, Gertrude Stein Collection.

———— to Henry McBride, 1913–1931. New Haven: Yale University, Gertrude Stein Collection.

—— to Virgil Thomson, 1927–1946. New Haven: Yale University, Gertrude Stein Collection.

Thomson, Virgil. *Film:* "Deux Soeurs qui sont pas Soeurs." Vocal Score, 1930. New Haven: Yale University, Gertrude Stein Collection.

——. Interview with Charles Amirkhanian. New Haven: Yale University, Gertrude Stein Collection.

——. Interview with the Author. New York: Chelsea Hotel, October 2, 1977.

——. Letter to the Author, September 6, 1977.

—— to William A. Bradley, May 6, 1933. New Haven: Yale University, Gertrude Stein Collection.

—— to Gertrude Stein, 1927–1946. New Haven: Yale University, Gertrude Stein Collection.

—— to Alice Toklas, 1947–1948. New Haven: Yale University, Gertrude Stein Collection.

Toklas, Alice to Henry McBride, August 6, 1960. New Haven: Yale University, Gertrude Stein Collection.

Van Vechten, Carl to Gertrude Stein, 1923–1946. New Haven: Yale University, Gertrude Stein Collection.

"What Happened," April 15, 17, 1947. New York: New York Public Library at Lincoln Center, Theatre Program Collection.

"When This You See Remember Me," by the Cardboard Alley Players, May 4, 5, 1967. New Haven: Yale University, Gertrude Stein Program Collection.

Zatkin, Nathan. Press Release, *Four Saints in Three Acts,* 1934. New Haven: Yale University, Gertrude Stein Collection.

Play Manuscripts and Typescripts (New Haven: Yale University, Gertrude Stein Collection.)

OMS = Original Manuscript
OTS = Original Typescript
TSC = Typescript Copy
MS = Manuscript
TS = Typescript

Accents in Alsace. A Reasonable Tragedy. 1919. OMS, OTS.

Am I To Go or I'll Say So. 1923. OMS, OTS.

At Present. A Play. Nothing but Contemporaries Allowed. 1930. OMS.

Bonne Année. A Play. 1916. OMS, OTS.

A Bouquet. Their Wills. 1928. OMS, OTS.

Byron a Play. But Which They Say Byron a Play. 1933. OMS, TSC.

Capital Capitals. 1923. OMS.

Captain Walter Arnold. A Play. 1916. OMS, OTS.

Capture Splinters. 1921. OMS.

A Circular Play. A Play In Circles. 1920. OMS.

Civilization. A Play. In Three Acts. 1931. OMS.

Counting Her Dresses. A Play. 1917. OMS, OTS.

A Curtain Raiser. 1913. OMS, OTS.

Daniel Webster. Eighteen in America: A Play. 1937. OMS.

Doctor Faustus Lights the Lights. 1938. OMS, OTS, Another TS.

Do Let Us Go Away. A Play. 1916. OMS, OTS.

Every Afternoon. A Dialogue. 1916. OMS, OTS.

An Exercise In Analysis. A Play. 1917. OMS, OTS.

Film. deux soeurs qui ne sont pas soeurs. 1929. OMS, OTS.

The Five Georges. 1931. OMS.

For The Country Entirely. A Play in Letters. 1916. OMS, OTS.

Four Saints in Three Acts. An Opera To Be Sung. 1927. OMS, OTS, TSC.

He Said It. Monologue. 1915. OMS, OTS.

An Historic Drama in Memory of Winnie Elliot. 1930. OMS, TSC.

Identity a Play. in The Geographical History of America or the Relation of Human Nature to the Human Mind. 1935. TSC.

Identity a Poem. 1935. OMS.

IIIIIIIIII. 1913. OMS, OTS.

I Like It to Be a Play. A Play. 1916. OMS, OTS.

In a Garden. A Tragedy in One Act. 1943. OMS, MS.

John Breon a novel or a play. 1946. OMS, TSC.

The King or Something. (The Public Is Invited To Dance). 1917. OMS, OTS.

Ladies' Voices. 1916. OMS, OTS.

Lend a Hand or Four Religions. 1922. OMS, OTS.

Lesson Sixteen. A Play. 1941. OMS, OTS.

A List. 1923. OMS, OTS.

Listen to Me. A Play. 1936. MS, TSC.

Look and Long. A Play In Three Acts. 1943. OMS, MS, MS.

Louis XI and Madame Giraud. 1930. OMS.

Lucretia Borgia. A Play. 1938. OMS.

Lynn and The College de France. 1931. OMS.

A Lyrical Opera Made by Two. To be Sung. 1928. OMS.

Madame Recamier. An Opera. 1930. OMS.

A Manoir. An Historical Play in which they are Approached More Often. 1932. OMS.

Mexico. A Play. 1916. OMS, OTS.

Monday and Tuesday. A Play. 1919. OMS, TSC.

The Mother of Us All. 1945-1946. OMS.

A Movie. 1920. OMS, OTS.

Not Sightly. A Play. 1915. OMS, OTS.

Objects Lie on a Table. A Play. 1922. OMS, OTS.

Old and Old. 1913. OMS, OTS.

One. Carl Van Vechten. 1913. OMS, OTS.

Paiseau. A Play. A Work of Pure Imagination in which No Reminiscences Intrude. 1928. OMS, MS, OTS.

Parlor. A Play. between parlor of the sisters. and parlor of the Earls. 1930. OMS.

Photograph. A Play in Five Acts. 1920. OMS, OTS.

A Play A Lion for Max Jacob. 1932. OMS.

A Play Called Not and Now. 1936. OMS.

Play I (III). 1930. OMS, TSC.

A Play of Pounds. 1932. OMS, TSC.

A Play without Roses. Portrait of Eugene Jolas. 1932. OMS, OTS.

Please Do Not Suffer. A Play. 1916. OMS, OTS.

Polybe in Port: A Curtain Raiser. 1916. OMS, OTS.

Reread Another. A Play. To be played indoors or out. I wish to be a school. 1921. OMS, OTS.

A Saint in Seven. 1922. OMS, OTS.

Saints and Singing. A Play. 1922. OMS, OTS.

Say it with Flowers. A Play. 1931. OMS.

Scenery and George Washington. A Novel or a Play. 1932. OMS.

Short Sentences. 1932. OMS, TSC.
Simons a Bouquet. 1913. OMS, OTS.
They Must. Be Wedded. To Their Wife. A Play. 1931. OMS.
They Weighed Weighed-Layed. A Drama of Aphorisms. 1930. OMS.
Third Historic Drama. 1930. OMS, TS.
Three Sisters who are not Sisters. A Melodrama. 1943. OMS.
Turkey and Bones and Eating and We Liked It. A Play. 1916. OMS, OTS.
A Village. Are You Ready Yet Not Yet. A Play in Four Acts. 1923. OMS, TSC.
What Happened. A Five Act Play. 1913. OMS, OTS.
White Wines. Three Acts. 1913. OMS, OTS.
Will He Come Back Better. Second Historic Drama. In the Country. 1930. OMS, TSC.
Yes is for a Very Young Man. 1944–1946. OMS, 3 MS additions, 2 TS.

Index